A Dog for All Seasons

Labrador Retrievers:
Hunters, Companions, and Friends

Copyright © E. Donnall Thomas Jr.
This book, or parts thereof, may not be reproduced in any form without the permission of the author.
Thomas Jr., E. Donnall
A Dog for All Seasons

1. Labrador Retrievers
2. Upland Hunting
3. Waterfowl Hunting
4. Dog Training
5. Dog care

ISBN: 978-0-9856912-2-6 (Paperback Edition)
ISBN: 978-0-9856912-4-0 (Ebook Edition)

Cover and interior design by: integrative ink.com
Photography by Don and Lori Thomas

Printed in the United States of America

1 3 5 7

Also by E. Donnall Thomas Jr.

Longbows in the Far North
Whitefish Can't Jump
Fool Hen Blues
Longbow Country
Dream Fish and Road Trips
To All Things a Season
The Double Helix
Outside Adventure: Fly-Fishing
By Dawn's Early Light
The Life of a Lab
Labs Afield
Hunting Labs
My Kingdom for a Lab
Redfish, Bluefish, Ladyfish, Snook
How Sportsmen Saved the World
Language of Wings
Have Bow, Will Travel
On the Wing

A Dog for All Seasons

Labrador Retrievers:
Hunters, Companions, and Friends

By
E. Donnall Thomas Jr.

Foreword by
Steve Smith

Dedication

To the Smith family—Steve, Jake, and Sue—without whom this would not have been possible. And, to Sky, Sonny, Jake, Rocky, Kenai, Rosy, Kiska, and Keta. And, of course, to my wonderful wife Lori.

Acknowledgements

While many good editors have helped me along the way, I would like to extend my special gratitude to Steve and Jake Smith at Village Press. Many of the essays in this volume appeared in two of the magazines they oversee: *Retriever Journal* and *Just Labs*
Other portions of this book have appeared in *Big Sky Journal, Montana Outdoors, Shooting Sportsman, Pheasants Forever, Alaska, Strung, Gray's Sporting Journal,* and a journal published by a wetlands conservation organization headquartered in Memphis, Tennessee.

Table of Contents

Preface xiii
Introduction xv

I. LABS AND WATERFOWL 1

1. All About the Dogs 5
2. All Good Things 9
3. Alpha Females 19
4. Child Prodigies 27
5. To Err is Canine 35
6. Young Dog and Helping Hands 39
7. On the Road Again 43
8. Mallards on Ice 51
9. The Beaver Pond 59
10. Training Day 65
11. Season Highlights 73
12. Lone Star Labs 79
13. The Best Laid Plans 87
14. Obligations 95

II. UPLAND LABS 105

15. Guns 'n Roses 109
16. Hell Holes 117
17. Early Season Surprises 125

 18. Our Glorious Tenth 133
 19. Mountain Grouse 141
 20. Winter Roosters 149

III. LIFE WITH LABS 159

 21. A Brief History of Labs 163
 22. The Curse of a Great Dog 169
 23. Aging Gracefully 177
 24. All in a Day's Work 185
 25. The Wolf at Your Side 189
 26. Current and Banks 197
 27. Bones and Beyond 205
 28. The Lab in Winter 213
 29. Forgive them their Trespasses 223
 30. The Power to Heal 231
 31. Don't Tread on Me! 239
 32. From the Yard to the Field 245
 33. The Big Chill 253
 34. September Heat 261
 35. A Dog for All Seasons 269
 36. The Amphibious Lab 275
 37. Beyond Words 281
 38. The End of the Road 287

Preface

As the preceding pages make clear, I do a lot of writing. Is it any good? The writer is the last person to whom that question should be addressed. All I can say is that someone seems to think so. Nonetheless, I am getting older and can no longer engage in many of the rigorous physical activities I formerly enjoyed. I recognize that my ability to produce coherent prose may be suffering the same fate. If so, I will not resent being told so.

Publication of my early books were joyous occasions. There followed a period of workmanship during which I still enjoyed the craft of writing, but without that initial sense of euphoria. When I finished *Language of Wings*, I told myself that would be my last book. Then I wrote *Have Bow, Will Travel* and made myself the same promise. Then came *On the Wing*, followed by another hopeless vow. Now I'm back again, as if by magic…

The reason I talked myself out of another self-imposed retirement was my affection for this book's subject matter. I grew up with hunting dogs and they have been a constant presence and source of joy throughout my life. Concurring with the English poet William Cowper that variety is the spice of life, I trained and hunted with a number of breeds including English pointers and setters, Brittany spaniels, German shorthairs and wirehairs, beagles, blueticks, and treeing Walkers. I also spent time in the field with two other celebrated waterfowl breeds, Golden and Chesapeake Bay retrievers. When I was facing early stages of burnout as a physician, I promised myself that I would find something to like about every patient I saw. I brought the same attitude to bear on that riotous smorgasbord of dogs. Sometimes that was easy, but all those breeds produced a dog or two that was a hard to like, with one exception…

By now readers should have no trouble identifying the dog in question. For that matter, the fact that you are reading this book suggests that you share my opinion. Greetings, brothers and sisters.

Some of us enjoy Labs primarily as hunting dogs, while others equally devoted to the breed don't hunt at all. I have intended this book for both parties. The first two sections are basically hunting stories highlighted by Labs, while the third focuses on the dogs independent of their roles as hunters. If you're reading this book because of your enthusiasm for Labs but do not hunt, I suggest that you begin with the third section, **Life with Labs,** before reading the preceding material with an open mind. That's my favorite section anyway.

I frequently describe my dogs in ways suggesting they have feelings and insights they almost certainly don't have—the definition of anthropomorphism. I'm too much a scientist to believe in those descriptions literally but too much a romantic to deny them. I apologize for any confusion.

The photos that accompany the text are weighted toward those dogs that accompanied us over the last 30 just because we didn't do much photography before then. Apologies to Sky, Sonny, and Rocky. I'll have to let words paint most of those pictures.

Don Thomas
Lewistown, MT

Introduction

When Don Thomas asked me to write this part of the opening of his newest book, I quickly agreed. But when I sat down at my keyboard, it quickly hit me: *Where do I start?* I've known Don professionally as his editor and personally as his friend for more decades than either of us would like to remember. Over those years I learned that no one—and I mean no one—knows the life and times of the Labrador retriever like Don and Lori Thomas.

As this book will show you beautifully, the Lab lives three lives. He—and I'll use this pronoun for ease of explanation and not for any other reason—hunts upland birds, where he is the boss. Nothing happens in the field in terms of birds in the air unless *he* makes it happen; *you* are along for the ride and to make retrieves possible. In a duck blind, he is a servant. Nothing happens in the marsh until *you* make it happen, and *he* is sent to retrieve the game. Finally, in the home, there is no greater companion, canine or otherwise, than a Labrador retriever. Period. There will be no discussion. I can say that because Labs have been keeping my family room couch from floating away for many years.

So, this dog is sometimes the boss and sometimes the servant, but he's always the best of friends. Having read this book before it became a book, I can tell you that no one shows you those sides of these great dogs as Don Thomas does in these pages.

It has been said that everyone has one good story. As a sporting magazine editor, I can tell you that a great writer has one every issue.

The epitome of a good article, a good story, is to send the reader away both entertained and with a useful nugget of information he didn't have before. Don's hundreds of articles in my magazines and others all do that, as do the chapters in this book.

But it's not all memories of days afield. There is a lot of practical advice here—hunting techniques in the uplands and lowlands, advice on dog training and care, and the art of simply living with these great animals, matters like a Lab's aging process, what to expect, and how—if you can—prepare yourself for what is to come. Oh, and raise your hand if your Lab has ever been a "counter surfer." This book is all about day-to-day life with a Labrador retriever: life in the field, life in the marsh, life in the home. No one looks at those lives—and our lives with these great dogs—like Don Thomas.

Enjoy.

Steve Smith
Traverse City, Michigan
Editor Emeritus
Retriever Journal
Just Labs

I.

Labs and Waterfowl

The best long-distance shotgun load for mallards is a fine retriever.

—Nash Buckingham

One of the Labrador retriever's most admirable qualities as a gun dog is its versatility, a concept we'll return to frequently throughout this text. However, I think most of the breed's enthusiasts who hunt with their dogs would agree that they shine their brightest in the pursuit of waterfowl. I wouldn't hunt ducks or geese without one.

While I would grant an exception to hunters shooting geese in a field, a good retriever can prevent unrecovered birds even there, as we shall see. If one drops a bird from a covey of quail or Huns, there is at least a reasonable chance of finding it without a dog even though recovery is by no means certain. In many waterfowl hunting situations, a downed duck might be lost as soon as the hunter pulls the trigger absent a trained retriever.

The dog doesn't have to be a Lab. Although I've had minimal experience with some of the other retrieving breeds, I have seen inspired performances from friends' Chessies. Our big male German wirehair pointer serves wonderfully from a duck blind in terms of results if not in style. With that said, for most serious duck hunters there is nothing like a Lab.

1.

All About the Dogs

The surface of the pond lay so still beneath the October sunrise that the reflection of the autumn foliage there seemed etched as precisely as the motionless leaves themselves. I'd already peeled off my wool shirt and was thinking about shedding another layer. This was hardly classical waterfowling weather, but we were there anyway, enjoying the Indian summer while we could and waiting for a few birds to drop by so we could call our morning a duck hunt.

With the great autumn flights still far away to the north we hadn't expected much shooting, and for the first hour that's what we got. Suddenly a little flock of mallards descended out of the sun unannounced. My thumb slid toward the safety as my eyes began to separate drakes from hens. Lori shot first as the birds flared over her side of the decoy spread, and I saw one tumble. I killed another cleanly with my first barrel but watched with chagrin after my second sent another bird dropping slowly. It splashed down a hundred yards away and began churning for the opposite shore.

Young Rosy had drawn retrieving duty that morning. This was just her second season. I knew we'd be fortunate to recover the wounded bird. The dog veered toward one of the obvious falls when I sent her, but she looked back at my first whistle blast, turned a few befuddled circles when I ordered her back, and finally continued across the pond. When she reached the far shore I anchored her with the whistle, signaled her over, and watched her hit the skids when she reached the point where I'd seen the cripple disappear. Then she put her nose down and vanished into a dense tangle of cattails and brush.

The dog was the first wild animal humans successfully domesticated, an event that took place, albeit with some controversy about the date, sometime between 15,000 and 30,000 years ago according to most authorities. Recent evidence from the fossil record suggests that it may have occurred even earlier. Our two species have been hunting together ever since. This cooperative relationship likely began in disorganized fashion as each recognized the advantages of hunting as partners rather than competitors, an understanding that began to reach its full expression with the development of our great retrieving breeds. Dogs probably began fetching thrown sticks as a source of mutual entertainment around communal cooking fires, but suddenly they were revolutionizing the way we hunted waterfowl—by salvaging game, enlivening duck blinds, and engendering pride in their owners and handlers.

I don't think I've ever known a serious duck hunter who didn't have a retriever, and most, like me, usually have several. The practical reasons are obvious. A trained retrieving dog will routinely recover countless birds that would otherwise be lost to scavengers. Many argue that hunting waterfowl without a capable dog should be illegal. I'm not ready to go quite that far, but it's certainly hard to recommend and not just because of unrecovered birds. Those of us who hunt with Labs consider their companionship in a duck blind an essential component of the experience.

Retrievers often develop closer bonds with their owners than hounds or pointing dogs. I know, because I've trained and hunted with all three since my childhood. The intensity of those attachments derives in part from practical factors like the physical intimacy of the duck blind and the long hours of company shared while waiting for ducks that have decided to go somewhere else. Then there are the intangibles: the intensity of a dog still scanning the sky after I've given up for the morning; the geyser of icy water that accompanies a spectacular water entry. As much as I love watching my wirehair lock up on a covey of Huns or listen to my blueticks take a cougar track over the top of a mountain, there's nothing quite like the way one of the Labs can turn an ordinary morning into something special.

Just as Rosy did that day… Twenty minutes had elapsed, and we'd passed up a flock of teal to avoid distracting the dog with gunfire. Suddenly she popped out of the brush at the extreme far corner of the pond and headed in our direction as fast as she could swim. She was so far away I had to squint into the sun to identify the greenhead's neck extending from the side of her mouth. Mission accomplished—somehow.

Duck hunting is a complex undertaking, and that complexity lies at the heart of its appeal. Sunrises, decoys, setting wings, shotguns, natural history, camaraderie, calls, cuisine, and above all the habitat waterfowl enjoy and share with such an astounding variety of wildlife. To emphasize any single element of the experience at the expense of all the rest is probably a mistake. Even so, whenever dogs are involved, it can be tempting.

Duck hunting may not be all about the dogs, but it often comes close.

2.

All Good Things

Heavy snowfall can make the long drive from our central Montana home to Washington State's Columbia River Basin a nightmare, but we encountered no such aggravation on our final trip of that season. Upon arrival however, we found typical late season weather waiting for us: temperature flirting with the freezing point; dense ice fog obscuring the sun; not even a hint of wind to breathe life into a decoy spread. While these conditions couldn't have been less promising, the number of ducks flying back and forth through the gloom overhead offered us hope for a busy morning yet to come.

We hadn't planned to be there for the final days of the Pacific Flyway waterfowl season. A severe cold snap had canceled our planned trip two weeks earlier by locking the ponds in ice and sending all the birds off to open water on the Columbia. However, when the cold front reached Montana and inflicted the same indignity on our local ponds, the flocks of mallards wintering in the valley all swarmed to the ice-resistant spring-fed creeks and sloughs that dot the area. Lori and I spent the final two days of the Central Flyway season standing in the bushes beside one such creek and shot limits of mallards as they tried to land on top of our heads. Rosy, by then gracefully aging, seemed to enjoy the experience just as much as we did, although it was hard for me to avoid the impression that I might be watching her last duck hunt.

We had cleaned and oiled the shotguns and put them away for the winter when friends called to tell us that the ponds in Washington were opening up again and the ducks were back in staggering numbers. With the Pacific Flyway season still open for two more weeks and next to nothing on our schedule, we hauled the shotguns out of cold storage, watched the dogs jump gleefully into the truck, and set out to close the season down in style. We hoped.

The morning following our arrival, I did some head-scratching about our choice of blinds. Some favorites remained iced over, but too much water had opened to concentrate birds around flowing inlets and outlets. As is often the case, my eventual decision was guided more by instinct than science.

I had barely returned to the blind after setting out the decoys when I spotted a lone greenhead approaching the spread on cupped wings. I hadn't had time to load my shotgun yet, so—hoping that Lori had—I whispered for her to "Take him!" The bird folded at the sound of her shot and fell dead in front of the blind, neatly demonstrating how effective a 20-gauge can be on decoying ducks. (Of course, gentleman that I am, I would have offered Lori the shot even if I'd been ready for it myself. Probably.) Full of pent-up energy after the long, boring drive, Rosy hit the water a moment before I told her to, but I didn't bother correcting her. Both the shot and the retrieve turned out to be the easiest we'd see for the next three days.

By this late phase of the season the birds had seen plenty of decoys, heard plenty of calls, and learned a lot about staying alive. For the next hour, we watched ducks circle just out of shotgun range as if we had a force field around us creating an invisible barrier the birds couldn't cross. Then a drake pintail that evidently didn't get the memo provided me with an opportunity to sound off about one of my pet wing-shooting peeves—the selective safety.

The bird arrived suddenly and unannounced, offering a lovely crossing shot at perhaps 25 yards. As I shouldered my shotgun I felt my thumb jam tightly against the safety, which I couldn't disengage. This happens to me once or twice every season when the safety gets stuck between "over" and "under" and winds up providing neither even though I make a continuous effort to keep the safety pushed to one side. For some reason this hiccup usually occurs on mulligan shot opportunities, making it doubly frustrating. I even have bad dreams about it. By the time I could communicate my problem to Lori the bird was out of range.

The next shot opportunity came courtesy of a drake gadwall that fell to a long, satisfying shot and dropped on a solid sheet of ice. While it was obviously stone dead, fulfilling my moral obligation to recover it was still going to require some tricky dog work. Our canine team was larger than usual on this trip because we didn't want to leave anyone behind to face the possibility of sub-zero weather in their outside kennels back at home.

Rosy will appear frequently in the pages that follow. In good writerly fashion, I'll try to show rather than tell about her many wonderful qualities as a waterfowl dog. Physically, she had started the slow downhill slide dogs inevitably face as they age, but she was still too eager to leave behind. Kiska, another yellow female, remained a work in progress thanks to an inexplicable aversion to water. Prior to the season, I had discussed this dilemma with several knowledgeable trainers, who offered good suggestions to supplement ideas of my own. We agreed that ice and winter weather did not provide an appropriate environment for a dog facing this challenge, and I would have left Kiska back in Montana except for the concerns just outlined. On this trip, we nicknamed her Miss Snowflake because of her comical refusal to get her feet wet even when she was standing at the waterline clearly eager to retrieve a duck floating in the decoys.

This brings us the most atypical member of the team: Max, a handsome, athletic male German wirehair pointer. During the previous season I had decided to see what Max could do in the water. Granted, he didn't look like a duck dog and didn't handle as well as some of my better Labs. However, based on enthusiasm, determination, and results, he knocked his early opportunities out of the park.

Because of concerns about Rosy's physical ability to handle ice, I decided the gadwall retrieve belonged to Max. The bird was lying 30 yards from the nearest bank or open water, and I didn't know if the ice was thick enough to support his weight. I did know it wouldn't support mine. I also knew that the water was shallow enough that I would be able to extract the dog if he got into trouble, although doing so would likely leave me too wet and hypothermic to remain in the field.

Max had marked the fall but sending him in a straight line would have required him to claw his way up onto the ice, which could have proved difficult. Instead, I gave him a line across the open water to the nearest shoreline and then casted him laterally until he could reach the ice from dry ground. After picking up the gadwall he took the direct route home across the open water, which provided him an opportunity to splatter me as he shook off and delivered the bird to hand.

There is nothing like being in the right place at the right time when hunting ducks, but that morning we weren't. While we shot a modest mixed bag and missed a few as well, all morning long we watched flock after flock of mallards ignore our decoys, over-fly us, and land a quarter mile away at the end of a long, narrow bay connected to one of the area's larger ponds. If there was a habitat or weather consideration that explained this determined behavior, I couldn't identify it. Although our duck straps were a handful of birds short of limits when we finally decided to retreat and warm up, we had fulfilled two important personal criteria for a successful hunt: neither of us had shot a hen mallard and the dogs hadn't lost a single bird.

Furthermore, I knew exactly where I wanted to be the following day.

After awakening to another cold, gray morning, we encountered difficulty as soon as we reached the new blind. Ice rimmed the shoreline for perhaps ten yards from dry ground. While plenty of open water lay beyond it, I had to cross the ice to set out the decoys and therein lay the rub. The ice was too thick to punch my way through but not quite strong enough to support my weight. Every time I took a step, a large plate of slick ice fractured underfoot and came to rest at a slanted angle that threatened to make me lose my balance and fall in. The ice was so enmeshed in aquatic vegetation that it was impossible to clear a path by pushing the broken plates aside. Only a last-minute decision to bring along a wading staff kept me upright and dry. I didn't want to make any more trips than necessary back out to open water.

To make matters worse yet, the waves of mallards that had teased us so cruelly the previous morning were standing us up. I have no idea where they were, but it wasn't where we were. Fortunately, nature provided us with an unexpected but welcome alternative: ring-necked ducks.

The nearby Columbia holds large numbers of divers. I have spent some pleasant days there shooting scaup, redheads, and canvasbacks as well as ringnecks. However, only the latter leave the big water for the ponds, and even they only do so occasionally. By first shooting light that morning, tight little flocks of ringnecks were roaring right down the centerline of the bay at high speed with air whistling through their flight primaries loudly enough to wake the dead. Coordinated as closely as aircraft on final approach to LAX, they flew a constant vector from left to right at low altitude but almost always just beyond shotgun range.

Situations like this invite the kind of magical thinking that suggests if you want the birds to be ten yards closer badly enough, they will be. I resisted that urge for nearly an hour. Lori responsibly announced that the ringnecks were out of range for her and waited for one of the teal circling the lake to succumb to our decoys' invitation. When the urge to shoot finally overwhelmed me, I mentally isolated one ringneck from the next flock, drove my barrels ridiculously far out in front of the bird, and watched it fall when I pulled the trigger. The wounded bird appeared to start swimming before it even hit the water.

I knew the fallen duck posed a problem. Since I had shot, it belonged to me. That blind lacks a dog platform, and Rosy couldn't mark the fall. Max, however, had learned to balance with his hind feet on the bench and his front paws on the blind's frame, a breach of protocol that I tolerated in the interest of practicality. The bird had fallen near the shoreline in a sparse expanse of grass covered with patchy ice too thin to support a dog's weight. Ignoring Rosy's whines, I called Max to heel and set out again through the treacherous minefield of ice plates. After reaching open water upright and dry, I gave Max the line and sent him down the shore.

Nothing evades capture with more determination than a wounded diver. The duck was perhaps 60-yards away when I last spotted it churning toward dry ground, where it vanished into a nasty thicket of Russian olive. When Max reached the spot where I'd last seen the duck, he spun on a dime and lunged into the thorns. When he emerged ten minutes later and began to return, he held the live duck in his mouth. His appearance may not have conformed to everyone's idea of a retriever, but he had just satisfied my own definition of a duck dog even though he wasn't a Lab.

Perhaps it is fitting that the Retrieve of the Year came on the last day of the season. By midday, we had a nice assortment of mallards, teal, ringnecks, and woodies hanging in the blind when I noticed a high-flying drake pintail cup its wings and begin a cautious descent. With the previous day's clown show still fresh in my mind, I began carefully working my safety back and forth. Then the bird broke off its approach and went around for another look, a process it repeated three more times before I declared it within shotgun range.

Perhaps I should have allowed it another pass, for after the shot the duck sailed down across the pond and hit the water with its head up.

Since the situation called for all hands-on-deck, I exited the blind with Max and Rosy at my side, holding my wading staff rather than my shotgun. A firearm can prove useful in recovery situations like this as long as due attention is paid to canine safety, but the footing was so tricky that I worried about slipping and dropping my favorite double into water deep enough to hinder its recovery. Soon after leaving the blind, I spotted the drake's white tuxedo bobbing away through an expanse of sparse marsh grass intermittently broken up by ice of uncertain thickness. Since Max had been able to mark at least the general direction of the fall from his elevated position in the blind, I sent him, keeping Rosy at my side because of uncertainty about her ability to navigate the ice.

Although I couldn't describe Max's handling as crisp, I eventually directed him to the right area. Because my eyes were higher above the waterline than the dogs', I could still see the duck even though they couldn't—the very reason why I'd accompanied them from the blind. Then the sound of Max splashing through the water made the duck go into sneak mode, and I lost visual contact. The real rodeo began when Max appeared to catch a whiff of scent and began a manic ballet, spinning and repeatedly thrusting his head underwater. By then I had determined that the ice posed no real threat, so I sent Rosy to join him in an effort sometimes better accomplished by two dogs than one. We must have conveyed a sense of excitement all the way back to the blind, for I was pleasantly surprised to see that Miss Snowflake herself had paddled all the way out to join us.

Rosy covered the open water with remarkable speed for a dog her age. Then she joined Max in a tag-team effort to secure the duck. I eventually spotted the tip of its bill tracing a delicate V across the water's surface as it tried to escape along the edge of the grass. A whistle blast followed by hand signals redirected the dogs, who had been unable to spot the duck on their own. Just as I lost visual contact myself, both dogs wheeled sharply back into the grass and began creating the loudest ruckus yet. Finally, Max emerged from the grass with the bird in his mouth.

Returning to the blind with the dogs swimming along beside me, I thought about the paradox of what our teamwork had just accomplished. Granted, all I had to show for our collective effort was one dead duck—a beautiful specimen, but still. On the other hand, I've hunted multiple species of big game all around the world, taking many nice animals with nothing but a traditional longbow. While I've never been particularly interested in trophies, whatever that word means, many of those animals would have met anyone's definition as such. Yet I couldn't remember leaving the field feeling more satisfied about any of them than I was about the pintail hanging from my hand. Aldo Leopold once advised that the value of a trophy arises not from its size but from the amount of effort invested in obtaining it. This was just what he meant.

Like all good things, another season had come to an end. I was already looking forward to the next one and hoping that Rosy and I would both be around to enjoy it together. We were.

3.

Alpha Females

There is something about a drake pintail that excites me more than any other kind of duck. As a kid beginning my wing-shooting career in the Atlantic Flyway I hardly ever saw a pintail, but I encountered them regularly when I settled in the eastern Montana prairie 50 years ago. I quickly fell under the spell of their grace on the wing, their wariness as they circled the decoy spread, and their exceptional table quality. Those were the days of the old Central Flyway 100-point daily duck limit, and pintails were what a stock analyst would call "seriously under-valued" at 10 points a pop. I frequently passed up drake mallards (over-valued at 35 points) so I could keep hunting ducks I'd rather shoot.

Those days were long gone by the time young Rosy met her first sprig. After years of population decline due to drought in the prairie pothole region, the daily limit had been reduced to one, and I meant to use it wisely. The old magic was still there however, and when the lone drake began to circle the decoys at the edge of shotgun range, I exercised the same restraint I would have used had a bugling bull elk responded to my calling by hanging up just beyond the range of my longbow.

In typical pintail fashion the drake continued to circle, periodically setting its wings and starting to descend only to pull up and go around again. Aware of how quickly an over-eager young dog can end an encounter like this, I kept murmuring softly to Rosy: *stay, stay, stay*. She was tracking the bird with her eyes, and I could feel her quivering in anticipation, but she never broke. Whatever was arousing the drake's suspicion about our setup, it wasn't the dog.

When the bird set its wings once again and made its lowest pass yet I finally rose and took the shot. Perhaps I should have waited longer, for instead of collapsing, it shuddered briefly and began a long glide into a dense reedbed at the far end of the pond. Aware that I was guilty of either poor decision making or poor marksmanship, I gave myself a mental kick in the pants and set about trying to make the best of a bad situation.

I really wanted to recover this bird, for it would be my one pintail for the day whether or not it wound up on my game strap. I just wasn't sure that I had the dog I needed for the job ahead. It wasn't as if there was anything wrong with Rosy, who had performed precociously throughout the season thus far. But she was barely a year old, and now she was facing a task that would have challenged a veteran.

After I led her out the back of the blind, gave her the line, and sent her on her way, I watched her crash away through the shallows until she reached swimming depth and started churning her way down the pond.

When I acquired my first Labrador retriever long ago, I picked Bogey, a male, from a litter of puppies chosen nearly at random. I didn't invest a lot of thought in the litter's bloodlines, and I invested even less in the choice of gender. I'd grown up with hunting dogs of various breeds, and they had all been males. That decision was largely a matter of habit.

There are rational reasons for choosing males over females, and my father had discussed some of them with me when I was young. We were not interested in whelping puppies. Females required either a trip to the vet for neutering or special care and attention when in season. However, I now realize that underlying these perfectly legitimate considerations was a form of gender bias affecting our society at large back then. I knew where I was headed when I set off for Montana, and that a gun dog's job description there would require mental and physical toughness, stamina, determination, and the ability to hunt under demanding conditions of weather and terrain. That meant I needed a male, right?

Well, wrong, although it took me a lot longer than it should have to recognize this truth about dogs, or people, as I am now ashamed to admit. In the long interval between Bogey, who if nothing else taught me to pay more attention to breeding in the future, and Kenai, all my Labs were males. One was great, a couple went to good country homes on local ranches after washing out as working retrievers, and the rest ranged from good to very good. I never seriously considered owning a female.

Slowly, I began to absorb contrary opinions. Although I rarely enjoyed an opportunity to hunt with girl dogs, friends who had raised and hunted with Labs of both genders assured me that females were easier to train, less easily distracted, and better house dogs.

However, those old biases still lingered in the background. I knew that my male retrievers could smash through ice, sit patiently beside a Montana spring creek at 10-below, and attack the thickest, nastiest pheasant cover around, all without losing enthusiasm and ready to jump back in the truck and do it again the next day. Could a female handle those same job descriptions? Of course they could, although I still wasn't quite ready to test that proposal.

It was a hound, of all things, that finally undid my groundless biases against female hunting dogs. I was doing a lot of cougar hunting then and knew that one or two good hounds could tree a cat just as effectively as a large pack. When my excellent male bluetick died of old age, Sadie came to me at age two when her original owner had to leave the area for a new job. I had always started with puppies on the assumption that no one ever sells or gives away a really good dog, but Sadie turned into a star. Even when running a track with friends' experienced males, she was usually the first at the tree, and she wouldn't leave it until I put her on a leash and hauled her away. Winter weather in the mountains during the Montana cougar season can be hard on man and dog alike, but it never phased her. Furthermore, she wasn't lifting her leg on Lori's furniture or trying to hump visitors' belongings. I was finally beginning to see the light. With Kenai starting to show his age, the time had come to start grooming his replacement. Around that time, a friend in Oregon who had an excellent yellow female contacted me with the news that a litter was on the way. I put in a request for a female. Months later, Rosy was wiggling around on Lori's lap on the long ride back to Montana while I looked forward to training my first female retriever.

What is an alpha female, anyway? As with many terms derived from sociology and psychology, its definition is imprecise and decidedly soft around the edges, especially now that it has made the species leap from animals to humans. At its most precise, its origins lie in the canine family of mammals. Our dogs' wild ancestors—the domestic dog is but a subspecies of the gray wolf—are pack animals that developed elaborate social hierarchies to facilitate group activities no individual could tackle on its own, such as taking down large ungulate prey.

The male and female pack members occupying dominant positions atop this social order—the alphas—also typically enjoyed preferential breeding rights as nature's way of propagating the most adaptive genetics. According to these criteria, I acknowledge that I have misused the term in reference to some of my earlier misconceptions about female hunting dogs. Now that some women are commonly referred to as alpha females (just Google it), the term suggests such character traits as confidence, assertiveness, tenacity, and a high capacity to learn. This derivative version suits my purpose better than the original definition provided by biologists observing the behavior of canine species in the wild.

One day earlier in Rosy's first season, Lori and I got to share a duck blind with a friend and his big male Lab. Birds were flying, and we knocked down quite a few in the first hour of shooting light. Rosy was young and his dog wasn't particularly steady, so the two of them spent quite a bit of time crashing around in the decoys under less control than they should have been. (I know I shouldn't have been working a youngster under those conditions, but we were all having too much fun to stop.) "Your dog is sure *aggressive*," our friend commented at one point. "Especially for a young female."

He clearly meant this observation as a compliment, and I took it as one. It also made me think, since that wasn't an adjective I would have used to describe my own dog. Eager, enthusiastic… sure, but aggressive? Then I acknowledged that he was right. The interesting thing about Rosy though is that her attitude was aggressive only when a retrieve was involved, whether the object was a downed bird in the field or a bumper on the lawn. Socially, she was the most submissive of the dogs that occupy our kennel then, the exact opposite of a true alpha female. This paradoxical aspect of her behavior actually suits my purposes well, since she is a ball of fire when I need her to be and a pussycat around the house.

The second female Lab to enter my world illustrates the mirror image of this distinction. My Oregon friend's dam produced one more litter before she died in an accident, and I missed out on that opportunity because Lori and I were traveling constantly then and weren't ready for another puppy. I felt disappointed when I learned of his dog's death, since I was looking forward to a puppy from the same breeding. (Because of our travel schedule I'd had Rosy spayed by then, a decision I've regretted ever since.)

When Rosy was five however, I learned that her father had sired a litter with another well-bred, highly recommended dam. I wasn't going to pass up another opportunity, and once again chose a female puppy. Kiska did not prove to be as precocious as Rosy, but she was easy to train, intelligent, and blessed with an exceptional nose. What she lacked was Rosy's intensity when it came time to retrieve and an inexplicable (for a Lab) aversion to water.

Strangely though, Kiska really was an alpha female according to the unadulterated definition of the term. Whatever the circumstances, she insisted on being the boss. She delighted in beating up (gently) on her older half-sister. Max was the toughest dog in our kennel, a big, powerful dog Kiska intimidated so badly that when I let all the dogs out for their morning run, he cowered in the back of his kennel until his nemesis was out of sight.

None of this assertiveness by Kiska involved serious fighting. She simply bowled her kennel mates over and nipped at their ears until they assumed a submissive posture in the kind of mock battle canines have used to determine their social pecking order for countless generations. Granted, Kiska was a big girl that stood an inch taller than breed standards for female Labs. But her dominance was clearly a matter of attitude rather than physique. Max could clearly teach her a lesson any time he wanted to, but he didn't.

I only hoped that Kiska would eventually bring some of that assertive attitude to bear on fallen ducks lying in the water.

Rosy swam the hundred yards down the pond as if she were training for the Olympics. A thin rim of ice had formed along the shaded edge of the far shoreline, but it barely slowed her down. I lost visual contact with her when she vanished into the reeds, but the morning air was calm enough to let me hear her splashing and crashing through the cover.

She had reached the area of the fall. Given the way the duck had gone down after the shot, I thought there was a reasonable chance it was dead. If that were the case, I anticipated that she would locate it quickly, but the odds of a successful recovery would plummet if the duck was alive and taking evasive action. Since I could be of no help from the blind, I unloaded and set off down the edge of the pond in the dog's direction.

Unnecessarily, as events soon proved. When Rosy popped out of the reeds 50 yards from her point of entry she held the duck in her mouth, its extended neck indicating that it was still alive. Somehow, the young, inexperienced dog had made a retrieve that I would have been proud of from any of my tough, veteran males.

As Rosy powered through the water on the return leg of the retrieve, I offered a silent but heartfelt apology to all the female Labs I never owned. I had made baseless assumptions about their gender, and the time had come to admit that I'd been wrong. Many subsequent seasons with Rosy by my side eventually taught me just how wrong I'd been.

4.

Child Prodigies

The first time I took Skykomish duck hunting, I left the blind convinced that I was the most brilliant retriever trainer in the world, even though I hadn't had time to teach the dog much of anything yet.

I had acquired Sky, a yellow male of no great lineage, as a puppy, during the end of my first year of assignment as an Indian Health Service physician in northeastern Montana. The previous season's upland hunting had exceeded even my high expectations despite having to labor through it with Bogey, my first and most hardheaded Lab I ever owned. The waterfowling came as a surprise, for two consecutive wet years had transformed the ordinarily dry prairie into prime duck habitat. There were ducks everywhere, and only Bogey's incompetence prevented me from enjoying them to the fullest.

Hence my anticipation as I set out through the darkness on opening morning with a decoy bag slung over my shoulder, Sky and one hunting partner by my side, and wings already whistling overhead through the gloom. A late-night encounter with a speeding car had spelled the end of Bogey, and I'd only had a few months to work with the new pup by the time duck season rolled around. I'd passed up a lot of shots the previous season, simply because I couldn't rely on Bogey to make any retrieve I couldn't make myself.

My family had some good retrievers when I was growing up, and I longed to recreate the special confidence I'd enjoyed back then—the feeling of not needing to worry about where a bird fell because I knew the dog would get it.

Sky was barely eight months old on that memorable opening day. Over the summer, I'd given him all the time my schedule allowed. He had performed well during basic training and had some experience on sharptails and Huns by the time duck season opened, but he was still a puppy. I had warned myself against holding high expectations for him that morning, or any expectations at all. Intellectually, I knew that the morning belonged to the dog, but I didn't know how faithful to that principle I could be when the season's first ducks started to work the decoys. I felt more unsure of my own discipline than I did about the dog's.

We were hunting a wonderful wetland that no longer exists, a legacy of the unusual wet weather I'd been fortunate enough to blunder into the previous year. Two friends had taken their dogs to another blind on the opposite side of the marsh. With that exception, I didn't think there was another soul within five miles of Sky and me. There certainly weren't any other duck hunters. In fact, over the course of two long seasons there I never heard a shot fired by someone I didn't know, which speaks to the loneliness of that corner of the prairie more eloquently than any fragment of census data.

Dawn had just started to break by the time I heard a succession of shots from the other blind. When a small flock of wigeons buzzed the spread moments later, I had just enough light to let me identify a drake near the end of the line. The bird folded at the sound of the shot and hit the water with a reassuring *splat*. A stone-dead bird right in front of the blind was just what I wanted for the dog.

As I broke my shotgun to reload, I glanced around to see what Sky was up to. I had expected him to break, but to my pleasant surprise he was still sitting at the far end of the bench, his eyes focused with laser intensity on the floating duck. Given Bogey's lackluster performance the previous year, I hadn't given much thought to an exit route for the dog when I built the blind out of chicken wire, fence posts, and reeds. When I gave Sky an encouraging command to "*Fetch!*", he solved the dilemma by jumping straight over the front of the blind from a standing start. By the time he swam back with the duck in his mouth, I had unhooked the crude chicken wire door on my end of the blind, and he entered holding the duck like a seasoned pro—just the first of many pleasant surprises he provided that morning.

As any parent, pediatrician, or retriever trainer knows, the young of any species develop at their own individual rates, whether they're toddlers or puppies. Guidebooks for both suggest approximate timelines identifying likely developmental milestones at various ages. As many liability-inspired warnings now put it, these data are for planning purposes only. Interpreting them too literally can lead to confusion.

There is wide agreement that the age of seven to eight weeks is the ideal time to remove a puppy from its litter and introduce it to its new home. Age three to four months is accepted as the age at which to begin some basic training. However, as the complexity of the tasks being taught increases, these guidelines begin to diverge, even among experts. Nothing begets confusion like disagreement among authorities, as illustrated during the covid pandemic. For example, in early editions of *Training Your* Retriever, James Lamb Free recommended virtually no retriever training before the dog was two years old. Richard Wolters, on the other hand, suggested a quite specific timeline for training during the dog's first year.

The usual subject in discussions of timelines vs. reality is the dog that is slow to develop as a working retriever. The sad fact is that some dogs just aren't going to get there, but I know of no firm rules establishing when that point has been reached. Some good dogs don't show signs of promise until their third season, and I have written elsewhere about the dangers of throwing in the towel to soon. No one enjoys the decision to wash a dog out, especially once trainer and family have grown attached to it. There is nothing wrong with turning your retrieving prospect into a family dog. However, I'm assuming that most readers share my own modest goal of a capable working retriever, if not necessarily a field trial winner.

Here I'm discussing dogs at the other end of the bell curve: those that hunt effectively at an early age. Of course, we'd all like all our dogs to be like that, but if they were, the bell curve wouldn't be bell-shaped. Some dogs are just born with what Tom Wolfe called "the right stuff." If I had the ability to pick out these dogs as soon as they are whelped, I'd look like the greatest trainer in the world. I don't, and I'm not.

I have already admitted my inability to identify precocious dogs in advance. If I did anything differently in Rosy's selection, it was paying more attention than usual to her parentage—not so much to her papers and family tree as to personal knowledge. The breeder was a personal friend, and I knew that the dam was just the kind of working retriever I wanted. Other than that, it was the usual crap shoot.

During her first few months, she didn't demonstrate any truly exceptional characteristics. She proved to be enthusiastic and eager but so have a lot of my young Labs. She also demonstrated a mischievous streak that went beyond the usual puppy antics. I always found her after her frequent excursions away from home and never understood why Lori needed all those shoes in the first place. When two of her littermates and their trainers arrived for a visit one summer day, Rosy's only notable performance came in the standing high jump.

She began to distinguish herself when waterfowl season lay a month away and I began working her intensely on hand signals and long-distance marking. I also took her afield during Montana's early sharptail season. With an excellent young GWP in the kennel I didn't see that as part of Rosy's ultimate job description, but she demonstrated enthusiasm, showed no hint of gun shyness, and had a naturally soft mouth. Once again, I found myself eagerly anticipating another waterfowl opener.

With Kenai still going strong, I didn't really *need* Rosy to do anything from the duck blind yet. But Kenai wasn't going to last forever—none of the good ones ever do. As soon as we reached the blind we'd chosen to hunt that morning, I realized I'd made a tactical error. There was only room for one on the dog platform. Based on experience and seniority—not to mention size— Kenai assumed the spot was his. This left Rosy sitting unhappily on the floor where she couldn't see, which all retrievers naturally want to do. Since I wanted her to obtain some marking experience, I boosted her up on the bench between Lori and me.

To focus my attention on the young dog, I left my shotgun unloaded while Lori did the shooting during the first hour. Rosy certainly seemed happier about her modified job description than Kenai felt about his, because I kept him verbally anchored on the dog platform while Rosy handled a series of easy retrieves. When

Lori sent a drake mallard down in some heavy cover at the far end of the pond, however, I decided that the recovery was beyond Rosy's pay grade and sent the old warrior. When Rosy finished the morning fault-free with a half-dozen easy retrieves under her belt, I felt delighted.

In fact, I felt sufficiently confident in what I'd seen to leave Kenai behind the following morning, much to his clearly expressed disappointment. It fell to a pintail drake to prove just what I had on my hands with Rosy. I can't blame the marginal shooting on Lori because I did it myself, leaving the wounded bird sailing down into dense foliage across the pond. Rosy was seated on the dog platform that day. When I looked down at her I saw her eyes focused on the area of the fall. I knew better than to set a young dog up to fail by assigning it an impossible task, but there we were. When I gave the word, she leapt off the platform with just the kind of water entry I continued to admire for the next decade.

She drifted off-line a couple of times during the long swim down the pond, but whenever I blasted my whistle, she turned obediently and looked back for directions. I admit some nervousness when I lost visual contact with her as she entered the cover. I exited the blind and began to slog in that direction, to what end I do not know. Before I was halfway to the reeds she popped out of the cover with the pintail in her mouth, still very much alive and well save for a broken wing. I didn't need the cheer that erupted from Lori back in the blind to confirm that I had just seen something special. That retrieve would have impressed me from a dog of any experience level, much less from one scarcely beyond puppyhood.

I wish I could somehow take credit for what I'd seen that day, but I can't.

Back on the Montana prairie that long ago opening day, Sky came up with a remarkably similar retrieve when I dropped a mallard in the sea of cattails surrounding my makeshift blind. When he turned up 20 minutes later carrying the bird, all my hunting partner could say was, "How did he find that duck?" Damned if I knew. It was an event later in the week, however, that established Sky's reputation as a prodigy.

That marsh didn't attract many divers other than redheads. I generally avoided shooting them because of the big bite they took out of my point-count daily limit, but when a small flock gave us a fly-by I couldn't resist a nicely plumaged drake. Once again, the duck was merely wounded, as is often the case in truly memorable retrieves. True to its species' reputation, it began to dive as soon as it hit the water. I considered trying to kill it with my second barrel, but by the time I spotted its head above the surface Sky—who admittedly had broken—was too close to allow a safe shot. Furthermore, I'd already decided that trying to "swat" wounded ducks on the water is a waste of time and ammunition. If the bird is close enough to give you half a chance of killing it on the water, the dog should get it anyway.

As Sky reached the area where the bird had submerged below the surface, he disappeared as well. I have no idea how many seconds ticked off my wristwatch before the duck's head reappeared several yards away from the site of its first dive, but Sky came up right behind it. By then, the duck was taking full evasive action, with nothing but the tip of its bill visible. To my surprise, Sky sussed that trick out quickly and swam on in furious pursuit, the redhead's swimming pace matched almost exactly by his own. Then the duck vanished again, and the dog disappeared right along with it.

I'd heard of trainers rigging up elaborate pulley systems to teach dogs how to dive in this situation and had considered doing so myself, but could never imagine a reasonable way to teach a dog to swim down wounded ducks underwater. Over the next ten minutes, I lost track of how many times Sky submerged completely in this version of submarine warfare, but he eventually came up with the bird in his mouth. Over the course of his long career, I watched him repeat that performance so often that I no longer thought it remarkable, although a lot of my hunting partners did. As much as I would have enjoyed taking credit for teaching him this behavior, I always admitted the truth.

It always helps to start with a child prodigy.

I'll discuss the issue again further along in the text, but I can't leave this chapter without an important footnote. One should never expect anything before a Lab's second season and certainly should not try to make a youngster do anything it's not ready to do. If you're fortunate enough to realize you have a precocious retriever, just settle back and enjoy the show.

5.

To Err is Canine

To err is human; to forgive, divine.
Alexander Pope

Many of us consider retrievers an essential part of the waterfowling experience, as important as our shotguns and perhaps even as important as the ducks. We routinely celebrate their accomplishments in paint and print. But you don't have to spend a lot of time in a duck blind to realize that retrievers, like kids and stock markets, don't always behave as desired. While there may indeed be no bad dogs as some claim, it's a rare retriever that doesn't challenge that rose-tinted theory from time to time. Unless you've learned to respond to those transgressions with all the patience and humor they deserve, you can't really call yourself a duck hunter.

Bogey, my first Lab, taught me this lesson one opening morning 50 years ago. I was eager—too eager, as events soon proved—to start another season with him after a long summer of training. At first light, I dropped a drake mallard on the far side of a deep but narrow prairie stream. Bogey took the line like a pro, scrambled up the far bank, sat down next to the bird, and refused to pick it up.

No amount of encouragement could break the stalemate. Meanwhile, to my hunting partners' consternation, waves of teal and pintails were flaring overhead as I tried to work the dog. In a splendid demonstration of magical thinking, I finally decided that I could cross the stream in my chest waders and backed up for a running start, an effort that only proved I really couldn't walk on water. By the time I emerged sputtering from the mud, Bogey had compounded the problem by eating the duck—in front of witnesses. So much for my self-esteem as a dog trainer.

In fact, one of Thomas's Laws (readers will hear about more) holds that a dog will always reserve his worst performance of the season for the presence of witnesses, especially those you'd like to impress with some crisp dog work. This principle applies most reliably to the steadiest, most levelheaded dogs in the kennel. Everyone expects puppies to be puppies, but nothing will turn a solid veteran into a decoy-fetching, mud-splattering fool like out-of-town visitors you haven't hunted with for several seasons, who in turn can be counted upon to remember every silly mistake your dog makes and recount those misdeeds over wine at the dinner table for years to come.

If anything invites canine misbehavior more than the presence of friends, it's the presence of other dogs. While I always council against working more than one inexperienced dog from a blind at the same time, retrievers love to dumb themselves down to their own lowest common denominator, a principle that can quickly reduce even the staunchest veteran to silliness. One of the steadiest Labs I've ever owned, Sky would never break from the blind… unless a hunting partner was working a novice retriever, in which case he would sneak out and try to rob the youngster of any bird he regarded as his by virtue of seniority. This obnoxious habit proved difficult to break even through extensive yard work with his kennel mates, and I eventually took to leaving him behind whenever someone else had a young dog they wanted to work—an excellent principle in almost all circumstances.

If retrievers reserved their trying behavior for the field we would at least be spared during the off-season, but that notion represents more wishful thinking. Another of Thomas's Laws dictates that family members will always store their most fragile and highly prized possessions on shelves just the height of a Labrador puppy's reach, just as the pup will always chew on new boots rather than old ones and family heirlooms instead of items headed to the dump.

As related in detail later, a family friend once gave daughter Genevieve a pet chukar, a gesture that must have sounded like a good idea at the time. Although Gen kept the bird securely stowed away in a Sky Kennel inside her room, we'd reckoned without Rocky's determination. While we were away from home one day, Rocky chewed his way through the kennel door, liberating the bird. I will leave the scene that greeted our return that afternoon to the reader's imagination. Trust me to report that you cannot appreciate what mayhem a determined flushing retriever can create when confined inside a house with a game bird all day unless you've experienced it yourself.

Perhaps it is time to redefine Pope's famous dictum about the nature of error and forgiveness. Let us accept that to err is canine and hope we can forgive our dogs without the need for divine intervention.

6.

Young Dog and Helping Hands

Autumn is the most ephemeral of Alaska's seasons. Sometime in late September migratory birds begin to congregate, and the tundra starts to glow in shades of orange and gold. Then in a matter of a few weeks the birds are gone, the warm fall colors have disappeared, and winter's long reign begins.

After two days of trout and char we awoke to northern lights and the first hard frost of the season, a certain omen that another glorious fall on the tundra was about to slip away from us. We'd seen ducks trading up and down the Naknek River right in front of the lodge the night before, and I wanted to bid them farewell before they headed down the Pacific Flyway. As light rose slowly in the southeastern sky, we braced ourselves against the chill, loaded shotguns and decoys into one of the skiffs moored at the dock, and pushed off, accompanied by Connor Scott and his chocolate female Lab, Ellie. For the second time that week, we found ourselves accompanying a young dog on its maiden duck hunting experience.

We already appreciated Ellie's fine manners and cover girl good looks—a block-headed blend of athleticism and femininity wrapped in a rich cocoa-colored coat reminiscent of the local brown bears. I had never enjoyed an opportunity to spend much time around chocolate Labs. As we finished setting out our decoy spread my eyes kept wandering to Ellie as if she were some exotic beauty. Her deportment kept pace with her appearance, for when we finally settled into the grass, she plonked herself down at Connor's side as calmly as a veteran of many seasons.

We quickly realized that the ducks weren't going to behave as admirably as the dog. Most wilderness waterfowl on the Alaska Peninsula have never seen a human hunter, making blinds more elaborate than natural vegetation unnecessary. The birds around the village of King Salmon seemed warier though, and the first two flocks of wigeons and teal flared on final approach to our decoy spread. Ellie needed a slam-dunk—a stone dead bird hitting the water with a splash in the middle of the decoys. When a single wigeon finally made a mistake at the edge of shotgun range I anchored it on the water with my second barrel. I rarely do that, but I wasn't sure the young dog could chase a wounded duck around the river. Fortunately, the borrowed 12-gauge got the job done, and it was finally time for Ellie to go to work.

Her lack of experience became apparent as soon as she reached the bird. After swimming several circles around it she used classical young-dog-meets-first-duck technique to retrieve it—by one primary feather gripped between her teeth as lightly as possible, as if the duck were an Ebola virus specimen headed for a laboratory. By the time dog and duck reached shore, I found myself on the horns of a difficult dilemma. Nothing can ruin a morning of duck hunting faster than unwanted advice, particularly when it's focused on someone else's dog. But I needed to convince Connor that the dog's education was more important to Lori and me than shooting ducks, of which there would be many more in the months ahead. So, I decided to offer some advice born of experience and hope for the best.

My first suggestion was that Connor eliminate as many confounding factors as possible and give the dog the chip shot she needed. With Connor minding the dog, I pitched the bird in a lazy arc toward the decoys. When it splashed down, she made a beeline for the bird and picked it up properly this time, but she dropped it at the waterline on the return.

Connor was trying to be polite by getting on with the duck hunt. However, I pointed out that accepting such typical puppy faults simply makes them harder to correct down the line, and that we were more interested in the dog than adding birds to the duck strap. We wound up calling time out to work on getting Ellie to deliver to hand. Her intelligence and natural enthusiasm made that job progress nicely, and she finished the morning a better retriever than she'd been at first light.

We weren't done with Ellie yet. As Lori and I warmed up back at the lodge prior to a fly rod assault on the Naknek's famous big rainbows that afternoon, I wondered if I'd violated the unwritten rules of duck blind etiquette by offering unsolicited training suggestions. Before I could reach any conclusions, Brian Sexton, the lodge's young chef, ran up the stairs to our room and announced in a worried tone of voice that Ellie had sustained a collision with an ORV and Connor needed whatever help we could provide. We arrived on the scene to find a frantic cluster of staff surrounding the dog, who was obviously a popular favorite around the lodge. Fortunately, things looked worse than they really were. A long, deep laceration on the inside of one foreleg was doing a lot of bleeding, but the underlying bone appeared intact and there was no evidence of injury to vital structures elsewhere.

Lori and I took care of people and not dogs during our former medical careers, but we were way out in the Bush with no veterinary care nearby. So, we rolled up our sleeves and did our best with some improvised suture and a hemostat from the front of someone's fishing vest. Ellie's fine manners saved the day, for she allowed us to clean, inspect, and loosely close the wound without sedation or anesthesia, which were unavailable. Lori applied her nurse's touch to the wound dressing, Connor and I improvised a head cone to keep the dog from chewing it off, and we cancelled our plans to fish the river that afternoon so we could keep an eye on Ellie.

The change in agenda didn't bother me a bit. It's all about the dogs anyway.

When we finally packed up and left Alaska for the year, I felt all my usual ambivalence about our departure. The weather that September had been spectacular, and a rotator cuff tear that prevented me from shooting my bow left me with plenty of unfinished business. On the other hand, I could already feel the season up north starting to slip away, and it had barely started back in Montana. Furthermore, my own dogs were waiting for me, and it was time they got the attention they deserved. As much as I enjoyed our experiences with other people's dogs, it was now time for me to spend some time with my own.

7.

On the Road Again

I just can't wait to get on the road again…
Willie Nelson

I have ranted elsewhere about the difficulties of traveling by air with dogs and once is enough. However, my subsequent resolution to boycott the airlines and travel by ground whenever possible received a stern test during the first six hours of a recent late season trip from our Montana home to Washington State in the wake of a widespread blizzard. Blowing snow rendered the highways treacherous, intemperate drivers kept the pedal to the metal anyway, and so many cars lay planted in the ditch that the road looked like the scene of a demolition derby. By the time we reached bare Interstate near Missoula, my knuckles felt as if they had turned permanently white, and I had to wonder if we shouldn't have stayed at home in front of the fireplace after all.

Well, of course not… While the prime purpose of our trip was an overdue visit to my parents in the Seattle area, Washington's Pacific Flyway duck season runs nearly three weeks longer than our Central Flyway version. After a disappointing late waterfowl season at home, I felt especially eager to watch some birds drop from the sky. So did Kenai, our then five-year-old male yellow Lab… a.k.a.

the Big Horse for reasons obvious to anyone who ever shared space with him in a blind, boat, or cabin. For several seasons, he'd suffered the indignity of playing on the second string, first in deference to his father, Rocky, and then, in upland cover, to our promising young wirehair, Maggie. After an unusually long layoff, he'd worked through most of his rustiness during two days of shooting over a Montana spring creek the week before our departure. I still wanted to give him an opportunity to end his season with a bang, not a whimper.

I've noticed over the years that no experience rebuilds neglected canine relationships quite like a road trip, another argument in favor of vehicles over uncooperative airlines. The Labrador retriever's ancestors were bred to endure protracted stays in small fishing boats off the coast of Newfoundland, where ability to work in concert with their handlers without fraying human nerves became a central feature of their character. Today, vehicle travel requires a certain amount of bonding between hunter and dog in that same spirit. Since the dog must be under constant control, a road trip serves much the same purpose as boot camp, with a happier goal waiting at its conclusion: a duck hunt.

Kenai didn't get his bang during our first stop. On our way to Seattle, we'd planned to hunt our traditional Columbia Basin duck camp, but the weather had left those ponds locked in ice. However, our old friend Michael Crowder had discovered a huge wad of cans and redheads on the Columbia, so we set out in his skiff at first light on a serious diver expedition. Unfortunately, the wind that had concentrated the birds in a bay a few days earlier had fallen to a dead calm. Most of the divers had disappeared, and the few that remained weren't flying. Four chilly hours yielded a grand total of one ring-necked duck.

At least Kenai's deportment left me pleased. He was an exceptionally big Lab, but his behavior inside the crowded skiff proved impeccable as he sat and scanned the sky patiently for birds. There is no sterner test of canine manners than hunting from a boat, but he passed with flying colors. He'd already adjusted happily to life on the road. Confinement to a familiar crate doesn't represent the hardship some naïve observers assume. Dogs are denning animals by nature, and they instinctively regard a comfortable travel box as a source of security rather than restriction. By the time we set off for the wet, western side of the Cascades, Kenai was acting like a dog born to the road.

Dogs played their own role in our welcome reunion with my parents. I offered to keep the Kenai out of everyone's way in the kennel behind the house, but my folks wouldn't hear of it. Longtime hunters and keepers of a dog-friendly home, they invited the big guy in to hang out with Folly, the female Lab that had become the light of my father's life in his old age. My parents threatened to spoil Kenai so badly that I made a point of tossing some bumpers on the lawn every day to remind him that he was on a hunting trip.

After three relaxing family days, we loaded up again and headed for a waterfowl venue I hadn't visited in nearly 50 years: Sequim Bay, on the northern shore of the Olympic Peninsula. As a kid I'd killed my first black brant there, and I felt eager (and a little anxious) to see how this prime saltwater habitat had held up in the face of a half century of development in the booming Pacific Northwest.

Accompanied by our friend Kevin Kennedy, who had arranged two days of shooting at a waterfront location belonging to a friend of his, we arrived to find the northern Olympic Peninsula surprisingly like the way I'd left it decades earlier: damp, green, rather deliberately rustic, and overall looking like a good place to be a duck. As we rolled in and organized our gear for an evening shoot, I chatted with the fourth member of our party, Bill Matthaie, whom I had not met previously. By coincidence, he had received a once lethal medical diagnosis two years previously and was now in remission by way of a hematologic technique my father developed on his way to winning the Nobel Prize in Medicine in 1990. Bill openly expressed the gratitude of a man who is lucky to be around to hunt ducks and smart enough to know it. His only regret was that my parents could not have accepted his invitation to join us.

When Hunter and Tater, Bill's two black Labs, came boiling out of the back of Kevin's rig, I received a stern reminder that Kenai's splendid manners in human company did not always extend to other dogs. An incorrigible alpha male, he immediately went into dominance mode, which looked far worse than it was to those who didn't realize that the threat was posture and growl rather than bite. Fortunately, I'd anticipated this development and, to Bill's relief, had Kenai both leashed and wired for good behavior. Nonetheless, I suspect that Bill and his two dogs breathed a collective sigh of relief when Lori, Kenai, and I set off for a blind on the inside of the saltwater cove while they headed out across the spit with Kevin.

While we'd been staging beside the vehicles, I'd noticed large flocks of widgeon accompanied by a few mallards, pintails, and teal trading back and forth across the cove, which lay sheltered from the breeze gusting across the bay. I'd barely finished setting the blocks when the first set of widgeons buzzed the decoys. Lori hadn't even had time to load her shotgun yet. Although I inexcusably missed the back half of the double, a nice drake lay kicking in the decoy spread by the time the rest of the flock departed. It was finally time for Kenai to do what he'd traveled all those long miles to do.

The easy retrieve offered just one point of interest: Kenai's first encounter with salt water. Despite the inland location of our current principal residence, this realization hadn't even occurred to me until he started swimming toward the fallen duck. Most of my Labs have spent plenty of time in the marine environment, in locations ranging from Alaska to the Texas Gulf Coast. While I've seen dogs react strangely to the realization that they can't drink the stuff they're swimming in, Kenai handled his saltwater baptism casually. After delivering the bird—a gorgeous male that eventually made it to our taxidermist—he sat down in the front of the blind and began to scan the sky patiently for our next opportunity.

However, the birds we'd seen earlier evidently had other things in mind. The breeze out in the bay had dropped off, leaving the surface of our little cove as calm as a suburban swimming pool. Although I foolishly hadn't checked the tide table (after years on the Alaska coast I knew better), I noticed that the rocks in front of the blind were getting larger rather than smaller. Although the water was falling at a glacial pace compared to the tidal currents up north, I've usually done better in salt water on a rising tide, at least for puddle ducks. For whatever reason, the ducks—save for a few buffleheads—had disappeared, and that left us with a problem.

Lori and I had volunteered to cook a duck dinner for our party that night. Although I should know better than to count on fish or game for table fare, Kevin's description of the waterfowl hunting the place offered had made *canard a l'orange* sound like a slam dunk. Lori and I had carefully loaded all the necessary ingredients into our rig prior to departure... except, of course, for the *canard*.

And one widgeon divided four ways wasn't going to make dinner for a Weight Watcher's menu.

To make matters worse my shooting felt off, an observation that warrants a brief discussion. While I can safely if immodestly describe myself as a very good shot on upland birds, waterfowl sometimes make me look bad, especially if I haven't been doing a lot of duck hunting recently. Since decoying ducks just aren't that tough, one must wonder why. Fifty-plus years of pheasants, grouse, quail, chukar, and the like have made me a quick snap shooter, with a style adapted to getting on birds quickly before they fly out of range or behind obstructions. The duck blind, in contrast, offers plenty of time to *think* about incoming birds, which are often coming down instead of going up. I'm not used to thinking about anything when I shoot except safety. It's an interesting conundrum, and I'd be interested to learn if other veteran wing-shooters experience the same problem in the transition from upland game to waterfowl.

All of which explains my frustration when a lone drake widgeon finally appeared and set its wings just beyond the outer edge of the decoy spread. "Take him!" I whispered to Lori while Kenai minded his manners and studied the bird through a gap in the weathered boards that formed the front of the blind.

"You take him!" she hissed back. "We need him for dinner."

Wishing that I shared her confidence, I did just that… or, rather, I didn't. As the bird flared and departed unscathed, a pregnant silence enveloped the blind. It did not help that both Lori and Kenai were too polite to comment.

The remaining hour of shooting light passed in much the same way. We killed a few birds, and we missed a few we shouldn't have. Kenai performed enthusiastically if unspectacularly. It was impossible to evaluate his performance further, since the retrieves were either easy or impossible. The impossibility, in the dog's defense, arose when I dropped a pintail with a long shot only to watch a bald eagle appear from nowhere and snatch it from the grass across the cove before Kenai could get there. I've never watched a retriever and an eagle fight over a duck, but I don't want to. In the end, we wound up supplementing our duck dinner with pork chops from the local market, as stern a lesson in humiliation as any I'd experienced in the field for some time.

The personal high point of our hunt the following morning again came quickly when a set of pintails appeared just as I finished setting out the decoys, and I dropped the drake. Our home county doesn't produce many of these sublimely elegant birds, and I hadn't killed one all fall. The duck looked so beautiful when Kenai delivered it to my hand that I felt perfectly content to watch Lori shoot the few teal that dribbled in over the next several hours while I handled Kenai and manned the camera. Of course, once we finally decided to pick up and head in for brunch, birds started barreling into the cove again as if they'd just been waiting for us to leave.

Nothing makes a retriever smell cleaner than work in saltwater. While the sea wasn't as chilly and unforgiving as the ocean I'd know in Alaska, it's still part of the North Pacific. That's no place for the faint of heart even if the subject is clad in a Labrador retriever's prime winter coat. Nonetheless, Kenai had handled the challenge with aplomb, and if he could talk, I suspect that his only complaint would be about my own inconsistent shooting.

Rather unexpectedly, Kenai finally got his bang when we stopped in camp on our way back home and found a few ponds with open water. In less than an hour we had a varied limit—woodies, green-wings, and the only drake mallard we saw—hanging from the duck strap. Coupled with the pair of birds that Lori dropped, Kenai enjoyed a brisk workout in the icy pond without losing a bird.

The long drive home to Montana and its bitter weather evoked ambivalent feelings. Our Central Flyway duck season was done for the year and there wasn't anything left to hunt at home but mountain lions. On the other hand, we were heading for Texas shortly for three days of shooting on the Gulf with old friends. Since that was too much driving for such a short trip we'd be traveling by air, which meant that none of our own dogs would be going along. I hoped they'd forgive us.

At least our road trip had given me an opportunity to reconnect with Kenai, and our next opening day wasn't all that far away.

8.

Mallards on Ice

Credit the dense, frigid air for the magical acoustics. Even though the creek still lay a hundred yards away, the gurgling progress of its current sounded amplified, as if it were running right past my ear. Gleaming through the crisp mountain air, winter constellations held their ground against the first swell of sunlight from the southeastern horizon: Cassiopeia, the Dippers, Orion with his Dog Star close at heel. I had to wonder if my celestial counterpart's canine friend felt as eager as my own.

Although only in his second season, Rocky, heir apparent after Sonny's long reign as my kennel's go-to dog, knew full well what was up. He'd been acting like a kid on Christmas morning ever since he saw me pull the shotgun out of the cabinet back at home. After the confinement of the ride, he was busy frolicking in the snow like a maniac. We'd been hunting the creek several days a week for almost a month now, but he still hadn't learned to contain that first burst of youthful enthusiasm. Save it for later, buddy, I longed to advise him. If things went right, he would need it.

By the time we reached the creek bank, cool morning light had started to bathe the valley, making the rime that accumulated on the brush along the creek overnight sparkle like fine jewelry. Now came the hard part. I'd lugged those same decoys around for nearly thirty years. Unlike many newer models, they weren't self-righting.

That meant I had to wade out into the backwater and set them all by hand, no pleasant chore when the mercury dipped into negative territory. I kept waiting for those old blocks to fall apart or spring leaks so I'd have an excuse to replace them, but for better or worse their durability exceeded the wisdom of their design. Studying the water below the bank like an Olympic platform diver, I finally sucked in my breath and took the plunge.

Right up through his final season, Sonny always insisted on "helping" me with the decoys, an aggravating habit I somehow never took the time to break. But after all those mornings of tangled lines and shaken dog water turning to ice on my coat, I learned my lesson and started Rocky out right from the morning of his first duck hunt. Studying my progress carefully from the bank he looked like the model of decorum, reminding me what a little extra training can accomplish. I only hoped he behaved as well once the shooting started.

Waiting for the arrival of spring creek mallards on a bitter cold morning goes better once you've learned two important tricks:

concentrating on the beauty of the surroundings and ignoring the cold. Discomfort will eventually visit you no matter how well insulated your waders or how many layers of wool you've piled on prior to setting out. Face and hands are the most vulnerable body parts, but a ski mask and beard – already coated with ice from my condensed breath – take care of the first while warm pockets manage the second. It's the feet that always get you in the end, because once they start to go numb there's little to be done but stomp them until it's time to retire from the field *hors de combat*. One only hopes the ducks will arrive first.

After an hour spent applying those principles as diligently as possible, I'd begun to have my doubts. Pacing back and forth along the bank and stomping my feet in the snow helped, but it was still only a matter of time. Then, thanks again to those remarkable cold weather acoustics, the whole mood of the morning changed as Rocky's ears perked up and he pivoted about to face downstream. His hearing was better than mine, and it took me nearly a minute to appreciate the reedy waves of feeding chuckles that announced the birds' return from the stubble fields where they'd spent the night stuffing themselves with grain.

If I'd done my homework properly—and I liked to think I knew our local waterfowl as well as anyone—some of these inbound birds should have been headed for the inviting backwater where my well-traveled blocks were turning lazily in the current. And sure enough; as the sound of setting wings filled the air, I began to feel like a genius. Suddenly, there were so many birds crowding the airspace above the decoys that neither Rocky nor I knew just which way to turn. From the standpoint of killing a limit, I would have preferred the birds to stagger their arrival, as my shotgun only holds two shells no matter how many ducks are in the air. But that morning, I gladly traded such practical considerations for the intangible value of watching the spectacle taking place overhead. I wouldn't kill any more ducks than I would have had a pair of drakes arrived by themselves, but the sight of all those mallards jockeying for position over a spot of water the size of my living room must rank among the greatest shows on earth.

Faced with such an overabundance of targets, the trick is not to blow it. The mental gymnastics begin with the visual separation of drakes from hens. I consider it important to make sure all my late season mallards have green heads. Legally, two of my hypothetical five-bird limit could be hens. Save for a few ounces of breast meat there isn't much difference between the sexes on the table. But hens are mothers after all, as American an icon as apple pie. I have always regarded killing one inadvertently as a failure.

Trouble is, trying to distinguish drakes from hens while in the act of shooting makes you raise your head from the stock, a compromise of form that in turn leads to embarrassing misses. So, I've learned to pick my drakes while they're still a way out and to concentrate on those birds to the exclusion of all others, no matter what is going on right in front of me over the decoys.

That much accomplished, I watched the pair I'd chosen circle the backwater with flaps extended. When they lowered their legs, I rose to take them. Both folded and dropped like rocks, confirming how little all this had to do with the technical demands of wing-shooting. Barking at Rocky to mind his manners and *stay*, I fumbled another pair of shells into the gun in case another member of the wheeling flock decided to do something foolish. But these birds had been at this all month just as we had. Moments later they were reduced to a scattering of black dots winging their way upstream in search of friendlier water.

Now—*finally*, according to Rocky—it was time for some dog work. I watched the second bird tumble into a swath of thick reeds on the opposite bank while the first lay belly up, riding the current in lazy circles through the decoys. No real challenge there, for which, given Rocky's youth and inexperience, I feel quietly grateful. Giving him a line on the floater—birds in the water always come first when hunting over current—I stood back and savored his entry, which generated almost enough spray to reach me despite the two deliberate steps backward I'd taken to avoid it. Moments later, one plump drake rested on my outstretched glove, creek water already turning to ice on its breast feathers.

The young dog handled the second retrieve in workmanlike fashion as well, but it was hard for me not to think about Sonny in his prime, churning downstream furiously to cut off birds threatening to drift away on the current. There is no substitute for experience in the development of such unorthodox skills. Rocky, while off to a solid start, would just have to invest a few more seasons in their mastery.

Somehow, in contrast to many of the chores on my agenda, I had a feeling this one would prove to be a pleasure.

Here on the high plains, waterfowl season usually does end with a bang. The days of warm prairie sunrises over broad marshes full of mixed flights of puddle ducks may be history, but some of the most exciting and reliable shooting takes place in December, during the final weeks of the long season. Assuming, of course, that you can do what must be done to enjoy it.

Another of Thomas's Laws holds that the nicer the weather, the worse the December mallard hunting will be. The explanation is simple: bitter cold deprives waterfowl of landing options as ponds and slowly moving creeks yield to the icy grip of winter. In any cold region, the key to late season waterfowling is local knowledge of the last water to freeze during winter weather. Such locations take various forms.

In our county, I know of a dozen isolated springs that seldom freeze. They don't hold much water, but they sometimes fill up with ducks packed together so tightly you couldn't pitch a penny into their midst without hitting one. A friend owns a spring-fed pond, part of which stays open during all but the bitterest cold snaps. Even when it does freeze, we've enjoyed fast shooting by kicking out a hole in the ice, setting out a decoy or two, and waiting for wintering mallards to investigate the pond as they leave the fields nearby. When visiting a friend in Alberta a few seasons back, we set up on the cooling pond at a local power plant and killed limits of decoying birds in some of the bitterest temperatures I've ever endured.

Locally, my favorite late season venues are the two true spring creeks that run through the hills I call home. Similar opportunities abound throughout the west wherever large volume springs emerge from the ground at constant water temperature. Often noted for the fly-fishing opportunities they provide during warmer months, these creeks rarely if ever freeze, and provide waterfowl with the reliable sources of open water they need to winter successfully in such inhospitable climates. While they receive some hunting pressure during warm weather, when the temperature plummets most local hunters sensibly retire from the field. That's the time to anticipate fast shooting, if you can survive long enough to enjoy it.

Typical late season duck hunting differs from its warm weather counterpart in several respects beyond the obvious necessity of appropriate dress. Large decoy spreads are seldom necessary, and I rarely carry more than a half dozen—an exercise in parsimony frozen fingers will appreciate when it comes time to set them out and pick them up. Most shooting takes place at close range, and I now do most of this hunting with one of my 20-gauges. Despite the small scope of the water, a capable dog is essential. Once you've gone over the top of your waders on a sub-zero morning, you'll understand why. Sending retrievers into fast current can make for challenging dog work, some details of which I'll discuss later in the text.

Quirky, challenging, and occasionally downright miserable, late season mallards aren't necessarily for everyone. But for those possessed of stout hearts (and perhaps a paucity of common sense), the rewards can be substantial: fast shooting, stirring dog work, prime game for the table, and the satisfaction of knowing that while most of the competition has retired to the couch in front of the television set, you've found a way to keep on hunting.

MALLARDS ON ICE

The last day of any season always produces a certain heaviness in the heart. On the closing day that year, the somber sky overhead seemed perfectly suited to the moment. Lead gray clouds obscured what might have been a gorgeous sunset and carried the promise of more winter still to come. But we were out here anyway, Lori and Rocky and I, watching the clock tick down on a season that began in shirtsleeves and was about to end in multiple layers of wool.

We were set up on a puny backwater kept open by nothing but the constant presence of the landowner's cattle. An old friend, he'd given us permission to shoot there despite the presence of his livestock, and I felt grateful for his trust. It was hard to ignore how much our decoys resembled the cow turds littering the bank, but despite those esthetic compromises I couldn't imagine a place I'd rather be. The night before, I'd watched mallards pour into that spot by the dozen at last light. Even if a fraction of their numbers returned, we'd end our season with a few minutes of frantic shooting and the essential ingredients of the duck dinner I'd promised friends.

The late season is always about promises in the end. The ducks promise to arrive, sometime, and you promise to last until they do. If nothing else, you will have held the end of yet another glorious season at bay for a little longer. That consideration alone justifies all the long, cold waiting.

Suddenly, Rocky turned his head to the sky. I felt sure I heard them coming....

9.

The Beaver Pond

I found the beaver pond while hunting pheasants that year, a welcome discovery during an upland season that could be described as ordinary at best. The dogs were working the heavy brush along a small creek that seldom holds more than an occasional mallard when I noted ducks circling downstream. Over the course of the next hour, several small flocks drop their flaps and spiral into the creek bottom. With nothing but a lone rooster to show for our efforts in the pheasant cover, Lori and our company broke for lunch at the vehicle while Rocky and I set off to investigate.

Armed with lead shot and clad in hunter orange, the expedition was purely exploratory. Only the possibility of flushing an incidental pheasant kept me from unloading my shotgun. As we approached the fence marking the boundary line between the ranch we were hunting and the adjacent property, ducks began to boil out of the willows. Feeling more curious than predatory, I simply stood and enjoyed the spectacle of their departure. Rocky whined his displeasure at my inexplicable failure to shoulder my gun and provide him a reward for his long morning's work.

I quickly discovered the source of the ducks' new interest in the creek. We'd always encountered some beaver workings along the little stream—enough to justify hip waders when kicking the cover for birds. Since the previous season, the industrious rodents had created an ambitious structure to rival Fort Peck dam two hundred miles away to the northeast. The stretch of flooded creek just above the property line now lay 30 yards wide, an attraction the local waterfowl couldn't ignore.

This fortuitous discovery took place mid-October, ordinarily too early in the season for me to start thinking seriously about duck hunting. Due to poor late spring hatching conditions, our pheasant season was largely a bust. Once our bird hunting visitors left for home, I called the patient who owned the ranch and asked if he'd mind Lori and me driving through his yard in the dark to set up for ducks the following morning. He didn't. He never does, but just as you can never be too rich or too thin, you can never be too courteous to friendly landowners.

We rose early the next day, loaded our gear, kenneled Rocky in the back of the truck (leaving young Kenai to howl in protest), and set off toward the Great Perhaps.

It's unlikely that any wildlife species had a greater influence on the course of American history than *Castor canadensis*. Lewis and Clark marveled at the abundance of beavers during their epic journey up the Missouri. Then, thanks to the whims of fashion, an insatiable 19th century European appetite for fur hats nearly did to the beaver what Paul Prudhomme's recipe for blackened redfish nearly did to Gulf Coast drum two centuries later. Long before gold appeared at Sutter's Mill in 1849, fur trappers had established a social and mercantile infrastructure throughout the mountain west. While Americans no doubt would have found their way to California without help from the beavers, the ubiquitous rodents certainly hurried the process along.

Reclusive, nocturnal animals that seldom reveal themselves to human observers except by alarm slaps from their flattened tails, beavers nonetheless exert profound influences on the habitat they call home. While both their industry and engineering acumen are probably overrated (they are, after all, just highly adapted rats), their ability to convert small watercourses into fertile wetlands remains nothing short of amazing. Granted, that amazement may be tempered by aggravation when they've dammed a culvert and flooded the only road leading to your house. But from brook trout to teal, many of our favorite species continue to benefit from the beaver's tireless impulse to tame moving water.

I first learned to appreciate this phenomenon as a kid in northern New York. Beaver ponds may not have provided the easiest opportunities to learn how to handle a fly rod, but they sure held fish. Some of my earliest waterfowling memories derive from evenings beside beaver ponds, waiting for flights of black ducks and teal. Even when the ducks stood us up, I realized that beaver ponds were more interesting places than their manmade counterparts. They were natural, and they felt alive.

In contrast to large marshlands that always seem to hold some waterfowl, hunting beaver ponds tends to be feast or famine. Seldom large enough to support more than a few resident ducks, they're more likely to attract migrating birds interested in nothing more than temporary lodging for a few nights on their way to other destinations. Hence my minor surprise at the amount of activity along the creek that October day, when most ducks still should still have been content somewhere to the north.

Beaver ponds provide some of the most challenging conditions I know for working retrievers. The surrounding habitat usually contains thick, formidable vegetation, which is why the beavers are there in the first place. From the dog's-eye point of view, fallen birds often disappear into dense cover that makes marking difficult and hand signals impossible to see. Even short retrieves can require a dog to negotiate water, ice, mud, cattails and willows, all laced with twigs and branches sharpened to points by the beavers' keen incisors. This is no venue for a young or timid retriever, and even seasoned campaigners can expect to be put to a serious test.

LABS AND WATERFOWL

At the beginning of his fourth season, Rocky had already evolved into something of a waterfowl specialist, an unusual development in our kennel since my retrievers spend so much time hunting upland game. The indifferent attitude he'd shown toward hitting heavy bird cover as a puppy hadn't changed much with time. Fortunately, he had grown so useful in the duck blind that I really didn't care, especially since young Kenai was rapidly turning into a pheasant's worst nightmare. Nonetheless, Rocky had seldom enjoyed an opportunity to hunt ducks in a setting quite like this. Was he ready? Were we?

I only hoped the ducks would give us an opportunity to find out.

An indifferent sky greeted us as we climbed out of the vehicle and began to organize our gear in the dark. The nearly full moon glowed through a thin overcast layer that might have heralded anything from snow flurries to shirtsleeve weather over the course of the morning ahead. Like all serious duck hunters, I secretly longed for the worst. But we were carrying cameras as well as shotguns, and I couldn't ignore the memory of the brilliant autumn foliage gleaming in the sunlight a few days earlier. Bouncing out of the truck in an explosion of canine enthusiasm, Rocky made it clear that he didn't care what the weather did.

As soon as we arrived at the pond, I recognized a potentially serious miscalculation. The new dam had backed the water up into the willows even farther than I thought. There was no way to determine the depth of the open water. I wasn't sure we could set the decoys out far enough for the ducks to see them. The good news: I owned three perfectly good sets of chest waders. The bad news: I'd somehow left all three at our Alaska summer home, reducing me to hip boots that suddenly didn't seem high enough. More good news: Lori had the foresight to wear her chest waders. More bad news: Lori has to stretch to reach five feet in height, making her chest waders not much higher than my hip boots. While the weather felt balmy compared to our usual sub-zero late season duck hunting expeditions, wet waders would still mean an unpleasant morning. Suddenly, it was *Honey, how much do you love me?* time.

In the end, I hung onto some willows while Lori hung onto me. We stayed dry while setting a half-dozen blocks out along the edge of the pond well short of where I wanted them. Displaying his usual impeccable manners, Rocky sat quietly on the bank and watched as if he were waiting for someone to explain the punch line of a joke. Finally, I chambered a pair of shells, and we settled back in the willows to wait.

But not for long.... Rocky picked the birds up first. When I saw his focus concentrate, I followed his gaze downstream and saw a pair of mallards beginning to set their wings. By the time I finished one quick chuckle on the call, they'd slid in right in front of us. I killed the drake and watched the hen fight her way back up into the sky. Then it was time for the dog to go to work.

Of course, a floater belly-up in the middle of the pond would have been just too easy. The bird had fallen only thirty yards away in the willow jungle, but I'd found it difficult to mark because of the height and thickness of the brush around us. The dog's visual perspective had to be even worse than mine. As Rocky crashed off and disappeared into the brush I realized there wasn't a thing I could do to help him, so I didn't try. When the sound of his enthusiastic panting yielded to silence, I knew he had the bird in his mouth. Think that sounds like a simple retrieve? You try it.

For fifteen minutes, we watched a coot and muskrat perform an oddball *pas de deux* in front of the decoys, reminding me why shooting a few birds over a beaver pond can be more interesting than shooting a lot of them in a stubble field. "Single!" Lori hissed suddenly, and by the time I tore my eyes off the ballet the bird was right in front of us. I thumbed the safety and shouldered the gun only to come to a grinding halt. Since 99% of the ducks we shoot in our home county are mallards, a head any color but green reflexively makes me hold my fire. But hesitation didn't last long this time around. "Widgeon!" I blurted out to no one in particular. Then the shotgun's report broke the spell, and the bird was tumbling toward the willows.

My satisfaction extended beyond the shot, which was easy, and the retrieve, which wasn't. Our Central Flyway limit allows a total of six ducks, including no more than five drake mallards. Because of the paucity of other species during the late season, that effectively translates into a five-greenhead limit, which is hardly generous considering the amount of effort required to set out decoys in cold weather. It also means that anything other than a mallard is essentially one free duck, which, in this case, Rocky promptly delivered.

As anticipated, we never saw the waves of ducks I would expect a month later. Thanks to the limitations of our spread, the birds we saw didn't decoy particularly well. But after another hour spent trading shotgun and camera back and forth, Lori and I had several more greenheads and a teal resting beside the widgeon and that was enough. As we began the awkward process of retrieving the decoys more flocks of birds inevitably appeared overhead, but they could wait for another day. I never regretted the decision to pick up early. I'm sure Rocky disagreed, but until he's buying his own dog food, he doesn't get to vote.

There are many ways to measure success in a duck blind, from the number of birds in the bag at the end of the morning to the number of pinfeathers on their breasts. Never a scorekeeper in the field, I usually remember details of particular shots and retrieves more than tallies. Sometimes you go for the circumstances more than the shooting, and so it was that morning on the beaver pond. For a moment, I could close my eyes, rest my hand on Rocky's head, and remember another dog and another day, when a kid sat beside another beaver pond waiting for ducks and trying to imagine what he would become.

In contrast to ducks, no limits apply to the human imagination.

10.

Training Day

By early December that year, I had to acknowledge that young Kenai was overdue for a seminal experience in the life of every working retriever: his first solo in the duck blind.

One and a half years old then, Kenai had developed into a handsome, athletic dog with a winning personality. Every aspect of his early training had proceeded on schedule. He'd tagged along on several upland excursions, during which he'd heard some shotgun fire, tasted a few feathers, and shown impressive enthusiasm for heavy cover. Ordinarily, I'd have had a dog like that in the blind long before the northern mallards began to arrive. In Kenai's case, the delay in this landmark event had nothing to do with shortcomings on his part.

I suppose he could blame his father. Distracted by my bow and arrows, I hadn't done a lot of waterfowling in October and November. When I did go, I just couldn't bring myself to leave Rocky behind. Already the elder of the kennel at age four, Rocky was turning into a delightful duck dog. However, he did have some minor faults I wanted to correct before they became major ones, a goal that didn't lend itself well to including a boisterous youngster in the hunting party. Furthermore, thanks to a habit of running off, Rocky had largely been confined to the kennel outside. I missed his company. The upshot was that whenever it came time to throw the decoy bag in the back of the truck and set off for a local creek or pond, Kenai had stayed behind.

But I've been at this long enough to know that failure to give a promising youngster its due can be a huge mistake. With the last of the big game tags filled for the season, I loaded decoys and waders once again, and when the alarm clock roused me from sleep before dawn, I left Rocky whining in the kennel and let Kenai out instead.

The weather had been unseasonably warm for a week, but I'd enjoyed fast shooting in the company of a friend—with Rocky handling the retrieving chores—one morning the previous week. Without bothering to obtain a scouting report from the landowner, I chose to set up on a slough some five miles south of the pond I'd hunted earlier. Except for Lori, I couldn't talk any of my regular hunting partners into going along. To be honest I didn't try very hard. I wanted the dog to receive my undivided attention on his first duck hunt, with no apologies to anyone for whatever canine transgressions might take place.

The good news: none did. The bad news: that's because there weren't any ducks. Kenai behaved in exemplary fashion, lying quietly at our feet while we scanned empty skies for three long hours, a virtually unheard of development here in December when limits of greenheads prove the rule rather than the exception. Finally, a lone mallard appeared silhouetted against the clear azure sky. When the bird turned to give our spread a look, I realized it was a hen, creating an instant moral dilemma. Daily Central Flyway limits allow two hen mallards, but I never shoot them deliberately. Did my desire to reward a young dog's patience with his first duck retrieve justify violating this principle? To my relief, the bird resolved the issue by circling out of range and departing before I could make up my mind.

Later that week, a sudden cold snap sent snow flying and more geese winging by overhead than I'd seen all year. Confident that the weather would bring birds pouring into the slough, I talked Lori into accompanying Kenai and me again. The radio reported a temperature of 8-below as we headed out of town in the dark with my wife questioning my sanity. "Lousy weather means great duck hunting," I countered cheerfully. But to no avail; after freezing for an hour, we finally picked up and headed home without firing a shot.

Obviously, I was going to have to do some scouting to get Kenai his first duck retrieve... and save my marriage. I left work early the next afternoon and headed to a spring-fed backwater just outside town to see whether the change in weather had shuffled the mallards' cards. While this was essentially an exploratory mission, I've found that I always scout better when I'm carrying a shotgun. Of course, if you're going to take a gun, you must have a dog. Not expecting all that much from a short afternoon hunt, I yielded to the pleading look in Rocky's eyes and opened his kennel door instead of Kenai's.

After a brief chat with the landowner, I shouldered a small bag of decoys and set off through the recently fallen snow, noting with interest flocks of mallards circling a winter feedlot a half mile away. Soon ducks were trying to land on my head as I set out the decoys. By the time I chambered a pair of shells and retreated to a nearby clump of brush, another small flock was descending toward me with red legs extended. I killed two drakes and Rocky made short work of the retrieving duties. After dropping another single, I paused to consider my mission. I was supposed to be organizing a training session for Kenai and a productive duck hunt for Lori, not treating myself to an easy limit of birds. After collecting the blocks and stashing the decoy bag in the brush, I stood still with my gun empty and Rocky by my side and enjoyed the show as wave after wave of plump northern mallards arrived for the night.

Tomorrow, I told myself as I abandoned the darkened slough to the sound of whistling wings and chuckling mallards.

This time around, I really wanted Lori to accompany me. I knew we were going to have a great shoot, and Kenai was her dog as much as mine. As sometimes happens in retriever families, odd distinctions had arisen in Kenai's loyalties to the two of us. Both of us fed him, spent time with him, and threw him dummies, but he came to me when he wanted to work and he went to Lori when he wanted to be a puppy, an arrangement that worked for all concerned. Nonetheless, Lori had a genuine stake in his education and training. She deserved to be there on his first real duck hunt, and he deserved to have her with him.

My enthusiastic invitation, however, initially produced a stony silence for which I had no one to blame but myself. Lori is a tough woman who can tolerate virtually any challenge in the outdoors save one: bitter cold. Fact was, she hadn't quite forgiven me for our last outing.

"Come on, honey!" I gushed upon my return that night. "There are ducks all over the place!"

"That's what you said last time," she pointed out.

"And it's going to be warm tomorrow."

"What does *that* mean?" she demanded. "*Five* below?"

But finally, my powers of persuasion prevailed, and early the following morning we set out together in the dark with Kenai romping happily along beside us. When we approached the tip of the slough, the sound of birds on the water rose ahead of us through the gloom, and as we pitched the blocks between the thin ice shelves lining the shore, wave after wave of departing birds filled the air overhead. "No worries," I whispered as we stood together and drank in the sights and sounds of the spectacle. "If we leave them alone, they'll all filter back after they've fed."

After listening to what sounded like a hundred birds depart, we settled back into the makeshift blind I'd beaten out of the brush the night before and watched the minute hand on my watch creep toward legal shooting light. Ducks arrived right on schedule, but the first two sets ignored us and pitched in to the far end of the slough several hundred yards away. I knew at once what had happened: a wad of birds had remained on the water while we were setting up in the dark, and now the naturals were outdrawing our decoys. Only one option remained: I was going to have to go jump the other end of the slough.

I ordinarily eschew jump-shooting during the late season, when I can usually kill as many birds as I want over decoys. But high banks offered a perfect opportunity, and Kenai needed to get that first mallard in his mouth. So, I brought him to heel and set off through the brush on a circular route that would bring us out on top of the birds. Lori stayed behind to guard the decoys and protect them from anything with a green head.

As we began to approach the water, the dog slipped off and disappeared into the brush. I was whistling him in when an explosion of noise rose behind me and a cock pheasant rocketed into view. Kenai obviously had an excuse for slipping. He'd been busy flushing out the rooster. I'd encountered pheasants along this creek bottom before while duck hunting in late December, often under the constraint of a closed season. But this year, regulations extended the pheasant hunting through the end of the month. By the time I had all this worked out, the bird was accelerating across the water ahead. At the sound of the shot, the pheasant crumpled as a dozen startled mallards took to the air. I congratulated myself for giving the dog a retrieve and clearing the water without having to jump-shoot a duck.

Kenai handled the retrieve in passable fashion, no surprise as he'd enjoyed some experience with pheasants earlier that fall. Back at the blind, I found Lori waiting patiently. With no attractions about other than our blocks, I felt confident the next set of mallards would try to land on top of us. I suggested that she shoot while I handled the dog.

Since our marriage a decade earlier (a timeline that has now stretched to 30 years), Lori had become very proficient at outdoor activities involving bows, fly-rods, and cameras, but she'd been a slow starter with a shotgun. I accept my share of blame: clay birds don't do much for me anymore and we hadn't spent as much time together at the skeet range as we should have. But sensing chip shots on the menu, I decided this would be an excellent opportunity to train two novices at once.

We'd barely agreed to this plan when a flight of six mallards circled the tops of the cottonwoods and plummeted toward the water. "The lead bird's a drake," I whispered as I steadied my hand on Kenai's collar. The dog remained steady and so did Lori. But when the birds finally flared, she rose and missed cleanly.

"You shot behind him," I commented helpfully – I thought.

"Why is it," she asked, "that whenever I miss a bird, you tell me that I shot behind it?"

"Because," I explained, "whenever you miss a bird, that's what you do." Before marital strife could begin to compromise such a promising morning, I called time out and told her how well I remembered similar discussions when I was learning how to shoot under my father's watchful eye, and how the light finally went on in my brain and I *believed* him.

"Fair enough," she finally acknowledged. "But Kenai needs to retrieve a duck. You take the next set."

Just like that, more birds appeared. I picked out a drake and dropped him easily at the edge of the decoys with a big, wet *splat* that sounded loud enough to hear all the way in town. Then I took a few steps through the snow, sat the dog down, and sent him on his first duck retrieve.

The colossal balk I received in return surprised even more than it disappointed. I'd realized early on that Kenai wasn't going to be as precocious as his father, who was retrieving ducks competently under actual hunting conditions by the age of nine months. Kenai had proved himself birdy on upland game. The sight of him sitting on the bank staring at that big fluffy mallard drake left me momentarily befuddled. Finally, there was nothing to do but coax him through the retrieve as if he were still a puppy back on the lawn and retreat downcast to the blind.

"What was *that* all about?" Lori wondered.

Before I could offer any explanations or excuses, I heard more ducks in the air over the creek. Then a lone drake was circling the decoys. Kneeling next to Kenai to ensure his maximum attention, I whispered a plea to Lori: "Honey, I'd really like you to drop this bird."

She did. The duck hit the water with a broken wing and not much else and promptly began to flap away down the surface of the slough, offering the kind of retrieve that can challenge a veteran. As it turned out, the commotion was just what Kenai needed. As duck and dog disappeared around the corner, I set off on foot carrying my shotgun and trying to balance my responsibilities between the dog's training and recovering the wounded bird. In the end I resolved to shoot the cripple if a safe opportunity arose, but it never came to that. Five minutes later, to my relief and amazement, Kenai reappeared with the mallard in his mouth. The fact that we flared another flock of birds during the subsequent round of praise, reinforcement, and celebration didn't bother anyone.

Kenai's initial spell of hesitation had broken, reminding me all over again how thin the line between despair and triumph is in the outdoors. For the next hour, we took turns shooting drake mallards and working the dog. He managed each retrieve with more polish than the last and by the end of the hunt was scanning the skies for incoming birds like a veteran. This is not to imply that he began the day a puppy and finished it a pro. Hollywood may work like that, but life doesn't. However, he had successfully negotiated an important rite of passage and left the field ready to continue his education.

Conclusions? I offer several. No amount of training can fully prepare a young dog for its first experience in the field, so be ready for anything. No matter how enjoyable the hunting with the stalwart of the kennel, all young dogs deserve their day. Above all, on a youngster's first solo, the dog must be the focus of attention. Don't invite anyone along unless they're willing to allow making the dog, rather than their own shooting, the highest priority. And if that means going alone, wait for a day when you don't care about shooting your own limit.

Duck season closed two days after these events. Winter still held the countryside firmly in its grip as duck season closed. Rocky was demonstrating symptoms of withdrawal as was I. I would find ways to compensate chasing cougars through the hills with my bow (happy hounds!), tying flies, finishing book projects, and plotting escapes to warm places full of game and fish. Rocky had to make do by lying in front of the fire and dreaming about next season.

By then I could imagine Kenai dreaming right along with him.

11.

Season Highlights

Sometimes I'm called upon to tell the story of a hunt in which everything goes spectacularly wrong to the point of comedy. No matter how embarrassing the events, I always try to accept my share of the blame, as a hunter, dog trainer, or both. Fortunately, Fate's balance scales have a way of creating a zero-sum game in which good days and bad come out even in the end. Thus, it only seems fair to share some memories of hunts that exceeded expectations—not necessarily because of what I shot (or, in one case, what I didn't shoot) but because of the special places they earned in the complex hard-drive of human memory.

I owe readers an explanatory note. Because these events took place over the span of many seasons and because I write a lot, it's possible that some of you have read versions of this material before. In that case, I hope you will remember that some stories really do improve with retelling, not because of dishonesty or exaggeration but because time often improves the clarity of memory just as age highlights the subtleties of good wine.

So here we go, right down memory lane.

The Whiteness of the Goose

Let's begin with another goose story. Lori and I had just spent a leisurely morning duck hunting on the Texas Gulf Coast at the kind invitation of old friends. We had a mixed bag of ducks hanging from the strap in the back of the blind, and I was enjoying the novelty of a December duck hunt in shirtsleeves instead of the bulky winter clothes I'd be wearing back in Montana.

Pleasantly distracted by something—perhaps the exotic birdlife, perhaps the glimpse of a redfish tail in the decoys—I glanced up to an unexpected sight: a trio of snow geese suspended motionlessly right above the duck decoys. How they got there unnoticed remains a mystery. Snow geese abound in this area at that time of year, but they are almost always either flying at altitude or gabbling noisily far out in the bay. During several previous trips, I'd never had one anywhere close to shotgun range.

Unexpected chip shots like this can sometimes lead to atrocious shooting, but each of us dropped a bird with our first barrel and we collaborated on the third. Stone dead on the glassy water, the geese didn't offer much retrieving challenge save for one point: young Rosy had never seen a dead goose before. She made short work of it though, and soon the first of the trio was in my hand. Although I've never been a dedicated goose hunter as discussed later, those were just the first of many accidental geese she retrieved over the course of her long career.

Remarkably, its plumage was neither bloody nor muddy, leaving me face to face with one of nature's purest forms of white. One of the more inscrutable chapters in *Moby Dick* is titled "The Whiteness of the Whale." I'll spare readers an English major discussion of just what symbolism Melville had in mind, but I knew I'd never seen anything as perfectly white elsewhere in nature—not in a Dall sheep's coat, a winter ptarmigan's plumage, or Alaska's miniature version of Melville's white whale, the beluga.

I've never forgotten the intensity of the whiteness in that goose's plumage.

The Tideline

The first time I visited our Cook Inlet Duck Shack that year, I was alone save for Sky. The flying weather was marginal, and I breathed a quiet sigh of relief when the Cub bounced to a stop in the grass next to the little cabin. Nothing reinforces one's personal insignificance in the vast universe like the silence that follows an aircraft engine's roar after a remote landing. As it happens, I have always enjoyed that sudden blast of solitude. Besides, I had the dog for company.

I hadn't arrived until late afternoon, and darkness was already gathering beneath a thick, gray ceiling. I thought about retreating from the drizzle and firing up the Duck Shack's oil stove. However, I had come to hunt ducks even though I didn't expect many until freezing weather in the Interior pushed birds down to the Inlet's open salt water. With the tide ebbing, I could have hiked across the flats to one of my customary spots. However, given the limited light I decided to set up on the pond right in front of the shack even though no one ever shot much there.

I tossed out a dozen decoys in front of a log the last high tide had deposited in the grass. I had barely sat down when a flock of teal flew by and turned into the wind. Sky handled the two retrieves casually. Next came a flock of wigeon, and then another, and by the time the light finally drained from the sky I had a limit of ducks resting beside me.

The rain had picked up by then, and after plucking the pair of teal I hung the rest of the birds and retreated to the shelter of the shack. Teal cooked in a cast iron skillet over a Coleman stove may not sound like gourmet fare, but they served the purpose that night. Finally, I curled up in my sleeping bag with the dog at my feet and listened to rain pound the tin roof overhead until I drifted off to sleep.

I'm not sure why the memory of that night always rises to the top when I think back to the Duck Shack. I experienced more spectacular shooting there on numerous occasions and always enjoyed the company of my two hunting partners when they were around. Chalk it up to the special ambience created by a combination of solitude, security against the elements, good shooting where I hadn't expected any, and the company of a great dog. Memory works in strange ways.

Unloaded Guns

At the time, I didn't appreciate what exceptional circumstances I enjoyed during my first two years on the Montana prairie back in the early 1970s. Ordinarily that country is dry enough to qualify as semi-desert, but exceptional rains had turned the landscape green, provided a bumper grain crop for local farmers, filled reservoirs to the brim, and brought forth a terrific hatch of waterfowl. I have never enjoyed better duck hunting.

The other two young physicians stationed at the Indian Health Service Clinic with me were also avid hunters. We were in the field as much as our work schedule allowed, two at a time since someone always had to stay behind to deal with emergencies. We had located what the map optimistically called a lake just a few miles from home. In fact, it was just a low spot in a muddy creek drainage that the unusual summer rains had turned into miles of ideal duck habitat. During the two years we spent there, we never saw another hunter.

I learned a lot about the chronology of prairie duck hunting during my first season there: a month of relaxed shooting for local ducks; a week of craziness when the northern birds arrived from Canada; and then back to the pheasant cover once the first arctic cold front turned all that water into ice. On the afternoon in question, Dick and I had left Ray in charge of the emergency room and headed out on a balmy Indian summer afternoon hoping for the best. Of course, Sky came with us.

An hour over the decoys produced nothing but a couple of scruffy gadwalls. Shooting light about to end and a long slog back through the marsh still ahead, we picked up early and set out for dry ground. We were halfway there when, as suddenly as if a switch had been thrown, a roar of wings began to build high overhead as vast vortices of migrating mallards descended upon the marsh. Evidently believing in the security of numbers, they behaved as if we were invisible and started landing right on top of our heads—literally. Twice I felt wings brush against my face. At some point, Sky jumped up and grabbed one out of the air. Fortunately, it was a drake.

Legal shooting light was almost over, although the spectacle left us both too stunned to shoot. When I finally started to raise my shotgun, I hesitated, lowered the barrels, and unloaded. Glancing over at Dick I saw that he had spontaneously reached the same conclusion. Some events are just too remarkable to interrupt with gunfire, and this was one of them.

That is the story of how I spent what may have been the most breath-taking half-hour of duck hunting I've ever enjoyed standing still with an empty shotgun.

It's no coincidence that two of these three vignettes feature Sky, who became great despite my own inexperience as a trainer. These snippets of memory offer examples of what can make a day in the field exceptional: spectacular outdoor settings; unique varieties of waterfowl; enjoyable canine company; remarkable wildlife displays. Furious shooting seems notable for its absence from this list. I won't pretend that I don't enjoy those days too, but if I've learned anything about the subject over the years it's that there is more to duck hunting than shooting ducks.

12.

Lone Star Labs

After growing up in the Pacific Northwest, the sight of the sun rising from the ocean in the morning always feels disorienting. I'm conditioned to watching the sun's disc meet the watery horizon on its way down at the end of the day, not emerge from it at the beginning. But there it came anyway, far out in the Gulf of Mexico, flooding the saltwater marsh with golden light and reminding us—Lori, the two dogs, and me—that it was time to start thinking like duck hunters instead of non-consumptive users of wildlife on a bird watching tour.

We had certainly enjoyed plenty of distraction as we set out the decoys and settled back into the blind. By the time the duck hunting gets good on Montana spring creeks in December most of the local birdlife has departed for the winter, leaving little to look at but magpies, ravens, raptors—and mallards, if you've done your homework. Here in South Texas though, the brackish wetlands were alive with bird species I hadn't seen in decades. The spectacle left me mesmerized, and I might have missed the first flock of teal completely if Rosy's body language hadn't alerted me to their impending arrival.

Rosy probably saw ducks better than I did back then and I know she heard them better. I could not determine whether the cue that caught her attention that morning was audial or visual, but when I followed her line of sight down the pond, I could see little dots silhouetted against the pink sky behind them. Given the way the ducks fluttered about erratically in formation, they could only be teal. By the time I'd reminded the dogs to *sit* and thumbed the safety on my shotgun, they were over the decoy spread. When we rose to meet them, green wings burst away in all directions like a Fourth of July fireworks display. I had to remind myself consciously to concentrate on one of them and ignore the rest. Moments later, Lori and I each had one bird down and kicking in the decoys and I knew my second barrel had sent a cripple sailing into the grass on the far side of the pond.

Now I found myself on the horns of a dilemma. I knew I needed to get Rosy started on the long retrieve, but 18-month-old Kiska had been a slow starter, and I wanted to give her a chance at one of the chip shots lying in the decoys. Against my better judgement—working a youngster simultaneously with another dog invites chaos, as I'll advise elsewhere in this text—I told Kiska to *sit* and gave Rosy the long line. I had to hand signal her *back* through the decoys and past the easy falls, but soon she was lined out and chugging for the far shore. Then I stepped out of the blind and sent Kiska paddling through the decoys.

All this turned out better than I had any right to expect. Kiska ignored the blocks and picked up one of the fallen teal while Rosy vanished into the grass a hundred yards away. By the time Kiska completed another lap around the spread and picked up her second bird, Rosy was headed for home with a live green wing in her mouth.

A chorus of goose-talk from the bay cut short the warm fuzzies for Kiska as we all scrambled back into the blind and I fumbled for my goose call. I remember feeling acutely aware of how glad I was to be in Texas.

The previous day, fatigue had left me blinded to the appeal of our surroundings. Since we were arriving from our winter quail hunting home in Arizona, we'd chosen to drive rather than deal with the airlines, which is why we'd been able to bring two dogs along. By then I'd decided that transporting dogs is such a hassle for the airlines that they discourage it by doing everything in their power to make it as expensive and inconvenient as possible. I can't prove that theory, although experience seems to support it. Perhaps I just need to get a friend in the medical profession to write a letter confirming that I suffer from some vague mental condition and need my Labs with me as "emotional support dogs." That wouldn't be far from the truth.

I'd been at the wheel for what felt like forever by the time we reached Victoria, Texas. Although I'd never been there before, I felt an odd historical resonance as we drove down its quiet streets. Nearly a century earlier, my mother had been born in Victoria. She left at an early age and never looked back, probably because her father was a violent, alcoholic sociopath. My grandfather had disappeared long before I was born so I never had the dubious pleasure of meeting him, but the few faded photographs that have survived the years show a tall cowboy built on a Marlboro Man template, the last guy you'd want to see bearing down on you in a barroom brawl. Apparently, he engaged in more than his share of them.

Don't worry—this really is a story about dogs and ducks, not dark family history, and we'll get back to them in short order. I just feel the need to ground the hunting in the personally complex setting in which it took place, if only because we owed our presence there to a different kind of Texan, the one that is hospitable, generous, and gracious. One can't truly understand the hunting without understanding the people who make it possible.

One fall day two decades earlier, I'd fielded an out-of-the-blue call from a visiting bird hunter who knew me as the editor of a bowhunting magazine and thought I might like to meet his father. He turned out to be Bill Negley, a gracefully aging legend within the bowhunting community. In addition to a distinguished career in the oil business and crucial work on the conservation of inshore Texas redfish populations, Bill was the first hunter to kill the Big Five of African dangerous game with a bow, mostly without rifle backup. Of course, I wanted to meet him. Bill, his son Dick, and Marshall Davidson came over for dinner, and we went pheasant hunting together the next day. The invitation to hunt ducks with them on the Texas Gulf Coast was a classic example of an offer one cannot refuse.

That Texas waterfowl expedition soon became an annual event. The shooting ranged from good to fast and furious, but the enjoyment Lori and I derived from the trip was always about more than what was hanging from the duck strap at the end of the day. In Texas hunting is a social event, and the company was always engaging despite political differences that never boiled over into arguments.

(Well, almost never.) Buckets of fresh Gulf Coast oysters invariably found their way to the dining room every night. And where else could I lay a fly line out through the middle of a decoy spread and hook a redfish while I was duck hunting?

The variety of birdlife in the marsh always left me fascinated. It included birds I wanted to shoot at as well as birds I simply wanted to observe. Late season duck hunting in Montana consists almost entirely of mallards—a nice problem to have according to most of my friends, but one that still left me longing for an occasional change of pace. On the Gulf Coast that was seldom a problem. Making a positive identification on inbound ducks was often harder than hitting them. Canvasbacks, redheads, and scaup were frequent visitors to our decoys whenever wind was kicking up out in the bay. On some mornings, the sky was full of pintails. I killed my first (and thus far only) mottled duck there and even identified it as such before I slapped the trigger.

Geese were abundant, although they usually spent most of their time rafted up in huge flocks offshore. However, as related earlier, enough lost singles and small groups traded up and down the marsh to justify including a few goose decoys in the duck spread. Most of the geese were snows, but there was a little bit of everything. One morning I managed a trifecta of snows, speckle-bellies, and a lone honker, which I've never done anywhere else south of the Alberta prairies.

The dogs always loved the trip, and not just because they got to fetch a lot of birds. The balmy weather provided them a welcome break from Montana winters, and the presence of other duck dogs always gave Dick's place the feel of a day care center for retrievers. No matter how tired the dogs appeared at the end of the morning hunt, they always summoned the energy needed to romp with new friends. Old Kenai, a regular companion on our early trips to the area, even developed a taste for wading alongside me when I grabbed my fly rod and headed to the bay for redfish after the hunting was done.

As appealing as the warm, ice-free water of the marsh must have felt to them after weeks of sub-freezing mallards around our Montana home, it came with an asterisk that I recognized the first time I spotted an eight-foot gator hauled out next to the airboat. Our hosts assured us that it was winter even though it didn't feel like winter to us, and the cold-blooded reptiles were too sluggish to be dangerous. Even so, the mere thought of one of my dogs disappearing in a boil like a surface popper vanishing into a pike's maw gave me nightmares. Despite our friends' nonchalance toward gators during the winter, they acknowledged that they kept their dogs on dry land during the early teal season.

The next flock of ducks to appear on the morning described earlier obviously consisted of something other than teal as they came barreling in low to the water in tight formation. When they turned into the sun, I could tell that they were canvasbacks and dropped the lead drake while Lori uncharacteristically missed. Since I wasn't sure the bird was dead, I sent Rosy after it while Kiska remained behind as an observer. My silent apologies to the youngster were sincere, but I wasn't about to let her lack of experience cost me a can. I felt confident that she'd soon have more opportunities to learn on teal lying dead in the decoys, and I was right.

We'd nearly reached the duck limit by mid-morning, when the birds seemed to stop flying. Lori and I remained relaxed in the sunshine, working on Kiska's grasp of the *hold* and *drop* commands and trying to identify the more obscure varieties of wading birds trading back and forth behind the blind.

By the time we heard the airboat approaching from the far side of the marsh, we were done. When Dick coasted in to pick us up, the boat's bow was awash in white geese. Current limits allowed hunters to shoot more snow geese in a day than I felt like plucking, a reasonable biological response to the species' continental overpopulation and the havoc the birds are visiting upon their fragile arctic nesting habitat. All of us felt delighted to have done our share to address this potential ecologic crisis.

I've never understood the poor reputation snow geese enjoy as table fare. I've eaten plenty of snows and always found them good even though I wouldn't trade a speckle-belly for one. Breasted, marinated, and grilled over coals that night those we shot that morning made for a memorable meal, although the redfish ceviche and freshly shucked local oysters that accompanied them certainly could have contributed to this impression. The dogs certainly found nothing wrong with the hearts and livers we added to their food dishes as a reward for their hard work and good behavior.

13.

The Best Laid Plans

Back during my childhood days in the Atlantic Flyway when my dad and I depended on our German shorthair to fetch what few ducks we shot, woodies were an important quarry. They weren't as challenging as black ducks or as tasty as teal, but they were beautiful, and they were there. I missed them when our family moved West, for I hardly ever saw one in Washington, Alaska, or Montana, the states I lived in following our westward relocation. While their resurgence in the Northwest has been gratifying, I rarely target them now. There are other ducks I'd rather shoot and eat. However, sometimes one makes us an offer we can't refuse.

Such was the case one bluebird early season morning in Washington several years ago. By then, Lori and I had decided we'd just as soon look at mounted ducks as stare into the glass eyes of big game animals we'd taken with our bows. Since reaching that decision, every season we'd look for a good specimen of a different waterfowl species to take to our favorite taxidermist, not because we were trying to build a museum but because good mounts of flying ducks are intrinsically beautiful. Now Lori wanted a wood duck, and who could blame her? Besides, it had been another slow morning, and young Kenai needed some work.

Perhaps these factors influenced Lori's shot selection. When the first drake wood duck of the year buzzed the outer edge of the

87

decoy spread, I thought the range was marginal for her 20-gauge. However, I couldn't fault her for taking the shot. Nothing seemed to happen to the duck when she took it. As it flew over the slough west of the blind however, I noticed it slowly but steadily losing altitude before it disappeared behind a dense clump of brush. It would have been easy to ignore this observation, but I couldn't.

As I've noted elsewhere, a great retrieve from a duck blind is like a field goal in football. If the team had done its job perfectly in the first place, the result would have been a touchdown on the playing field or an easy retrieve in the marsh. I'm not criticizing my wife's shooting. Lori is quite capable with a shotgun, and few of us are sharp during the first week of the season. No one likes wounded birds, but she didn't do anything I haven't done, as have the rest of us.

However, this was not a job for a puppy. I had nothing but a general sense of where the bird might have gone down, if it had gone down at all. I told Lori to keep Kenai with her and guard the decoy spread while I stepped out of the blind and gave Rocky the line, which he took in his usual laconic manner. Anticipating that he might need some help, I walked the shoreline next to a nasty wall of flooded Russian olive. When I rounded the first corner, I saw the dog staring intently at a patch of aquatic grass in in knee-deep water. Then the rodeo began.

I had already decided that the duck would likely be dead if it was down at all, and that if it were merely wounded it would likely have headed deep into the brush. I was wrong on both counts. Rocky looked like a fox chasing a mouse is he pounced up and down at the bird, which was diving and swimming in circles underwater. As I closed the gap between us, I noticed a faint wake heading across a stretch of open water beyond the dog, interrupted occasionally by the tip of the duck's bill. After securing Rocky's attention with a whistle blast, I cast him in that direction. The duck led him on a merry chase through the brush on the far side of the pond, but eventually he was back at my side with the drake cradled in his mouth. Some field goal.

THE BEST LAID PLANS

Working dogs in hunting situations is very different from working them in the yard, where it's possible to control many of the variables that can affect a dog's learning and performance. In the field, strategies don't always follow the script. As Robert Burns once put it (in Scottish dialect), such plans "gang aft agley".

A long list of factors can contribute to the unpredictability that underlies most of these busted flushes, with weather often at the top of the list. Modern technology has greatly increased our ability to predict tomorrow's cloud cover or wind direction. However, such prognostication is always vulnerable to surprise simply because no one really understands the weather. It's one thing to note that a cold front is moving in from the Pacific, but it's much more difficult to explain why. Perhaps last week a butterfly in China beat its wings faster than expected? Since it's logically impossible to prove a negative, that explanation would be difficult to refute.

Some years ago, soon after Lori and I got married, we set off with two friends on New Year's Day to hunt geese near some open water on the lower (to us Montanans) Missouri River. We expected typical Montana winter weather, but the forecast didn't call for anything colder than the mid-20s. After a four-hour drive across the prairie, a productive afternoon of scouting led us to a stubble field loaded with geese and permission to hunt it the following morning.

We didn't have much choice in lodging that night, but the only motel within 50 miles was right across the street from the bar and the manager of both establishments cheerfully gave me permission to bring my dog inside with us. By then, Rocky had grown into a tough, weatherproof yellow Lab with plenty of experience under his belt and I knew he would have been fine sleeping in the back of the truck. Even so, I thought that after a long day of driving he deserved a comfortable night inside.

The first thing I noticed when I stepped out into the dark the following morning was how cold it felt even though I was bundled up head to toe in layers of high-quality outdoor clothing. My old truck didn't have an Outside Air Temperature gauge (otherwise known as a thermometer) but I didn't need one to know that lying motionless in a frozen wheat field wasn't going to be a comfortable way to spend the morning. The good news, from the perspective of comfort if not the shooting, was the total absence of breeze. After discussing the amount of time and effort we had already invested in the hunt and the number of geese we'd seen trading in and out of the field the previous day we unanimously agreed to proceed as planned. Since this was Lori's first goose hunt, I felt proud of her resolve.

Since there was absolutely no cover around the field, after dumping off my hunting partners and a big pile of decoys I drove down the dirt road and parked the truck sufficiently far away that it wouldn't flare educated late-season geese, or so I hoped. By the time I walked back the decoys were in place and the gabbling from the nearby river was building to a slow crescendo. Since our layout blinds weren't any more comfortable than anticipated, I did the gentlemanly thing and let Rocky curl up next to Lori to provide her with a passive external heat source.

Despite the imminent departure that the racket from the river suggested, the birds took their own sweet time getting wheels up. But as often happens on goose hunts (although not nearly often enough), the excitement level redlined quickly once the birds got airborne. The first flock's pass left five big Canadas stone dead in the decoys while one more waddled off faster than I could run. Rocky chased the cripple down however, silencing some low-level skepticism I'd heard about bringing a dog along on a field hunt.

We killed three more birds on the next pass, but by the time we had them added to the pile my hands were so cold I couldn't feel my shotgun's trigger. "I think we have enough geese," Lori said. "We still need to clean them."

After making a great show of counting the dead birds I said, "We're limited out anyway," even though I knew we weren't. No one objected.

The hike back to the truck was a nightmare, as a newly arisen breeze in my face kept freezing my eyelids shut. I wound up walking backwards most of the way. At least the truck's heater provided some temporary respite from the cold as we picked up our gear. The bar across the street from our motel served breakfast, and the friendly owner invited Rocky inside to join us as we warmed up. "I thought you said you checked the weather!" one of our hunting partners complained. "It wasn't supposed to be colder than the mid-20s!"

"I've thought it over and recognized my mistake," I said. "I think the report really said mid-20s *below.*" The thermometer outside the window supported this explanation of events.

"Help me understand," Lori said as her shivering fingers spilled coffee all over the table. "We're doing this because it's *fun?*"

Absent a ready answer to this question, I turned my attention back to the best, warmest omelet in memory. The fact that Lori didn't balk when someone suggested staying over to hunt again the following morning convinced me that I had married the right woman,

One October day long before that sub-zero goose hunt, two friends and I set out from our homes on northeastern Montana's Fort Peck Reservation for one of the variety-pack days of hunting we used to enjoy regularly during those great times. Dick, Ray, and I constituted the entire medical staff of the local hospital and knew every rancher for miles around. With few exceptions, we could hunt anything anywhere we wanted. Since Dick still had his antelope tag, he threw a rifle into the back of the truck, and I did the same with my old recurve bow even though I had no realistic expectation of shooting anything with it. We all brought shotguns and boxes of shells. One bag of decoys went in, and I brought waders in case we had an opportunity to set them out. Sky and Lester, Ray's hardheaded Chessie, rounded out the team.

Late that afternoon, Ray and I watched Dick fill his antelope tag and added the buck to the three limits of pheasants and scattering of sharptails and Huns in the truck bed. Although the weather was pleasantly crisp, we decided we should work our way back in the direction of home so we could care for the antelope carcass properly. We were driving down the kind of backroad known only to locals when we passed a tiny pond and noticed a flock of teal sitting in the lee of old WPA era earthen dam. Should we? Of course we should.

However, we immediately recognized a tactical problem. There was no brush around the pond, and even the grass had been grazed down to the dirt. The only cover was the dam itself, which we could reach undetected by walking up the gully below it. By this time, however, the teal had drifted out of range from the dam. The only way to make this work would be by sending two of us behind the dam while the third circled around the other end of the pond in plain sight. With luck, he would flush the birds over the top of the dam and into shotgun range for two of us. A quick game of rock-paper-scissors determined that Ray would play the part of the sacrificial lamb.

Dick and I executed the sneak flawlessly, and once we were in place I cautiously raised my gun barrels over the top of the dam as a signal to Ray. Five minutes later we heard him yell, "They're up!" Then, as we began to rise into shooting position, we watched the whole flock execute a quick 180-degree turn and fly right back over Ray, who doubled smoothly. "Some sacrificial lamb!" I growled at Dick.

A few minutes later, we were standing together at the open end of the pond watching the dogs complete two easy retrieves. Dick had recently purchased a new shotgun several pay grades above anything any of us had ever owned—a Pigeon-grade Browning O/U, as I recall. Ray hadn't even had an opportunity to see it yet, much less shoot it. "Mind if I have a look?" he asked as Sky crawled out of the mud with the first downed teal, and then the two of them exchanged shotguns.

After accepting the bird from Sky, I glanced up and spotted an event in progress that only teal would ever consider. The whole flock was returning to the pond on a vector that would carry them right by us. Ray hadn't reloaded his shotgun, which was now in Dick's hands. I had emptied mine because I'd seen no reason not to. Dick's new gun was the only one still loaded, and Ray was holding it. The story wouldn't be nearly as good had he missed, but he wasn't about to let that happen. "Nice shotgun!" he said as he handed it back to Dick and we watched the dogs crash into the water to clean up his second double.

With that, the "Sacrificial Lamb" became a regular part of our hunting lexicon, where it remains to this day. Newcomers to our circle can't understand why we use it to describe a desirable job description rather than one to avoid.

Is there a deep inner meaning to these stories and others like them lurking in my memory? I hope not, for one of the joys of being in the field with friends, family, and dogs is the opportunity to avoid worrying about factors beyond our control. However, it's worth remembering how unpredictable life afield can be and how easy it is for even the best of our plans to "gang aft agley," as Burns put it. In fact, uncertainty is one of the factors that helps keep the combination of dogs, shotgun, and wildlife so interesting.

14.
Obligations

The morning had largely been uneventful and dreary, offering the kind of duck hunting experience writers generally avoid describing. The time was late November, and a listless mass of gray scud lay over the valley, turning the landscape into monotonous shades of gray. It wouldn't have taken much wind to push the overcast away, but the air lay still. Our decoys looked lifeless as they rested on the calm surface of the pond, and the ducks weren't flying.

By mid-morning, we had a grand total of one greenhead hanging, a result of the only shot I had fired since shooting light arrived. Even perpetually intent Rosy was growing fidgety. Kiska, still a youngster, hadn't enjoyed enough experience to know the difference between duck hunting and sitting in the rain. Leave it to my wife to produce an adventure on a morning like this.

The lone mallard appeared from nowhere over the decoys after approaching from the brush-choked blind spot behind us, offering a tough shot at best. The bird was already climbing when I heard her shotgun bark, and it kept on flying despite her second barrel. Had I realized she'd hit the bird I would have fired as well, but I didn't. Then I saw it slowly begin to lose altitude over the far end of the pond and disappear behind a berm separating us from a larger body of water behind it.

The berm lay over 100 yards away, but I couldn't see over it and I couldn't tell how far the duck had flown before it went down. I had marked the bearing to the fall reasonably well but had no idea of the range. However, I felt reasonably certain it was dead as most birds that go down despite having two intact wings usually are. The berm's eclipse would make it impossible for the dog to see hand signals even if I'd known where to send her. Although the chance of recovering the bird seemed slim, I felt an obligation to try.

After unloading my shotgun and leaning it safely in a corner of the blind, I set out with Rosy at heel. Since the berm was the only dry ground around and offered the best opportunity for the dog to pick up scent, I began by casting her through the thick brush along its banks. After she covered the whole berm thoroughly without smelling anything of interest, we walked back to the point of beginning.

As I tried to form a plan, I began to wonder if one duck that might not even be there was worth all this effort. Then I noticed something out of place far out on the surface of the large pond. It could have been just a clump of aquatic grass, but it could have been a dead duck. Perhaps my brain simply registered the presence of something I hadn't noticed there before. Whatever it was lay in open water three times shotgun range from shore. I lined Rosy up and sent her.

From there it was nothing more than a couple of hand signals *back* until the dog saw what I was seeing and retrieved Lori's mallard, our second and last on an otherwise unremarkable morning. There wasn't anything epic about Rosy's performance. Technically, it didn't require much beyond enthusiasm and some basic handling ability. However, that retrieve left me thinking hard as we picked up the decoys and walked back to the Duck Truck. Why do we fret so much about the recovery of a single bird? Why do we invest so much energy in our dogs and lost game even when it isn't necessary for our survival?

OBLIGATIONS

I came by this obsession the true old-fashioned way—I inherited it. Despite his accomplishments later in life, my father grew up poor in rural Texas during the Great Depression. Dad started hunting for the most basic reason of all—to put meat on the table. He never forgot those hard times. I was raised to believe that recovering what you shot was even more important than shooting it. In the days before my family acquired its first capable retriever (Bits, a German shorthair pointer introduced elsewhere in the text), when someone knocked a gamebird down, we searched until we found it or exhausted all possibilities of recovery. Waterfowl hunting was limited to small water no deeper than our boots.

That first shorthair changed our wing-shooting lives. We no longer had to interrupt an afternoon in the grouse cover to search for a fallen bird. We could hunt ducks wherever we could find them. (Bits was remarkably capable in the water, an observation I put to good use with a GWP decades later.) There was a downside. While childhood friends who hunted without retrievers developed the ability to mark downed birds accurately as a matter of necessity, I neglected that skill. I didn't need it, because the dog always found what we shot.

When Labs began to enter my life, I experienced a subtle change in attitude toward retrievers. No longer simply a matter of utility in the field, they became an end unto themselves. During the off-season, I spent more time working with them than I really had to, and once autumn rolled around I either couldn't or wouldn't bring myself to hunt anything that flew without them. The deep, underlying sense of obligation to recover every bird I shot became even more powerful. I would have much rather spent a morning in a duck blind without firing a shot than go home with a limit of mallards after losing one. I still feel that way.

This discussion circles us back to central questions about how our dogs came to be what they are today and why we have retrievers in the first place. While our Labs' ancestors came from North America, they became the dogs we know today in the British Isles, where much of their job description involved retrieving driven grouse and pheasants for the landed gentry. Their owners obviously didn't depend on the dogs' performances for their dinner. Instead, they were a matter of convenience and style once the gunfire had stopped at the end of a drive.

Leave it to us hardscrabble colonials to introduce a mercenary element into the dogs' lives. Back in the market hunting days, a good Chesapeake Bay retriever could mean the difference between profit and loss when a day of commercial canvasback hunting ended. While I certainly don't feel any nostalgia for those bad old days, I suspect that the pressure to perform that they created influenced the genetic makeup of the retrievers we know today.

I'm confident that no one reading this book is a market hunter or an entry in *Burke's Peerage*. Our crowd enjoys a variety of motivations for the effort and enthusiasm we invest in our hunting retrievers, ranging from companionship in duck blinds to improved field trial performance. All are valid. But at some level, I suspect that most of us who hunt with our dogs share the motivation that matters most to me: an underlying sense of obligation to recover what we shoot and turn it into food for family and friends rather than an unexpected treat for scavengers. The best of our retrievers seem to feel the same way.

The following year, Rosy produced another Retrieve of the Year nomination from a blind less than a mile away from the one just described. Lori and I had invited our close friend Glenn Elison and his young female black Lab on that trip to our Washington State duck camp. Like me, Glenn had deep roots in Alaska, where he served in the Fish and Wildlife Service and managed several important National Wildlife Refuges during his long career. We had both developed the habit of giving our dogs names with Alaska themes. By total coincidence, we had both named our up-and-coming young females Kiska after an island near the end of the Aleutian Chain. On this trip Glenn's dog was performing well for her age, but I had left our Kiska at home because she had seemed reluctant to work in cold water.

The events that follow took place on an afternoon hunt in early December. With an hour of shooting light remaining, we had a half dozen mallard drakes and a brace of teal hanging in the back of the blind. The ducks had been trickling in as singles and pairs all afternoon when a nice little flock of mallards surprised us from behind the blind. Everyone shot something although we never did determine just who shot what. The good news was that none of us had mistakenly killed a hen in the confusion. The bad news was that the bird I shot with my second barrel made a long, slow descent over the top of a dense Russian olive cluster a hundred yards away at which point I lost sight of it. These events reminded me of the situation the year before as described in the beginning of this chapter, with one important exception. Something told me that this bird was still alive.

With the heart of the evening flight due to start arriving at any time it would have been easy for me to forget the long cripple, reload, and get ready for the fast action expected soon. I couldn't and I didn't.

As Glenn's dog started to work on the birds lying in the decoys, I noticed that Rosy's line of sight remained focused in the direction of the long fall. After some consideration, I sent her. I decided to exit the blind and explained my intention to Lori and Glenn. I wanted to be well out of the way so they could safely shoot incoming birds. Another factor further complicated my plans. The year before we had lost Rosy in the same area and almost didn't get her back. I wanted to remain as close to her as possible.

At the beginning of that fiasco, I'd had her on a leash inside the blind because I was working with young Kiska. When Rosy broke on a retrieve the leash came untied, and she dragged it along behind her as she tore off into a vast tangle of Russian olive. I knew she wouldn't give up on the duck. When she failed to return, I assumed that her leash was tangled in the brush. Everyone in duck camp spent two days looking for her. We flew drones overhead and left what felt like pounds of flesh behind us on thorns. Lori and I finally had to abandon the search and head for home for some complex family reasons. I felt heartbroken.

That sad story had a happy ending though when one of our friends found Rosy tangled up but otherwise well a quarter mile from the blind. She was sitting quietly without making a sound. Lori and I had each walked by within 50 yards of her but couldn't spot her because of the thickness of the brush. I wasn't about to go through all that anguish again.

The terrain into which that afternoon's duck had disappeared was close to the site of her disappearance the previous year, minus some of the thick brush. I knew Rosy wouldn't give up on the bird unless I made her. The only thing to do was to go along and stay ready to keep her out of trouble.

I had lost visual contact with the dog by the time I worked my way around the line of Russian olive that had obscured the fall. A gravel track ran along the far side of the open water farther ahead. Reeds and grass dotted the open water in front of it. I couldn't see Rosy. At that point I wanted the dog a lot more than I wanted the mallard. I began to whistle and wade across the open water toward the gravel track. Just as I reached it, I saw Rosy emerge from the far side of the track with the live mallard in her mouth.

Light was starting to fade as we started back toward the blind. I saw ducks circling the decoys, but no one shot until I rounded the brush and they saw me. Lori later explained that they' had several opportunities to shoot while I was gone but held their fire because they didn't want to confuse the dog, wherever she was. I certainly appreciated their courtesy and concern.

Experienced duck hunters will likely finish the story feeling admiration for the dog's performance and skepticism about mine. Rosy had covered over 300 yards of water and brush based on nothing more than marking a fall without seeing its conclusion. I probably shouldn't have let her go. All this took place in the days before sophisticated locator collars were available. Young Keta now has an air tag in hers.

These two vignettes illustrate the underlying reason why ethical hunters hunt with trained retrievers. They also taught me why my obligation to recover what I've shot should not outweigh my obligation to the dog.

II.

Upland Labs

When the Labrador retrievers' ancestors recrossed the Atlantic from the British Isles to the breed's New World homeland, their initial job description was largely limited to retrieving waterfowl on the East Coast. Labs fetched duck and geese along the coast for both market hunters and recreational shooters. Grouse and quail hunters continued to rely on traditional pointing breeds. Labs just didn't seem to have a role to play in upland cover.

That changed with the introduction of ring-necked pheasants from their Asiatic homeland to Oregon's Willamette Valley in 1881. Because of their size, striking appearance, and outstanding table quality, pheasants soon became the country's most popular upland gamebird.

Because of their behavior and habitat preferences, pheasant hunters soon recognized the need for a different kind of gun dog. Ringnecks preferred cover dense to the point of impenetrability. A canine nose that could find the bird was no longer enough. The dog had to flush it too. Rather than holding for a point like a gentleman, pheasants loved to run out ahead of dogs and guns. Recovering a wounded pheasant could be impossible without a capable retriever.

The arrival of German gun dog breeds like the shorthair and wirehair approached the latter issue from one direction, by introducing pointing dogs that retrieved as well as they pointed. Meanwhile, the Lab's ability to deal with new upland challenges gave rise to the concept of the versatile retriever. Despite my own enthusiasm for Labs, I can't deny the joy of walking up on a dog frozen on point. Over the years, while hunting upland cover with numerous pointing breeds, I developed special enthusiasm for shorthairs and wirehairs, some of which proved as capable in duck blinds as they were in the field.

There's still nothing like a Lab. The first section of this text was a tribute to their waterfowl hunting abilities, about which most of us already knew. Now I'll explore the other half of the versatile retriever's job description. I've hunted virtually every gamebird on the continent with my Labs, from quail in our desert Southwest to ptarmigan on the Alaska tundra in addition to the smorgasbord of gamebirds where I now live in the Mountain West.

While I can't pretend that I don't miss those points when I leave my wirehairs behind, if I *had* to shoot a limit of pheasants from any given cover on any different day, I'd take one of my Labs. However, there's more to the upland Lab's job than ringnecks, as we'll soon see.

15.

Guns 'n Roses

Every day, the license plates on my truck remind me that I live in Big Sky Country. But if A. B. Guthrie wanted to experience a real blast of high plains agoraphobia he should have traveled a couple of hundred miles farther north, out of Montana and across the border into Alberta. I've never seen the sky look bigger than it does there, even on the open ocean. I'm not sure how to explain this phenomenon. Perhaps it derives from the way the terrain invites you to walk on and on toward a horizon you know you'll never reach. Such temptations are hard to resist, especially when carrying a shotgun.

The first time I hunted birds on the southern Alberta prairie, the energy boom that began in the oil sands to the north had barely started to trickle down to that part of the province, occasional natural gas wells notwithstanding. It was still grain and cattle country at heart, just as it was around our Montana home. But despite—or more likely, because of—its isolation, I know few areas that offer so many of the things I like to do come hunting season. The coulees and river bottoms are home to big mule deer and whitetails. The reservoirs fill up with ducks and geese once the first hard freeze starts the waterfowl moving south. But as much as I've enjoyed these wildlife resources, it's the upland bird hunting that has left the most lasting impression. There's no better way to come to terms with remote prairie habitat than by walking seemingly endless coulees behind a dog, waiting for the next explosion of wings.

On that first Alberta prairie hunt, I met Edmonton resident Jeff Lander, an old bowhunting partner, southeast of Calgary. We were driving back to camp after spending another morning proving that mule deer were smarter than we were when a covey of Hungarian partridge rose from the roadside grass and sailed away down a brushy coulee. After three straight mornings of frustration involving longbows and deer, I suddenly realized how satisfying it would be to pursue a quarry I might actually catch up with and kill. Jeff evidently experienced the same epiphany. Before I could say a word, he was turning into the driveway that led to the nearest farmhouse.

"Do we know these folks?" I asked.

"No, but we're about to," he replied.

A huge, overall-clad man answered our knock. His build suggested a professional wrestler's, but his weathered face looked friendly. After some preliminary introductions, we asked about hunting the coulee behind his barn. "Go right ahead," he replied. "You fellas wouldn't care to stay for a bite of lunch, would you?"

I felt a bitter pang of nostalgia as we politely declined. I remembered when receptions like that were routine in my part of Montana, back before public wildlife became *de facto* private property on so many local ranches. I could not escape the irony of having to cross an international border to rediscover the hospitality I had once enjoyed at home. It's a long way between towns on the prairie, and there's not much to those towns when you find them. That kind of social isolation will either turn you into a sociopath or enhance your appetite for human company. In a welcome display of courtesy, most residents of Wild Rose Country have opted for the latter.

Fifteen minutes later, Rocky, then still a novice flushing Lab, finally got to leave his kennel in the back of my truck and do his job. Halfway to the draw where I'd marked the Huns, he nosed an entirely different covey from a tangled patch of grass and wild rose bushes. I'd only brought one shotgun with me on the trip, the long-range full-and-full I'd packed in anticipation of serious goose shooting. Now, this unlikely choice of upland guns proved ideal by serendipity. When the Huns flushed at the edge of shotgun range, I needed all the choke I had to reach out and drop one. I didn't bother with my second barrel.

Despite my sentimental affection for native sharptails and sage grouse, few elements of the prairie upland experience stir me like the explosive racket a covey of Huns makes as it erupts from the grass. (Yes, I know that *Perdix perdix* is properly known as the gray partridge, but I've never heard them called by that name anywhere other than the printed page. So, Huns they shall remain.) Enthusiasts throughout the birds' North American range owe a special measure of gratitude to the Alberta prairies. Sporadic introductions of Eurasian Huns took place at various locations throughout the American West around the time of our first pheasant releases in the 1880's. In contrast to the ringnecks, the Huns fared poorly for reasons that remain unclear. However, Hun releases in the Calgary area during the early 1900's proved successful. Most American Hun populations today derive from Alberta birds that wandered south across the border on their own accord.

Rocky and Trigger, Jeff's Lab, had found three more coveys for us by the time we circled back to the truck that morning carrying enough Huns to feed our deer camp. Never mind the heavy-racked mule deer buck I'd unsuccessfully stalked earlier in the day. Bird hunting that good didn't deserve to be considered a sidelight to anything. On that trip, I never thought of it that way again.

When I headed north the following year, I carried a real bird gun in my truck. Almost unnecessarily, as it turned out—this time geese took up most of the slack time between mule deer. Then one day Jeff mentioned that he'd seen sharptails flying into a shelterbelt north of camp. Late the following morning, Jeff, Lori, and I set off to explore the grouse cover.

Prairie grasslands are seldom as homogenous as they seem. Any terrain feature that offers wildlife a bit of extra cover can concentrate game, including structures of human origin: windbreaks, old barns, stock ponds, and abandoned homesteads. As soon as I saw the shelterbelt rising from the sea of grass and grain stubble, I knew we were going to find birds there. Killing enough for dinner should have been easy, at least in comparison to all those long, agonizing stalks that ended just short of bow range from bedded mule deer. I should have known better.

We found the birds holding tight in the brush, and walking its margins while the dogs worked the cover seemed an obvious tactic. But the 12-foot-high bushes were too thick to see over or shoot through, and the birds proved remarkably adept at flushing on the wrong side of the cover. Jeff and I unwisely decided to hunt the shelterbelt from opposite directions, theoretically to push birds toward each other. In practice, driving grouse turns out to be a lot like herding cats; how they do it so effectively in Scotland baffles me. Neither of us ever pushed a bird within shotgun range of the other. When I walked the inside of the shelterbelt, the birds that Rocky flushed escaped to the outside, and when I fought my way through the thorns and walked the outside… well, you get the idea. We heard a lot more chattering sharptails than barking shotguns, but there were so many birds that we still took a grouse dinner home for the camp.

Dedicated upland hunters may raise their eyebrows at my choice of a Lab on these hunts, especially since Huns and sharptails are such wonderful birds to hunt over pointing dogs. I appreciate that opinion myself. Nowadays, I do most of my upland hunting over our wirehairs, although I usually have a Lab with me as well. We'll explore that kind of teamwork later in the text. In Alberta, geese were usually our principal shotgun quarry. The hassle of taking more than one dog across the border and caring for them once I was there didn't seem worth the effort. Consequently, I left the wirehairs behind on these trips. One thesis of this text is that the Lab's versatility in wildly different circumstances is one of the breed's most valuable attributes. No setting I know illustrates that principle better than the Alberta prairie.

Among the pantheon of prairie upland birds, I have always been partial to the sharptail grouse. Several Native Plains tribes called them the "hairy-footed bird" in recognition of the ptarmigan-like feathered feet that help both species walk across snow during the long northern winter. Sharptails are quicker on the wing and more rewarding on the table than sage grouse. In contrast to the admirable but non-native Hungarian partridge and ringneck pheasants, they belong to the prairie in a way only thousands of generations of natural selection can fit any given species into a particular habitat niche. While I have certainly shot plenty of sharptails on our own high plains, their distribution can be erratic and prone to inscrutable local fluctuations from season to season. I know no better place to find sharptails consistently than the southern Alberta prairie. Its oases of cover attract and concentrate birds from vast swaths of habitat rich in foods as diverse as leftover grain, grasshoppers, and the fruit of the wild roses that give the country its name.

Food and cover... food and cover. This is the place to see Aldo Leopold's mantra played out in nearly infinite scope and variation.

It's Saturday night in the little farming hamlet just outside the Saskatchewan border where we traditionally headquarter on our forays into Wild Rose Country. Nearly a dozen pickups stand parked outside the town's single, bare-bones watering hole, instead of the usual two or three on weeknights. Covered in dirt, studded with cactus thorns from the morning's deer hunt, and sprinkled with blood and feathers after a quick afternoon limit of Huns, we enter in search of a cold beer and the final innings of a World Series game that might as well be playing on another planet. Turns out it's Hockey Night in Canada on the tube, a sacrosanct event north of the border. I make one polite request to turn the channel to the

Series before realizing that the Calgary Flames are playing. After spending my medical internship year in Montreal, I don't even consider asking twice. When one of the locals offers to do so anyway, I don't hesitate to decline. It's enough to learn that Canada is still that kind of place

Granted, the Alberta landscape has changed over the previous decade. Those vast reaches of grain and grass turned out to overlie equally vast reserves of fossil fuel. Now rig traffic rattles down new networks of gravel roads. So many new wellheads sprout like mushrooms that is hard to avoid the impression of a visit to an OPEC nation. To their credit the Canadians seem to have done it right, and the net impact to wildlife habitat appears remarkably small. The game is certainly thriving as we had already proven that day.

Alberta allows no Sunday big game hunting, so tomorrow will be all about birds. Fine by me and even finer by Rocky, who has remained patiently kenneled longer than he probably liked. We have every intention of addressing that complaint tomorrow by hunting near the northern limits of the ringneck's New World range.

While I've never killed a rooster here, Jeff has located a creek bottom full of them and obtained permission to hunt it. Pheasants are a novel quarry for him and hence an official Big Deal of the same order as Himalayan snow cocks. Lori and I, on the other hand, have already enjoyed two weeks of Montana pheasant season and have a freezer full of roosters back at home. So, I'm trying to reconcile the gentlemanly obligation to indulge our friend with my own interest in the waves of geese I saw pouring into a pea field an hour after sunrise that morning. Once the hockey game is over it takes a late inning pitching duel and another round of Molson's for us to arrive upon a remarkably simple solution. We'll set up for geese in the morning, hunt pheasants in the afternoon, and hope we have time to heal by Monday.

The country lends itself well to such ambitious agendas. Some bird hunting expeditions wind up being all about the shooting, others about the dogs, others still about the company or the quarry.

But hunting the prairie here is always about the landscape and the SPACE, the latter spelled large for the same reason Melville scholar Charles Olson spelled it large at the beginning of *Call Me Ishmael*. More than distinctions of language, history, or culture, open space is what makes us different from the French or the Japanese. You're not really a citizen of North America until you've looked it in the eye and felt it make you blink.

There's no better place to do that than Wild Rose Country, and no better excuse to be there than a shotgun in your hand and an eager dog leading the way up yet another endless coulee.

16.

Hell Holes

The autumn air lay crisp and still above the creek bottom as we unloaded the dogs and set off along the grassy swale that ran from the stubble field down toward the heart of the cover. In the best of all possible worlds, we would have caught some roosters up in the grass where the going was easy and the shooting unobstructed. That was too much to ask for, and we knew it. By the time we reached the bluff above the creek, the dogs had nosed a single hen into the air and nothing more. The birds were hidden in the hell hole below us, as we had known all along that they would be. Now there was nothing to be done except go in after them.

While Lori positioned herself strategically at the apex of large bend in the creek, I called Sonny and Rocky to heel and set out to circle the cover. As soon as I dropped down into the creek bottom to begin the push back toward Lori, the comforting azure sky began to recede beyond the tops of the willows. The beavers had been busy over the summer, and I couldn't find a place to get across the creek without getting wet. I had to fight my way through the brush for 30 yards before I came to a beaver dam over which I could walk dry-footed.

As I began the precarious balancing act that would lead me to the other side of the creek, I glanced down and saw a #2 double long-spring practically underfoot. With both dogs clamoring across the dam right behind me, I had no choice but to drop my shotgun, grab their collars and heave them around the trap. By the time we reached the opposite bank, my favorite shotgun and I were both wet and covered with mud, and our hunt hadn't even started.

As soon as I began to work my way back toward Lori, both dogs disappeared. It wasn't their fault; the dense thicket of willows and reeds simply restricted the visibility to a matter of feet. In fact, the Labs were doing exactly what they were supposed to be doing, which was to use their legs, hearts, and noses to coax some roosters from the cover. As we closed slowly toward Lori there was little to do but let the willows slap my face and hope.

The creek bend ahead should have given us the defining terrain feature we needed to flush birds in range of someone, but the season was s month old, and these pheasants were educated. When birds finally began to erupt from the cover, the first wave split the defense perfectly. Lori couldn't shoot because the birds were out of range and I couldn't shoot because I couldn't see past the brambles, so I listened in frustration as wings thundered and roosters cackled in what sounded like mockery.

Then one made a mistake. "Rooster!" Lori cried helpfully from her purchase on the bluff, but her assistance proved unnecessary. As the bird passed overhead, I could see plenty of color and nothing behind the bird but blue sky. Then as I brought the gun to my shoulder, the barrel snagged an inconveniently placed willow that disrupted my swing completely. Aware that it was futile to try manufacturing a shot that wasn't there, I slid my finger off the trigger and watched the bird sail passed unscathed.

"What about that last bird?" Lori asked when we finally regrouped on opposite sides of the creek.

"Don't ask," I replied glumly just as the dogs appeared, covered with mud and panting heavily from their exertion. They had done their job, and none of us enjoys playing well in a losing effort. But while I believe Labs measure success in the field by the number of retrieves they get to make, they also accept their occasional share of disappointments. The failures on this hunt—whether viewed as unfired shells in the vest or brush slashes across the face—were on us and not the dogs. They both seemed ready and eager to keep hunting. We owed them the favor of honoring their wish.

Back when I was a kid in upstate New York, we regularly hunted grouse and woodcock in a vast alder-infested bottom known simply as the Hole. Despite its formidable appearance and inhospitable character, it eventually became a personal favorite. I killed my first bird on the wing there, a ruffed grouse that exploded in front of the family shorthair and took a bit too long getting behind the nearest tree. When migrating flights of woodcock settled in overnight, the Hole offered the fastest shooting I'd ever experienced then. We never saw anyone hunting there other than members of our own party. Dense, wet, and brambly, the Hole could be punishing, but it also taught me a valuable lesson. Good hunting and pleasant hiking don't always go together.

My appreciation of the hell hole phenomenon accelerated once my family moved west. This was pheasant country, and nothing gravitates toward horrific cover quite like wild ringnecks. While chukar and blue grouse can challenge the hunter physically in their up and down terrain, no western game bird habitat produces *Why am I doing this?* frustration quite like pheasant cover. This is especially true when roosters have been hunted for several weeks and learned from the experience.

That education is an important part of the equation. Opening weekend pheasants can be found in casual cover, but that dignified situation seldom lasts long. After the first wave of cherry-pickers has swept through the cover the birds will either be smart or dead. If you want to find the survivors, you'll have to start looking in less accommodating places. That, in my opinion, is when real pheasant hunting starts.

What makes a good hell hole? To qualify, cover first needs to be, well... a hole. While you can find unpleasantly thick brush just about anywhere in rooster country, depressions gather the moisture needed to make it flourish. Real hell holes should cut you off from the surrounding terrain, enforcing the feeling of descent, as into you-know-where.

Not just any kind of brush can make a real hell hole. It should be tall enough to obstruct your vision and thick enough to impede your progress on foot. It should force you to your hands and knees intermittently, to give birds an opportunity to flush when it's impossible to shoot. Dense reeds and willows meet these basic requirements. However, the brush in fully developed hell holes should sport industrial strength thorns in a variety of shapes and sizes, from big ones stout enough to punch through your britches to sharp little ones to carry home in the skin on the back of your hands. That way, you'll know you've been pheasant hunting days after the event itself. Here on the prairie, buffaloberry and hawthorn serve that purpose well.

Hell holes should contain some water, for it's hard to appreciate them properly with dry feet. While the depth may vary, it should always come two inches above the top of whatever boots you're wearing and should tempt you to slog through it repeatedly even when you know better. The presence of beavers practically guarantees wet feet. Our largest rodents also love to leave numerous sharpened stobs underfoot to puncture boots and impale the flesh of the careless hunters.

Since it's so difficult to shoot from the middle of this kind of cover, hell holes are tough to hunt alone. Working them effectively requires teamwork among hunters and dogs alike. The best approach is to break them up into manageable pieces, with edges defined by terrain features like bluffs and creek bends. With a gun or two situated strategically near the open where it's possible to see and shoot, some sacrificial lamb (see Chapter Five) gets to take the dogs into the heart of darkness. When things go well, those on the outside shoot some birds while the sacrificial lamb builds character.

While cover like this proves difficult to hunt with only one gun, it's impossible to hunt at all without willing dogs. In fact, no terrain better showcases the utility of experienced flushing retrievers. This kind of dog work should not be confused with rocket science, and enthusiasm and able noses are the only absolute canine requirements. Since it is all but impossible to teach a dog how to hunt such cover effectively save by doing it, there is no substitute for experience. Since the physical demands this kind of cover imposes can be great, hell holes are often where dogs first begin to show their age. The result can be a painfully narrow window of opportunity between the ages of five and eight when the dog knows what to do and still maintains the capacity to do it—another argument for a high-capacity kennel.

Another day, another dog, another hell hole. With the season already a month old, I should know better than to believe Lori's order for a pheasant dinner will come easily. But there hasn't been much hunting pressure out here in the middle of nowhere, and I've convinced myself that a quick run through the thick grass between a stubble field and a brush-lined creek bottom will produce the three-bird limit needed to feed our company. The easy going produces just what it deserves—nothing. By the time the dogs and I wind up empty-handed on the bluff overlooking the creek our options have been reduced to two: return home humiliated and feed our visitors elk burger or gird up our loins and give the real cover our best.

Kenai's gracefully aging chassis isn't going to allow him to crash through the willows the way he did a few seasons past. But even in an effort as physically demanding as the pursuit of wild ringnecks, brains can still trump brawn if they're exercised properly. After scouting the tangled cover from above, I finally settle on an oxbow with a relatively civil patch of cattails at the end. With a little luck, Kenai and I will arrive there together with the pheasants, and they will flush with enough shooting room to produce the pheasant dinner we're supposed to provide.

As we climb down the bank to begin our push, the cover demonstrates all the qualifications of a classic hell hole: thorns, tangles, treacherous footing, water of unpredictable depth, and beaver workings. Within moments of entering the cover, my right foot is wet, and one hand is full of thorns. Somewhere up ahead, Kenai snuffles along faithfully. I can mark his progress by the sound of cattails breaking and the eager whines he makes when he's hot on the trail of running birds. The hunt has been reduced to a footrace as I struggle to reach the open area next to the oxbow before the birds flush, leaving me with nothing to do but crash my way forward like a foraging bear.

An explosion of wings finally announces the first rise, but there is nothing I can do about it even though it takes place right in front of me. Then I break out next to the creek just as Kenai noses another rooster into the sky. Hanging airborne above the oxbow, the bird seems to realize he's made a mistake, but it's too late for a second guess. At the sound of the shot the rooster drops into the cattails with a satisfying crash.

I've been caught with my gun open too many times to let it happen to me today. Instead of reloading at once, I stand patiently with my second barrel ready while Kenai works his way through the last of the cover. This time, technique earns its just reward. When the next rooster bursts from the cover I'm waiting with my second barrel ready instead of a useless open gun. After the dog completes both retrieves seamlessly, I only need one more rooster to make our pheasant dinner complete. It comes when Kenai noses one tightly holding bird into the air as we circle our way back out of the brush.

As we climb back up the bank, the pheasants resting in my game vest feel even more gratifying than most, and why not? I've learned over the years that measuring success in the field by numbers of birds or inches of antler comes with limitations. The real satisfaction of any bag must reflect the effort required in its harvest. That concept seems difficult enough for hunters to master, let alone our dogs. But as we crest the bank and set off across the field toward the truck, Kenai seems to be carrying himself a bit more proudly than usual. I know that's just sentimental anthropomorphism, but it's enough to make me wonder.

So, let's all reserve a spot in our hearts for hell holes. The cover that presents the greatest challenges also provides the greatest rewards, a principle that enjoys applications elsewhere in life. Now we're going home, Kenai to his rug on the dining room floor and me to a pheasant dinner with family and friends. Tonight, that will be enough.

17.

Early Season Surprises

The storm had followed me all the way down from Alaska like a lost puppy. I'd spent two weeks hunkered down on the Alaska Peninsula in wind and horizontal rain. At the conclusion of a successful season guiding bear hunters my need for some Indian summer Montana weather almost exceeded my desire to see Lori and the dogs. But when I finally got out of the Bush and checked the computer, there it was: the same ominous low-pressure system bearing down on the high plains like a mass murderer wielding an axe.

I'd barely had time to kiss Lori and unpack weeks' worth of mouldering hunting clothes laced with rancid bear fat by the time the rain began to fall. Then we woke up the following morning to find the foothills behind our house coated in snow. Although I could think of a dozen reasons to spend the day curled up in front of the fireplace, my desire to hunt eventually overruled my common sense. In Alaska, a guide cannot hunt at all while accompanying clients in the field, and after all that time worrying about other people's bears, I desperately needed to head into the field with my own agenda. Besides, I sensed an impending rebellion in the kennel if I didn't take the dogs hunting soon.

I could have headed for old, reliable cover, but there's always something exciting about exploring new ground. During my absence Lori had come up with a promising lead. One of her girlfriends had told her about all the sharptails she'd been seeing on the ranch she and her husband owned, and she had extended a gracious invitation for us to hunt the place. I've certainly set off into the unknown based on less promising intelligence.

"At least I *think* they're sharptails," she said when we arrived at the door to review the lay of the land and its boundaries. I momentarily felt my heart sink, since pheasant season didn't open for two more weeks.

"Maybe they're Huns?" I asked.

"All I know is that they scare the hell out of my horse when I'm riding the coulees," she replied. Since Huns were certainly the most likely of our prairie upland species to spook a horse by flushing suddenly, I felt my spirits rise once more. I'll trade a limit of sharptails—or just about anything else—for a good Hun hunt any day.

When I dropped the tailgate on the truck, I took a long, hard look at the dog boxes inside. I'd brought Maggie, our young wirehair, along just so she could sniff a few birds and hear some guns go off, but I wasn't ready for any puppy antics yet. Anticipating sharptails in open cover, I'd left young Kenai behind to pout in the kennel back at home. That meant that the workhorse for the day would be Rocky, who was more experienced and obedient. He came boiling out of the truck like a dog half the age his papers claimed him to be.

I couldn't pretend I'd made a similar visit to the Fountain of Youth as we began to slip and slide our way along the steep coulee behind the barn. However, I did appreciate the conditioning my legs had received during my long stay up north. With Rocky dutifully hugging my side in his role as a no-slip retriever, I began to wonder if we'd dressed warmly enough for the freak storm. We hadn't climbed 50 yards before the buzz of wings and a chorus of avian squeaks rose above the sound of the wind. The mystery birds were Huns after all.

Thick brush screened me from most of the covey, which looked as if it contained a good 20 birds. But a pair of stragglers finally peeled off in my direction, and I dropped the first before missing what should have been the back half of a tough but makeable double. Rocky ran down the fallen bird as if he'd never endured a long summer layoff. Then I suggested that we crest the rise and work the next draw, where I felt sure the bulk of the covey had settled.

We almost didn't make it that far. No cattle had grazed the native grass on top of the hill, which made it prime Hun cover. We'd barely started across the field when we flushed a fresh covey. This time I bore down and completed the double. Lori was having an uncharacteristically bad shooting day. All I could do was remind her to get her cheek back down on the stock once she'd isolated a target from the covey and compensate for the birds' speed in the wind by driving her barrels even farther forward than usual. When Rocky started to nose up singles from the two scattered coveys, those suggestions seemed to help.

Over the next two hours, we enjoyed the best Hun hunting I'd experienced in years. I'd guess we flushed eight or ten separate coveys, each containing 15-20 birds. Although the brush-choked coulee bottoms looked like ideal grouse cover, the only sharptails we saw were two singles that flushed out of range. After completing my limit (I'd call it an easy limit except that there is no such thing on Huns), I swung back by the truck to give Rocky a rest, pick up Maggie, and let the pup romp while Lori kept hunting.

Rocky, the old warrior, had certainly done his job. Granted, retrieving Huns isn't as difficult as retrieving pheasants, but a wounded Hun gone to ground in tall grass can still be hard to find without a capable dog. We finished the morning with a dozen Huns, no lost birds, and the makings of a real wild game feast riding in our game vests.

By the time we stopped back by the landowners' house to express our appreciation for their hospitality, the snow was already disappearing, the clouds were rolling back, and the countryside was starting to look like Montana in September again. My welcome home from Alaska concluded with two unlikely surprises: winter weather weeks ahead of schedule and "sharptails" that mysteriously morphed into an abundance of the best game bird the prairie has to offer.

Out on the tundra, I'd been seriously considering leaving Montana and moving back to our Alaska home fulltime. No such pipedreams could survive a morning like that.

I still wanted some sharptails, and Lori, no slouch herself when it comes to ferreting out bird cover, soon came up with a second plan. Another of her girlfriends—all our wives should have girlfriends like these—called to report large numbers of sharptails in the brush around their rural home north of town. And Dee, the lady of the house and a novice bird hunter herself, had just acquired a new 28-gauge. Would we mind coming out and offering her some instruction while we hunted her property together? As Br'er Rabbit once pleaded, please don't throw me in that briar patch (or, more accurately, those buffaloberry bushes).

But the following morning was the opening day of duck season. Our local early waterfowling opportunities are limited, but my personal reverence for the opener extends all the way back to my childhood. I always try to set up somewhere on opening day, even with modest expectations that seldom exceed a duck dinner for two. As it happens, Dee and her husband Bill had a one-acre pond on their place that occasionally attracts a few flocks of early season waterfowl. Thus, my plan crystallized: sunrise in a duck blind by the pond, followed by what sounded like a guaranteed run through the sharptail cover.

Dawn broke clear, crisp, and still. Since we were hunting ducks, I found myself longing briefly for the ideal waterfowling weather we'd endured two days earlier. As usual, Lori hung in there with me like a trooper. Since Rocky had just enjoyed a good workout in the upland cover, Kenai provided our canine companionship. After

EARLY SEASON SURPRISES

living in Rocky's shadow for several seasons, he deserved a crack at the limelight. I couldn't imagine a better point of beginning.

Coyotes were serenading the impending sunrise by the time I finished pitching the blocks onto the glassy surface of the pond. Our timing had been perfect. I'd no sooner settled into our makeshift blind when I glanced at my watch and announced the arrival of shooting light. And there, right on schedule, came the first flight of the year.

The half-dozen mallards caught me flat-footed the first time they circled the decoys, but when they returned with their wings set, I barked "Pick out a drake and take him!"

"I'm not even loaded yet!" Lori protested.

But time, tide, and circling ducks wait for no man, and for no woman either. With silent apologies to my wife for whatever breach of etiquette I was committing, I picked out the nearest greenhead and dumped him. Then as the flock climbed back into the sky, I dropped a second. "Sorry, Honey," I mumbled as I led Kenai out in front of the camo netting hanging from the brush in front of us and gave him the line. "It was my fault for not being ready," she replied, and that admission assuaged my guilt a little.

Despite his size and athleticism, Kenai never demonstrated a striking water entry, and I found myself shaking my head as he minced his way through the reeds in front of the blind. But then he kicked it into overdrive, and moments later the year's first brace of ducks lay resting in the grass beside us.

My manners weren't all bad that morning. The sun had just risen over the mountains behind us to the east when another pair of mallards buzzed the spread. I didn't even touch my gun when I encouraged Lori to take the drake. Kenai already seemed to be gaining enthusiasm and confidence as he blasted into the pond and completed the morning's third retrieve in style.

Shortly thereafter, Dee walked down from the house with a fresh thermos of coffee. I knew our duck hunt was over for the day, a point we spent the next hour proving. Finally, we decided it was time to get after the grouse that had supposedly been our quarry all along.

After walking Dee through the mechanics of her new shotgun I cased my own at the truck, leaving me free to focus my attention on Kenai and our hostess. We did flush some grouse during a mile-long circuit through some great looking cover surrounding their house. Every one of them rose wild and hopelessly out of range, unusual behavior for sharptails so early in the season. For the second time in three days, we ended a promising sharptail hunt without popping a cap at a grouse.

Conclusions? First and foremost, don't be limited by your expectations in the field. Both of our "sharptail" hunts sounded like slam-dunks based on preliminary intelligence, but neither turned out that way at all. In both cases we were able to save the day by taking advantage of surprising alternatives. If we hadn't gone prepared for the unexpected, we would have missed some fine action—in the first case a spectacular morning of Hun shooting, in the second a neat little duck hunt that managed to keep the sacrosanct tradition of opening day alive for another year.

Second, appreciate all the possibilities of wing-shooting on the prairie, where variety really is the spice of life. A hunt for eastern ruffed grouse or southwestern desert quail is unlikely to produce anything else. Out here, you just never know.

Finally, how about a tip of the hat to the dogs that can do it all: our versatile retrievers. Sure, it would have been nice to have a polished pointing dog along when we got into all those Huns. But I know that Rocky didn't let us walk by many tight-holding singles, and we finished a morning of fast shooting without an unrecovered bird. And where would we have been with three mallards bobbing around on the surface of that pond without Kenai?

Now as I write, the season is still refreshingly young, and I can only begin to imagine what the next three months will bring for our team before we head for Arizona in January. But I do know that I have a mess of birds hanging, and I'll have to start cleaning them soon before Dee and her family arrive for the wild game dinner we promised them.

And it doesn't bother me that there isn't a single sharptail grouse among them.

18.

Our Glorious Tenth

After a shake, rattle, and roll landing on remote gravel bar west of the Alaska Range (the rocks always bigger than they look from the air), I shut the engine down and let old Sky pick his way down from the Cub's back seat. I was flying in supplies for a caribou hunt, but it was the opening day of ptarmigan season. I'd seen no reason why the cargo should not include a shotgun, a box of shells, and a Labrador retriever. After unloading a duffle full of heavy canned goods, I climbed back in the Cub and dug out my old 12-gauge pump, which I planned to leave behind as a camp bear gun. After throwing some shells in my daypack, the dog and I set out to climb through the brush to the open tundra above the riverbed.

Tundra may seem featureless to the inexperienced eye, but as with the sagebrush prairie of the Lower-48 the monotony of its treeless terrain proves illusory. Each of the many species that call it home will identify and inhabit their own favorite parts. The willow ptarmigan I expected to find prefer low ridges, where good drainage provides dry footing. With Sky at my side, I picked my way around the edge of a bog and began to climb.

From the top of the gentle rise, I could see a herd of caribou off in the distance, but Alaska's same-day-airborne restriction made them of informational interest only. The state's prohibition against hunting and flying the same day does not apply to small game, as

I soon had an opportunity to appreciate. I've never billed Sky as a pointing Lab, but he would usually slow down rather than speed up at the first whiff of game. When he began to mince around at the edge of a scrub willow clump, I fixed him to the turf with a whistle blast.

I hadn't even bothered to load the gun yet and couldn't remember whether I'd removed the magazine plug after the previous waterfowl season. When the fourth shell came up against a brick wall, I reminded myself to turn it back into a bear gun later. I've spent countless nights outside in grizzly country without ever having to reach for a firearm in the dark, but should the need ever arise I wanted the gun to give me my money's worth.

By the time I chambered the first shell, I could hear low, reedy clucks issuing from the brush ahead. Fully loaded at last I urged Sky forward, precipitating a slow, rolling eruption of wings. Conveniently staggering each rise, birds went this way and that at a measured pace as if the whole encounter had been choreographed. I had plenty of time to kill two birds and miss a third, perhaps because I was pointlessly wondering whether the circumstances would qualify as a legitimate triple. I didn't even bother to chide myself for the last, lousy shot, because I already had what mattered most: dinner and a chance to work Sky after a long off-season.

Ptarmigan are neither tough nor tenacious. Downed birds aren't difficult to locate when their camouflage plumage is out of synch with the season, as these birds' would be in another month. But the pair I dropped were still dressed for summer. Since I'd been too busy shooting to mark them accurately when they tumbled on the opposite side of the little ridge, I was glad I had the dog. If Sky had suffered from inattention during the previous months, he was too polite to show it. Both birds were resting in my pack in less time than it takes to tell.

Then I faced a decision. With a happy dog at my side, I could hike back down to the gravel bar and tackle some camp chores, or I could continue up the ridge shooting ptarmigan and let my late arriving friends worry about setting up camp. The choice did not prove difficult. It was the 10th of August, the opening day of bird season, and the dog was still eager.

Besides, what are friends for?

Ptarmigan enjoy a circumpolar distribution without regard for distinction between Old World and New. Three species inhabit North America: the willow, the white-tailed, and the rock. While I've killed all three in various locations, the vast majority have been willow ptarmigan, Alaska's state bird. (Some would argue that this honor properly belongs to the mosquito, but that's another story.) Although a separate subspecies, the willow ptarmigan is essentially the same bird as the Scottish red grouse, the subject of great adulation by our wing-shooting counterparts in the UK as celebrated on their traditional Glorious Twelfth. While ptarmigan seasons vary among Alaska's 26 Game Management Units, most in the South-Central part of the state open on August 10th. I may have been rough shooting back when I lived up north full time, but I always appreciated my two-day head start on the gentry across the pond.

No game bird I know changes its habits during a season as predictably or as quickly as the willow ptarmigan. It's impossible to tell someone unfamiliar with the species what the quarry will look like without reference to a calendar. On the tundra, this transition takes place between opening day – the Glorious Tenth, if you will – and late September. Understanding the changes ptarmigan undergo during this period will help make anyone a better tundra bird hunter and help to explain the birds' growing allure among serious wing-shooters.

Opening day ptarmigan are usually still organized in small family groups of a dozen birds or fewer. Superbly camouflaged in their summer coats, they'll stick to the tundra like glue, often letting you walk right past them unless you're hunting alongside a dog with a nose. Twenty-gauge shotguns, light loads, and open chokes are reasonable choices given the relatively easy, largely close-range shooting.

Which seldom lasts long... By late August, birds have started to acquire their winter dress and will show plenty of white on their wings when they flush. Perhaps because they feel more vulnerable while their camouflage plumage is out of phase, they rapidly become more wary. Later in the season family groups coalesce into progressively larger flocks, which usually contain several designated sentries. In a matter of a few weeks, ptarmigan can go from being one of the easiest upland targets on the continent to one of the toughest. Expect long shots and plan accordingly. By the end of August in South-Central Alaska, I seldom regretted the full choke on my camp pump when it came time to put ptarmigan stew on the table.

Winter is still another story. Short days and arctic weather can make hunts a real challenge then, but by February shooting hours have started to lengthen. A late season ptarmigan hunt can provide a great cure for cabin fever blues. Most visiting wing-shooters aren't going to choose this time of year to hunt Alaska, but the possibilities are still intriguing. Stable arctic highs can produce some of the most inviting hunting weather of the year and the sight of pearl white ptarmigan rising against a clear azure sky can be breathtaking. Expect extremely wary birds however, often gathered in flocks of hundreds. Being there is often more rewarding than the shooting.

What role do retrievers play in this complex, seasonally variable wing-shooting experience? During the weeks following the Glorious Tenth, a retriever with a good nose can be very helpful locating and flushing birds that have gone to ground in the scrub willow that dots the tundra. Since downed birds look so much like the ground cover beneath them and rises often lead to multiple falls in various directions, a seasoned retriever can also be useful once the shooting is done.

By September, most birds won't need a flushing dog to get them airborne. Because of the birds' progressive wildness, a flushing dog that is not under complete control is more likely to be a liability than an asset. However, when large flocks of ptarmigan are flushing wild, most of the shooting may come from the few stragglers that elect to hide rather than take to the air prematurely. You may have trouble finding them without a dog's nose to assist you. Because of the increasing amount of white in their plumage downed birds are relatively easy to locate then, but a ptarmigan with a broken wing can still walk faster than most of us can across broken ground. A trained retriever will solve that problem in a hurry.

But the most valuable aspect of a retriever's presence on a typical Alaska ptarmigan hunt may derive from intangibles. The tundra can be a lonely place. While there's no substitute for wilderness, I always found a Lab's company an ideal compromise between too much company and not quite enough. Nothing stokes enthusiasm like an eager hunting dog in the field, and nothing reassures in camp at night like the same dog sleeping peacefully. From pulling sleds to guarding camps from bears, canine companions have been an essential part of the human experience in the Far North since both species crossed the great land bridge together 20,000 years ago. There's no reason why retrievers shouldn't continue that tradition today.

What a difference a few weeks make. Our caribou hunt is history, with my longbow accounting for a freezer full of steaks and another rack for the wall. Soon northern ducks will start to arrive from the interior to crowd the potholes on the tide flats. Today I arose with modest goals: a fresh silver salmon for the grill back home across Cook Inlet and a few more ptarmigan to fine tune Sky's manners before the waterfowling turns serious. The first proved easy enough even on a light fly rod, but the birds were another matter.

The problems certainly weren't biologic. For the third time in an hour, I just watched a flock of ptarmigan rocket up out of the willows a hundred yards ahead, white wings flashing against the rich tableau of autumn colors splashed across the foothills behind them. The airborne birds made a dramatic sight, and under different circumstances I might feel content just to enjoy it. But today I'm armed with a shotgun—a double no less, rather than the clumsy beater with which I began the season. I want to hear its report and watch a pair or two of those beating white wings tumble from their place in the line. Next week I'll be back across the mountains with my bow hunting moose. I can wait until then to enjoy the aesthetic experience of an autumn ptarmigan rise from a distance. Today I'm a bird hunter, and I've got a bird hunting dog at my side just as eager to hear the shotgun bark as I am.

I've marked the willows from which the last birds rose but as so often proves the case up north getting there proves more difficult than it seems. I must pick my way across a low patch of wet tundra,

OUR GLORIOUS TENTH

and by the time I emerge on the other side I have a soaking foot to compound the afternoon's frustrations. Sky obviously doesn't care about the bog and its consequences. Neither should I, a rationalization that sounds better than it feels as my wet foot begins to slip uncomfortably inside my boot.

The point of this exercise is an old observation concerning ptarmigan behavior: even the wildest flocks will often leave a few stragglers behind. Up close, the willows prove thicker than they looked. Venturing down into them to try kicking up birds will likely leave me without a shot even if I find a few left behind. Fortunately, the solution to this dilemma rode across the Inlet with me this morning in the back seat of the airplane. Climbing up on the tallest tussock I can find for the best available view, I check the safety and send in the dog.

Sky has served primarily as a duck dog since our move north simply because that's what we spend most of our time hunting. As well as he serves this purpose, he was raised and trained on the plains of Montana and remains a flushing retriever as well as a water retriever. This kind of chore is right up his alley. Every time I send him into the willows after reluctant ptarmigan, I remember the way he used to hit the buffaloberry for sharptails back when he was a puppy. I suspect that he does too.

This time our imported grouse tactics work to perfection. After a lot of canine thrashing down in the hole below, I hear a ptarmigan cluck and then its wings are practically in my face. I almost get my feet tangled up as I turn to take the bird going away, but the shot is just too easy to miss, and I don't. I even guess right in its aftermath, holding the gun closed on one loaded chamber rather than scrambling to reload immediately. When Sky nudges a second straggler into the air, I'm ready for it.

The mile-long circle back to the gravel bar where the airplane waits produces two more wild rises. One leads us to another pair of cooperative birds that leaves my game vest as full as I want it. We had to work to earn the fowl course planned to compliment the dinner party back at home that night, but I haven't minded in the least. The hunting has been a challenge, the teamwork with old Sky gratifying. With the easy ptarmigan of early August little more than a memory I ready the Cub for the flight back to civilization, grateful as always for the birds that have provided me an excuse to escape it.

19.

Mountain Grouse

October marks a time of grand transition here in the foothills of the Rockies, beginning with warm, accommodating days and ending with the kind of weather that invokes the feel of serious winter about to come. The promise of change in the air imparts an urgency shared by gathering waterfowl, whitetail bucks stirred by the impending rut, and hunters eager to log as much outdoor time as possible before the thermometer plummets. That mid-October day a clear, azure sky stretched above the hills' golden mantle as Kenai and I worked our way uphill, although it was hard to avoid the impression that we were enjoying favors that could be withdrawn at any moment. Experienced outdoorsmen know enough to savor these times. Not even the relentless drag of the steep slope against my legs could compromise enjoyment of the day.

Which is not to say that the appearance of a bird or two would have felt unwelcome. Climbing hills has a way of magnifying the expectation of a flush, as if crossing contour lines represents an investment that deserves a return. This morning my anticipation felt especially keen, for the rolling terrain that holds the usual October bounty of pheasants, sharptails, and Huns lay far away on the prairie below. We had left the easy going behind as we climbed in search of something out of the ordinary by local standards: mountain grouse—ruffs and blues—birds most western hunters occasionally behead with rifles during elk season and ignore during the rest of the year.

As I paused to catch my breath and plan our route of attack along the remainder of the ridge, Kenai spun mid-stride and disappeared into a clump of aspen with the intensity of a detective who has stumbled upon a solid clue after a long, frustrating search. Since the dog was too far past the puppy stage to generate many false alarms, I already had my feet planted and the shotgun at port arms by the time the sound of wings erupted from the cover. Even so the flush came as a shock. After a month of sharptails on the prairie I had grown accustomed to sedate rises in open terrain, with ample time to pick targets and track them against a plain background of sky. This time there was nothing but noise and trees leaving me open mouthed as I studied the tangle of cover ahead. For a moment it seemed as if the effort of the long climb might produce nothing more than frustration.

Then a dark form appeared hurtling through the aspens ahead of all that thunder. I spun and fired. The conviction that I had killed the bird stemmed from feeling more than evidence, for the foliage consumed the grouse before I could watch it fall. The mountain air lay still and empty, but the sudden geometry of the shot felt perfect the instant I slapped the trigger. Kenai confirmed this impression moments later when he bounded up the sidehill with a limp, dark form cradled gently in his mouth.

As the dog scrambled toward me, I broke the double, snagged the empty from the air, and reloaded in case the cover held another pleasant surprise. However, the mountain's silence soon confirmed that more shooting would mean more climbing. This realization convinced me to pause to appreciate what the dog had brought me. The bird was a mature blue, and its weight felt more like a turkey than a grouse as the dog dropped it in my hand. I hesitated for a moment, admiring its rich, dusky plumage before I reached back and eased it into my vest. Perhaps it was the effort of the climb and perhaps it was the bird's generous heft, but killing this grouse had the feel of big game. I found myself imagining as one does with elk or deer that one might just be enough for the day.

"What do you think?" I asked Kenai as I shifted my weight and eyed the climb upward toward the head of the ridge.

That was a foolish question, of course; no good Lab ever thinks one is enough. As the dog started ahead, I shouldered the gun and began to pick my own way uphill through the rocks. Why not? All those Labs can't be wrong.

Most upland bird hunting in the American West takes place in wide open spaces where broad horizons and empty skies offer an ideal venue for the wing-shooter's craft. I spend a lot of time every autumn enjoying miles of civil walking and unobstructed shooting when I find game. For a dedicated minority though, the West's mountain grouse strongholds provide a special opportunity fueled by the demands of steep terrain, challenging shooting, and in my own case a personal sense of history.

The first game bird I ever killed on the wing was a ruffed grouse. This seminal event took place in an alder thicket in upstate New York more years ago than I care to remember, with my father standing by my side and our German shorthair doing the honors before and after the shot. While the pace of the bird hunting we knew back then seems tame compared to what we found after moving to the West, hunting grouse in close quarters carries the special appeal that comes from doing things the way you did them in the beginning. In deference to my own bird hunting roots, I still make a special effort every season to reproduce that experience even though it may cost me a day or two in classical, user friendly western bird cover.

In the hills around our Montana home, hunting mountain grouse means chasing ruffs and blues. Spruce grouse, the definitive fool hens, sometimes occupy the same habitat although I rarely target them deliberately. They are too dumb to offer much challenge on the wing—if they fly. I shot enough of them with my bow as camp meat when I lived in Alaska.

Large, noisy, and quick, the blue can be an impressive game bird although it too occasionally operates in fool hen mode. Sometimes blues flutter up into the nearest tree and stare at you rather than providing an honest rise. But at their best they offer all anyone could ask for on the wing, with explosive flushes and rapid flight at the snappy angles that make even experienced gunners appreciate a successful shot. They do so often enough to make a good day of blue grouse hunting as challenging as wing-shooting gets.

Now for a brief biological digression lest astute readers accuse me of ignorance. Officially, there is no longer any such bird as a blue grouse. Based on genetic evidence, in 2006 the American Ornithological Union divided the blue into two separate, distinct species, the dusky and the sooty. Quite similar in appearance, they are best distinguished by their ranges, which scarcely overlap. Sooty grouse live by the sea, a useful mnemonic. I did shoot some sooties when I lived on the Alaska coast. Most of my experience has been with the inland dusky of the Mountain West, which maintained its original scientific name, *Denragapus obscurus*. However, old habits die hard. In this chapter I'll refer to dusky grouse as blues simply because that is the term I've always used. I've never heard any local hunter of my generation refer to them otherwise.

If western mountain grouse hunting offers any disappointment, it is most likely to come—alas—from the ruff. Those raised to regard the ruffed grouse as the noblest game bird in the New World often grow dispirited at the sight of a western ruff waddling away through the autumn leaves rather than flushing. I suspect that this naïve behavior stems from lack of hunting pressure rather than genetics, adding a bold stroke to the environmental side of the ledger in the timeless nature versus nurture debate. Perhaps the cagey New England version of the ruffed grouse simply reflects what two hundred years of shotguns have made it. Fortunately for those of us who live out here, some western ruffs do know how to act like real pa'tridge even in the foothills of the Rockies. When they do, the explosion of a close rise can make up for all sorts of foolishness at other times.

The role of the flushing retriever in the pursuit of western mountain grouse may seem questionable. I will admit my own initial skepticism about the idea of hunting ruffed grouse without the services of a capable pointer. Remember that this is big country. A morning spent chasing blues may require the hunter to cover more ground than a week of eastern grouse hunting. Locating birds in habitat this size always goes better with good canine help. Holding cover for mountain grouse tends to be thick but scattered, lending itself well to the use of a dog that can be handled tightly from the hunter's side. Anyone who has tried to kick a reluctant bird from thick thorn brush will soon appreciate the enthusiasm of a dog willing to provide this service. While a retriever may not be a classic grouse dog, a good Lab will translate into more shooting and more grouse in the game vest at the end of the day.

In my opinion, blue grouse make some of the best table fare of any gamebird on the continent. Anyone who loves to eat grouse as much as I do should be willing to sacrifice a bit of style in the name of substance.

There are many reasons to be climbing the hills behind the house tonight, including aerobic exercise, drop-dead autumn scenery, and the appearance of the first active whitetail scrapes of the year. But none of these excuses requires the presence of a gun and dog, without which even the most casual walk in the fall woods would feel incomplete. Sonny is full of bounce as usual. After a month and a half of chasing everything from elk to Huns my own legs have toughened enough to feel younger than their true odometer reading. All this adds up to a fine evening to be outdoors even if the relentless march of the seasons has left me with little more than an hour of shooting light between the end of my working day and nightfall.

I have not come expecting one of the big shoot-em-ups that lie at the heart of western bird hunting's appeal. In my haste to get out of the house before dark, I even forgot my game vest, but the single handful of shells I found in the truck's glove compartment feels perfectly adequate for the occasion. Just as there is a time for the feel of big hunts in big country, so is there a time for the opposite: a quick turn through nearby cover motivated more by the desire to be outside after a long, confining day than by any need to shoot.

Left to my own devices I might have settled for that, but Sonny has always been the kind of dog who hunts first and philosophizes later. While I'm busy walking, looking, and letting the business of the day loosen its grip, he's busy looking for birds. If you're going to bother carrying a gun when you go for a walk in the woods, he's just the kind of companion to take along.

A quarter mile uphill from the truck, he suddenly disappears into a tangle of brush, a golden dog perfectly camouflaged by the last of the year's golden autumn foliage. I'm not paying as much attention as I should. When the bird flushes I stand momentarily flustered even after all these years spent waiting for rises like this one. But the grouse—a mature ruff the color of dark beer—hasn't been paying attention either, and when Sonny noses the bird from its hiding place it cuts straight downhill in my direction, leaving me plenty of time to turn and take the shot going away.

The retrieve proves as easy as the shooting, even though Sonny insists on pretending he has done something heroic at its conclusion. In fact, the two of us have spent too much time together in the field for either of us to take his attempts at self-promotion seriously. But as I accept the bird and admire it briefly in the last moment of light before the sun slides away behind the hills, a remarkable transformation takes place. Drinking in the grouse smell and feeling the warm press of the dead bird's feathers against my hand, I am no longer a middle-aged man standing in the shadows a mile from his house but a kid in an alder patch half a world away. The impression lasts no more than an instant but that is enough to remind me of the gratitude we should feel toward both the birds and the dogs that find them for us.

The light has started to fail by the time I turn back up the hill with the empty gun over my shoulder and the dead bird hanging easily from my grip, but the end of shooting light is the only element of the evening that invokes regret.

20.

Winter Roosters

Back when I labored beneath the unjust burden of a day job I could only hunt when my schedule allowed. When pheasants were the quarry, that meant every day from the early-October opener through the end of December when I wasn't stuck at the hospital working. I didn't get to pick and choose. If I was free on a day with winter storm warnings in effect I usually went hunting, even if that meant chains on the truck, dressing for an Arctic expedition, and visibility limited to shotgun range or less. The Labs were often the only company I could talk into coming along. When the dogs were wet or tired at the end of the day, I let them ride up front with me, even if that meant driving with an ice scraper in one hand to clear away the frozen condensation from their breath to see the road.

That's all behind me now that I work when I feel like it. During yesterday's blizzard, which provided an appropriate introduction to the month of December, I stayed inside eating cold turkey sandwiches and reading a book. I felt guilty, and the dogs didn't seem to enjoy lying in front of the fireplace as much as I thought they would. The weather was forecast to improve, and so it has. Granted, the thermometer on the porch was dropping toward zero when I left the house, but the wind is dead calm and the sunlight falling on the fresh layer of undisturbed snow makes the entire countryside glow.

Arrived without incident at a friend's ranch, I drop the truck's tailgate to a chorus of excited canine whining, flip the latches on the dog box, and release the A-team to frolic in the powder until they have calmed down enough to hunt. Today, I've brought along the odd couple. Maggie is a six-year-old German Wirehair that looks like a GSP. Her mission is simple: find the birds, point them, and hold them long enough for me to reach her.

A precocious three-year-old, Rosy, in contrast to some of my previous flushing retrievers, hunts from heel in upland cover. Her first duty today will be to provide backup if needed should Maggie face an especially difficult retrieve. Maggie is a capable upland retriever, but a long blind that requires hand signals or a barely wounded rooster running off at high speed through thick cover can justify some help from a Lab. Second, if Maggie's locator collar indicates a point down in some truly nasty cover, I'll have a better chance of killing the bird if I stay out on the edge where I can shoot and send Rosy in to flush it. Third, a small, ice-resistant spring creek meanders across the ranch's southernmost pasture. With most ponds in the county locked in ice, the late season mallards know all about it. If we do our bird hunting on the other end of the property and leave the creek undisturbed, we should have a chance to end the day with a mixed bag. When it comes to water retrieves on frigid winter days, nothing gets the job done like a Lab.

WINTER ROOSTERS

My choice of clothing this morning would make me a lock for Mr. Halston's Worst Dressed list. Instead of my regular hunting hat, I'm wearing a wool ski mask in case the wind picks up and makes face protection necessary. My body is protected by a polypropylene wicking layer next to my skin topped with several more layers of wool, some of which I can shed if need be. Because of other spring fed streams I'll have to cross to reach the best pheasant cover, I have insulated hip boots on my feet. A light leather glove covers my left hand. While it doesn't provide much insulation, it does allow a better grip on the fore-stock than most alternatives. I have a fingerless wool glove on my right hand that leaves my fingertips exposed because I've always been fussy about being able to feel my safety and trigger. I can keep that hand in a coat pocket when I'm walking. I'm also carrying heavy wool gloves in my game vest in case saving my fingers from frostbite becomes more important than shooting my shotgun.

After double checking my game vest to be sure it contains no 20-gauge shells that could drop into a barrel with disastrous consequences and adjusting Maggie's collar, the three of us are off into the last month of pheasant season.

I love hunting pheasants in December for many reasons.

1. There is hardly anyone else in the field then (most other hunters having passed their IQ tests).
2. The roosters are all fully colored and flying strong.
3. I love the winter landscape on the high plains, even when it's cold. Pheasant hunting is a great cure for cabin fever.
4. Labs do better in cold weather than hot.
5. I'm no longer distracted by bowhunting big game.
6. Tracking snow helps me locate pheasants.
7. The birds are usually concentrated in well-defined cover.

Finally—and most important of all—I derive more satisfaction from shooting one wary late season rooster than I do from shooting an easy limit on opening day. By December, I'm hunting the wiliest of the wily, the cream of the Darwinian crop. The easy pheasants are all dead by the end of October. I'll have to be at the top of my wing-shooting game, since educated roosters don't offer many chip shots. Every late season pheasant is a trophy even if I'm going to do nothing more with the bird than cut it up and eat it.

Now for some practical considerations. Pheasant hunting in December is not the same game as it was during the first week of the season, and not just because the birds are smarter. Cold weather increases their caloric requirements, and late season birds spend a lot more time feeding in the open then than they do earlier. Where they do their feeding depends upon terrain and locale. Where I hunt, that usually means grain stubble. Feeding pheasants are easy to see against a background of snow, and it's not unusual to drive past a stubble field holding dozens of pheasants in plain sight.

There's a catch to that scenario, however. Pheasants know they are vulnerable when they're feeding in an open, snowy field where every raptor, coyote, and bobcat in the area can see them. They are almost impossible to approach then, and it's usually a mistake to try. If you push them out of the field and into the nearest cover, they'll be on full alert and difficult to locate even if they haven't run into the next county after landing. It's amazing how dozens of pheasants can flush from a field, fly into a little patch of willows, and disappear forever. The best tactic in this situation is usually to ignore the obvious birds and return once they have bled back into the cover on their own.

Outfitting yourself for a late season hunt is different, too. We've already reviewed some of my clothing choices, not that I expect everyone to agree with them. One thing has changed during the years since that hunt. As much as I love wool, its bulk can make it difficult to shoulder a shotgun smoothly. These days, I rely more on layered synthetics, which keep me just as warm with less inhibition of movement when it's time to shoot.

One cannot overstate the importance of proper hats, gloves, and footwear. Choose whatever works for you but remember to plan for the possibility that the day may end a lot colder than it began. I never go anywhere at that time of year without having all the winter survival essentials in my truck: extra clothes, sleeping bag, tire chains, tow rope, scoop shovel, flashlight, hi-lift jack, and at least some food and water for both me and the dogs. Sometimes I even remember to carry my cell phone, as much as I loathe it.

I've always been a nihilist about shotguns, chokes, and loads. In my experience most poor shots are due to poor shooting, not poor choices in firearms. However, late season ringnecks often offer shots at longer ranges than they do in October, and pheasants are tough birds. By December, I've usually traded my 20-gauge for a 12.

To understand how the dogs' job description changes throughout the pheasant season, one must appreciate a paradox in the birds' behavior. Late season pheasants are prone to flushing wild, but the ones that decide to hold *really* hold, especially with deep snow on the ground. I've taught myself to ignore the 90% of the birds that flush 60 yards ahead of the dogs and hunt the 10% that don't. When they have burrowed into an impenetrable mat of frozen vegetation beneath two feet of snow, they won't be coming out without a lot of encouragement. I don't want my wirehairs digging away at snow and ice like terriers when they should be pointing. Such situations are ideal for a flushing retriever, if the dog will stay at heel without running off to bust up points. My wirehairs now do most of the heavy lifting early in the season when I'm hunting Huns, sharptails, and naïve pheasants, although I usually have one of the Labs with me just to get the dog some exercise and make an occasional retrieve. By Thanksgiving though, I want a Lab at my side every time I load my shotgun.

Now, back to that bitter day in December…

Bright sunlight has brought an impression of warmth to the countryside, but I think that is largely an illusion. The recent snowfall has covered old frozen drifts that will not quite support my weight, and they are difficult to identify beneath the blanket of powder. While the dogs can scamper across them easily, I invariably break through, leaving me mired in what is known locally as "posthole snow." At least I'm hunting instead of reading a book, and the dogs are both acting particularly well behaved.

A 300-yard walk along a ribbon of barren hawthorn produces just one point, a sharptail that flushes out of range. Finally, we reach the beginning of what I consider the real pheasant cover: a glorious tangle of cattails covering a 20-acre spring fed marsh. A few weeks earlier wind pushed many of the reeds down onto the ice, where they froze like jackstraws as the thermometer plummeted. A hundred pheasants could be hiding in the resulting tangle. So could a hundred whitetails. Fortunately, tracks in the snow confirm that the first option is more likely.

The good news is that the old snow hasn't drifted in the cattails. The bad news is that in some places warm water from the springs has left the ice soft and rotten. I can't tell good ice from bad beneath the snow. After breaking through twice in the first twenty yards, I retreat to the bank. The dogs are going to have to do it all.

As if on cue, Maggie's locator collar begins to beep out in the mess. I can't see her, and there is no way to reach her without risking a fall that could leave me soaking wet and done for the day. Rosy is just where she is supposed to be, sitting beside my right ankle. I give her the line and send her.

I know now that Rosy can key off the sound of the locator collar on one of the pointing dogs. In retrospect I think she probably had it figured out even then. She makes quite a racket crashing through the reeds as she converges on Maggie. Then I hear her rooting around like a pig, and the sound of wings beating against frozen cattails rises above a freshening breeze. It sounds as if the noise is coming from a lot of wings, an impression soon proved correct.

Hen. Hen. Try as I might to conjure up some color on those first two birds, I just can't do it. While they don't form true coveys, late season pheasants often congregate in large groups. This behavior likely represents a response to ever shrinking sources of food and cover coupled with the value of more eyes remaining alert for predators. By December, pheasants are less randomly distributed than they are in October. By the end of the season, it's not unusual to walk all morning without flushing a bird, only to find dozens in one small patch of brush.

Another hen, and then, finally, a rooster. Although it's flying almost straight into the weak December sun it's lit up like a neon sign, and it folds neatly at the sound of the shot. My ears tell me that both dogs are moving now, but since I can't see them and they can't see me I decide to let the two of them work out the retrieve themselves.

To no great surprise it's Rosy who climbs up the bank with the bird in her mouth, but now I can hear Maggie's collar beeping again. This time a rooster flushes on its own and flies straight over my head. I have my gun broken to reload after the chip shot that follows when all hell breaks loose down in the cattails, as if a dam has burst. I snap the gun shut in time to pass up two roosters at marginal range before receiving an offer I can't refuse. Rattled by all the birds in the air, I must admit an embarrassing miss with my first barrel. Fortunately, doubles provide second opportunities.

Limited out on pheasants, I whistle the dogs in and head back toward the truck. My hope that Maggie can locate a cooperative sharptail along the way prove to be wishful thinking. Then I notice several small flocks of mallards circling the creek at the other end of the property. I've got my duck vest and steel shot inside the truck. Should I or shouldn't I?

Hey, it's not *that* cold.

III.

Life with Labs

I've written a lot about hunting with Labs because I've done a lot of hunting with Labs. However, I recognize that many Lab enthusiasts do little or no hunting with their dogs. I didn't want this book to ignore them. Despite their performances in the field Labs make wonderful companions and family dogs. I'd have Labs even if I didn't hunt.

Some hunting vignettes appear in the following chapters, but only to illustrate observations I've made over five decades with Labrador retrievers. Several focus on training topics that I hope will be of interest whether you hunt or not. Full disclosure: I am not a professional trainer and don't pretend to be. Pros can draw conclusions from experience with far more dogs than any amateur. I respect their knowledge and never hesitate to recommend consulting a professional trainer. Training requires a significant time commitment. Readers unable to make that commitment should consider sending their dog to a professional.

The degree of training a dog requires varies with the intentions of the owner. If the goal is a field trial champion, the training will have to require more time and rigor than most of us are willing to invest, me included. I'd love to have a Lab that lived up to those standards, but I want to do my own training rather than sending to a pro and I'm not motivated to do it myself. On the other end of the spectrum, some of us want nothing more than companionship from their Lab and aren't interested in training at all. While I'm sympathetic to that viewpoint, I would point out that a dog with at least some basic training will be a safer dog and a more enjoyable companion around the house and yard.

By now readers should recognize that I fall between those positions. While I certainly value my Labs as companions, as I hope I've made clear, I also need them to be capable of meeting modest performance standards in the field. Not all my hunting companions even aim for that modest goal. A dog with instincts can retrieve downed game with minimal input from the handler. I do allow my dogs to behave in ways that would earn them demerits in a field trial—running the bank on a retrieve in running water, for example, or veering offline to find its own way around an obstruction. As long as the dog is safe and trying to complete the retrieve, I don't worry about such details.

Why bother with advanced training at all? By now, readers should be aware of my abhorrence of unrecovered game. A dog that will obey hand signals, sit to whistle, and take a line will prevent that better than a dog that doesn't. However, my reasons for spending time training my Labs aren't all practical and should be of interest to readers who don't hunt with their dogs.

I believe that the training process helps develop the bond between dog and handler for which Labs are so well known and respected. Dogs, like teenagers, *want* a certain amount of discipline and direction in their lives even if they don't always admit it. While training my dogs is meant to improve their performance in the field, it also reenforces a bond that can be described as love without hyperbole.

The following segment isn't all about training. Labs are complex creatures. Understanding their personalities is as important to the relationship between dog and owner as teaching them to fetch ducks. While I certainly don't know everything about Labs, I have spent most of a lifetime trying to figure them out.

That process has brought me more joy than I deserve.

21.

A Brief History of Labs

I have presented this outline of the Lab's history before and apologize to those who don't feel like reading it twice. However, I think this material is so central to understanding the breed that I'm repeating it for the benefit of those to whom it is new, with apologies to those already familiar with this fascinating story.

Labs flush pheasants and fetch ducks, guide the blind and sniff out drugs, lick faces and enrich lives. At some point, every Lab enthusiast must wonder about the origins of the remarkable animal that became the most popular dog in America for decades. The Lab's history turns out to be laced with enough intrigue to fuel a spy novel, reflecting the difficulties of reconstructing events that took place over four centuries, one ocean and two cultures divided, as one sage noted, by a common language.

Archimedes observed that given a fulcrum he could move the world. In similar fashion, unraveling historical mysteries often goes best by starting with an event generally accepted as true, even if that means beginning in the middle of the story. The British Col. P. Hawker probably provided the first written description of the Lab in his 1814 treatise *Instructions to Young Sportsmen*. Referring to the St. John's dog in distinction from the larger, more familiar Newfoundland, he wrote: "The other, by far the best for every kind of shooting, is oftener black than of another color, and scarcely bigger than a pointer. He is made rather long in the head and nose; pretty deep in the chest; very fine in the legs; has short or smooth hair; does not carry his tail so much curled as the other; and is extremely active in running, swimming… " All of which sounds a lot like a dog we know we know.

While it's relatively easy to follow the trail forward from the British St. John's dog of the early 19th century to the modern Lab, tracing the Lab's ancestry from the coast of Newfoundland to Hawker's day proves more involved. Writers, alas, must bear their share of responsibility for the confusion. When the Lab returned to the New World as a popular East Coast sporting breed in the 1900's, commentators created a history to accompany it. In the process, they perpetuated two central ideas: that the Lab derived from the Newfoundland and that the Newfoundland in turn derived from indigenous New World canines. Both ideas are probably untrue.

Abundant evidence confirms that Native Americans lived and hunted with large dogs. But British explorers reached the coast of Newfoundland as early as 1494, and there is no reliable record of dogs in the area until cod fishermen arrived from England two centuries later. The romantic notion that our Labs' genes originated here in North America enjoys little objective support. On the contrary, the breed's ancestors almost certainly crossed the Atlantic as working dogs employed by Devon fishermen plying their dangerous trade along Newfoundland's rugged coast.

As for the derivation of the Lab (then known as the St. John's dog) from the Newfoundland, the late Richard Wolters has done a brilliant job of proving it was probably the other way around. In the face of sketchy direct evidence, Wolters argued that the dog's original job description favored the smaller breed, which had to crowd into cramped dories while waiting for a chance to fetch lines, nets, and fish for its handlers. The appearance of the larger Newfoundland coincided with the later development of permanent settlements along the coast, when colonists needed large, powerful dogs to haul heavy loads of firewood and perform similar chores on land.

What were the origins of the dog that crossed the Atlantic to the New World in the first place? The most likely candidate for the title of Lab's Ultimate Ancestor is the St. Hubert's hound, originally of French origin but popular in England at the time Newfoundland's first settlers embarked. Definitive answers remain elusive, but both the written descriptions and drawings of this breed in George Turbervile's *Booke of Hunting*, published in 1576, bear a striking resemblance to modern Labs.

By this complex route, the St. John's dog became a popular British sporting breed in the early 1800's, as evidenced by Delabere Blaine's description of the breed in his 1840 *Encyclopedia of Rural Sports*. "The St. John's breed is preferred by sportsmen on every account, being smaller, more easily managed and sagacious in the extreme. His scenting powers are also great.... Gentlemen have found them so intelligent, so faithful, and so capable of general instruction that they have given up most sporting varieties and content themselves with these..." Along the way the breed acquired its enduring name, when the popular sporting artist Edward Landseer painted *Cora. A Labrador Bitch* in 1823.

Unfortunately, the Lab's reputation fared better during the 19th century than the dogs themselves. American independence and changes in the fishing trade decreased direct commerce between the breed's point of origin in Newfoundland and the new market for them among the British aristocracy. Attempts to promote a sheep industry in Newfoundland led to new restrictions on dog rearing there. No matter how highly English sportsmen suddenly valued Labs, they couldn't get enough of them to maintain breeding stock and the Lab faced the threat of extinction.

But there are no friends like friends in high places, and the Lab was fortunate enough to enjoy the favor of just the right people. During the first half of the 18th century, the 2nd Lord of Malmesbury, the 5th Duke of Buccleuch, and the 10th Earl of Home, all avid sportsmen and Lab enthusiasts, established breeding programs and went to considerable lengths to import what fresh stock they could from Newfoundland. All fortunately had children interested in maintaining the family kennels, and while none seemed particularly interested in sharing their blood lines with anyone but each other, they managed to preserve the Lab during the most precarious period in the breed's history.

While all modern Labs derive from limited bloodlines developed and maintained by a few aristocratic British families, by the beginning of the 20th century they had started to thrive in England and Scotland. The British Kennel Club officially recognized the breed as distinct in 1903. Labs began attracting serious attention in field trials and bench shows, and Viscount Knutsford and Lorna Countess Howe established the Labrador Club in 1916. Back from the brink in England, it was time for the breed to realize the next formative step in its development, which it did by crossing the Atlantic once again.

Charles Meyer registered the first Labrador retriever in the American Kennel Club in 1917. Because American wing-shooters of the day approached the field so differently than their staid British counterparts, they viewed their sporting dogs differently as well. They routinely taught their pointers and setters to retrieve as a matter of course, leaving no defined job description for the pure retriever in the pursuit of upland game. Chesapeake Bay retrievers, derived from Newfoundlands that arrived during a shipwreck in 1807, handled the serious work in the water. The Rodney Dangerfields of the sporting world, retrievers didn't enjoy a lot of respect. As late as 1927 there were fewer than 30 retrievers registered with the AKC, all – Labs, Chessies, Goldens, Flat Coated and Curly Coated – lumped together under the single category of "Retriever".

In characteristic fashion, the amiable Lab—backed by a new generation of enthusiastic American admirers—set about gaining the respect it deserved. Initially, the Lab's reputation as a favorite of the British aristocracy helped fuel the breed's popularity among

A BRIEF HISTORY OF LABS

America's status conscious *nouveau riche*, the social class to which most early Lab importers belonged. But it was only a matter of time until the breed's reputation began to disseminate to the general sporting public, largely as the result of the dogs' performance in field trials. The new American Labrador Retriever Club held the breed's first trial in 1931. Although the tests were hardly demanding by today's standards, the event drew considerable attention. By the end of the decade, Lab trials had become popular, well-publicized events attended by amateur handlers as well as the professionals who originally managed dogs for their wealthy owners.

The history of the Lab's development as a field trial star during the middle of the last century is well documented. Meanwhile, to considerably less fanfare, other events were taking place that in my opinion contributed just as much to the breed's eventual development into the Lab we know today. First introduced to Oregon in the 1880's, the ringneck pheasant had expanded its range across the Midwest, attracting a major following among American sportsmen in the process. In contrast to the quail, woodcock, and grouse that defined upland gun dogs' original American job description, pheasants favored heavy cover, ran relentlessly before flushing, and proved exceptionally difficult to recover after the shot. The explosion of interest in outdoor sports that followed the end of the Second World War found American upland hunters in need of a new type of gun dog that could beat the wily ringneck at its own game. The demands of pheasant hunting practically defined the previously unknown concept of the flushing retriever, and the Lab proved ideally suited to perform this complex new job.

As Labs began to supplant Chessies in the duck blind and pointers in the field, a subtle change took place in the everyday relationship between the dogs and their owners. In 19th century Britain and even during the early years of the Lab's introduction to America, sporting dogs largely existed to entertain the wealthy. Cared for by servants and trained by professional handlers, Labs of that era enjoyed a distant, largely impersonal relationship with those who owned them and determined the future of the breed. But as Labs grew more versatile in the field, they became popular among Americans of all walks of life. Rather than retiring automatically to the kennel at the end of the day, they rode around in trucks, lounged in front of fireplaces, and played with kids. In short, they became family dogs, and the personality traits that suited their new role in life became as highly regarded as the courage and tenacity that had made them popular in the field.

It doesn't take a genius to recognize the Thomas residence as a Lab haven. As I finished this piece in its original form, Sonny, the Grand Old Man, lay upstairs on his favorite corner of the dining room rug taking a nap, which is what he did best by then. Rocky was circling the house looking for the sharptails that occasionally drop in over the winter. The birds weren't around that day, but he didn't seem to care. Kenai, the pup, was picking through a box full of fly-tying materials looking for something to eat. (He found it, leaving a chewed-up hackle neck and a trail of feathers around my office floor.) Each in his own way, they were all being Labs, and knowing where they came from helped me appreciate them just a little bit more.

22.

The Curse of a Great Dog

By definition, great dogs don't come along often. My dad and I were fortunate enough to stumble across one early in my wing-shooting career. The dog wasn't a Lab, but the lessons I learned from him illustrated several important points that helped me when I began to raise and train retrievers on my own.

I was around eight years old when we acquired Bits. My family was living in upstate New York with lots of grouse nearby. Although my father had grown up hunting, he had almost no experience with gun dogs. A friend of his who raised shorthairs took pity on us and gave us the runt from a litter. We named him Bits and watched him develop quickly into a terrific bird dog.

This was not just our own biased evaluation. By the end of his second season, the opinion among our circle of hunting fiends was unanimous: We had the dog of a lifetime. We entered him in a few field trials where he did well, although we didn't much care. It was his remarkable ability to find grouse and woodcock that mattered to us. I don't remember investing much effort in his training, which we handled ourselves. Of course, we assumed that his performance in the field reflected our ability as trainers. I think we even took credit for his exceptional nose.

In addition to his pointing ability, Bits was a great retriever. His marking ability was uncanny, and as an unfortunate result, I began my wing-shooting career without learning to mark fallen birds down reflexively. I didn't have to, because Bits found them no matter what. I remember hanging on to one end of a check-cord while my father introduced him to the basics of hand signals. Our methods must have worked, because by the time he matured he handled as well as many Labs I've subsequently owned—although not as well as all of them.

One night, Dad and I were sitting next to a beaver pond hoping some black ducks or woodies would arrive at last light. When the sound of wings setting overhead roused me from an adolescent daydream about a girl who set beside me in our 7th grade science class, I saw a large, dark, unfamiliar waterfowl descending above the tops of the alders. My dad correctly identified the bird as a brant even though neither of us had ever seen one before. When he shot it, the wounded bird glided down on the far side of the pond and began to swim for the brush as soon as it hit the surface. The chase lasted well into the darkness of a moonless night, but Bits eventually emerged from the gloom with the bird in his mouth. He really could do it all.

During our move West in the early 1960s, the lugs on one of our Suburban's rear wheels inexplicably failed at highway speed somewhere in the middle of Saskatchewan. The ensuing rollover nearly killed us all, including Bits. I think Dad was more worried about the dog's injuries than he was about his own, and probably mine. All of us survived with no lasting sequelae, but the incident made us realize that it was time to start grooming an eventual replacement for Bits. That's when we came face to face with the curse of the great dog, although we weren't astute enough to recognize it at the time.

Once we settled into our new home in Seattle, we bought another GSP puppy. (One corollary of the great dog curse is that once you've had one you'll return to the same breed repeatedly no matter how well those subsequent dogs perform.) In retrospect, Dos (as in Dos Equis), was a capable, biddable dog that never got the chance he deserved simply because he wasn't Bits. When he ran through several coveys of quail during his puppy season, we decided his nose

THE CURSE OF A GREAT DOG

was weak. When he shook up the first pheasant he ever retrieved, we accused him of having a hard mouth. Time was limited then, with Dad hard at work and me busy with school. When we did have an opportunity to hunt we wanted to make the most of it, so we took Bits. In retrospect, I think Dos would have made a good gun dog, if only we'd given him a chance. The problem wasn't the dog; it was our expectations.

I was in college when Bits died at a ripe old age. That was the only time I ever saw my father in tears. With room for another dog in the kennel, we went with another shorthair. We devoted more time to her, and she turned into a capable dog even though she still labored in the long shadow Bits cast. By the time Dos finally went the way of all dogs, I had developed some insight into our problem and suggested that we strike out along new lines entirely. It was time to accept the fact that there simply wasn't going to be another Bits. This realization eventually led to a long line of Brittanies that behaved wonderfully, pointed, retrieved, and left everyone in the family delighted. We had broken the curse, but it took years to do it.

While all this was evolving back home in Seattle, I was completing my long medical education and thinking about a dog of my own. There had never been a Lab in the family until I bought a yellow male puppy in Montreal at the completion of my medical internship. I was setting off for an Indian Health Service assignment in a remote corner of Montana, where I anticipated two-years of challenging medical practice and some great hunting. I was right on both counts.

Bogey turned out to be a blockhead. I can think of no other single adjective to describe his remarkable combination of stupidity, belligerence, and incompetence. I didn't have any kids yet, so I spent a lot of time working with him, all to no avail. I was visiting my parents in Seattle when a friend back in Montana called to tell me that the dog had been hit by a car and killed. I felt devastated. However, while no one likes to lose a dog that way, parting company with Bogey turned out to be a blessing in disguise.

Faced with the prospect of starting my next bird season with no dog, I picked up a copy of the Seattle paper, scanned the classified ads, and bought the male puppy that turned into Skykomish, named after a favorite steelhead stream. While this impulsive decision violates nearly every principle regarding the selection of a hunting dog, it soon made me look like a genius.

My change of fortune became apparent from the start, during Sky's early puppy training. I decided that I had become a brilliant teacher by magic, a folly I recognized only in retrospect. As with Bits, it was all about the dog, right from the start. By now, I've had enough experience to know that the surest way to look like a brilliant trainer is to start with a brilliant puppy.

The country was loaded with both upland birds and waterfowl, and he was the only dog in my kennel. Pressed into service in the field at an early age by circumstances, Sky began the season at age six months and performed remarkably. With the wisdom of hindsight, I realize that asking him to do too much too soon presented a great opportunity to ruin a young dog, but Sky was bomb-proof. He didn't just fetch ducks. I hesitate to think how many we shot over him during his first year back in the days of the 100-point Central Flyway daily limit. He marked, handled, and crashed through brush and ice, all with one of the softest mouths I've ever seen. He also proved tenacious and capable in upland cover, and my friends and I may have killed even more pheasants, sharptails, and Huns over him than ducks.

Sky only improved with the passage of time. When I moved to Alaska, he went with me. There, he learned to ride in the back of a Super Cub, avoid bears, flush ptarmigan, and fetch ducks from the frigid North Pacific. When we moved back to Montana, he enjoyed two more years of waterfowl and wild ringnecks before dying quietly in his sleep at age fifteen. Unfortunately, his hip x-rays had shown significant dysplasia. I didn't know anything about the problem when I bought him, and I don't think the breeder did

THE CURSE OF A GREAT DOG

either. While his bad hips never affected his ability to hunt, I was responsible enough to neuter him, and he never sired a litter.

I had made plans for his succession though and was working with another young male at the time Sky died. There was just one problem. Luke wasn't another Sky. Neither were Jake or Becca. They all went to good rural homes to become pot-lickers, cow dogs, and family pets. I wasn't overjoyed with Sonny at first either, for the same reason as I now realize. I did stick with him though, long enough to enjoy his company as a capable retriever for the duration of his long life. By the time Rocky and Kenai came along, I was finally over it. Neither of them was going to be another Sky either, but by accepting that fact, I was able to give them more of the time they deserved, and they became good working Labs. Not great, mind you... but good.

Going all the way back to Bits and Sky, I've had five hunting dogs I consider great: two Labs, one shorthair, one wirehair, and one blue tick hound. (Since I first wrote this piece, it seems likely that young Keta will join this list.) Lucking into an exceptional dog early in your career as a trainer can leave you with unrealistic expectations for years to come. Comparing all subsequent dogs to such high standards usually just sets them up to fail. Facing a dog's inability to meet expectations, no matter how unrealistic, inevitably leads to questioning one's own competence as a trainer. We need positive feedback during training sessions just as much as dogs do. When training leads to frustration and disappointment instead of reward and satisfaction, one tends to do less of it. That can be the beginning of a vicious cycle in which less effort on your part leads to less learning by the dog, which leads to even less effort from you.

One mark of an accomplished trainer is the ability to derive the most from dogs with differing degrees of natural talent. That requires a level of experience with a number of dogs that only professional trainers are likely to attain. I'm not one, but I have nothing but high regard for those who are. I have learned that every young dog deserves patience, optimism, and an honest investment of time, especially when the bar has been set at unrealistic levels. If you hunt a lot and expect good performance from your dogs in the field some will wash out no matter what, but that decision should be made based on that dog's abilities, not on those of a great one that preceded it.

I was eventually dealing with the curse of another great Lab. Rosy became a terrific waterfowl dog, perhaps even better than Sky. I really didn't give her a chance to prove herself in upland cover for two reasons. Her retrieving talent was so obvious I wanted to leave her free to concentrate on the breed's original job description, and both of my German wirehairs proved excellent upland retrievers. If Sky still holds the title as my best flushing Lab, he may not hold it indefinitely. Little Keta is still very much a puppy, as I must remind myself when she acts like one. However, during her first upland season her enthusiasm and talent suggested unlimited potential.

She may or may not be another Sky or Rosy, but I'll give her every opportunity to become what she can.

23.

Aging Gracefully

It's unfortunate that all Lab owners don't have an opportunity to experience the unique atmosphere of a duck camp, even if they have no interest in hunting ducks. Dogs will likely outnumber people, frolicking everywhere like kids at a swimming pool. There may be a Chesapeake Bay retriever or two and perhaps a golden, but most of them will be Labs, getting ready to do what Labs were meant to do and making no secret of their excitement.

It's hard to keep track of your grown kids when they live a thousand miles away, the distance that separated son Nick in Seattle from our rural Montana home. It felt wonderful to see him and his wife, Shannon, when they stepped out of their car in the middle of our eastern Washington duck camp one November evening. In some ways I felt even more excited to see the third occupant of their vehicle: Folly, an eleven-year-old female yellow Lab whose credentials as a family member ran as deep as any.

Bird dogs and retrievers had always been a part of my parents' household. As a rebellious teenager I once considered asking my mother if she loved the dogs more than she loved me but decided I probably didn't want to hear the answer. Mom and Dad were in their early 80s when their last Lab and German shorthair died during the same year, and they announced that they were too old to get another dog. I trumped that gloomy view by presenting them with the wriggly yellow puppy that became Folly.

That was the second-best idea I've ever had in my life (the best being marriage to Lori). My father's health began to fail first, and I will never forget smuggling Folly past the sympathetic and briefly myopic eyes of the head nurse on the ward where he lay recovering from his first major surgery. I think that visit did as much for his recovery as the excellent medical care he was receiving. When it all caught up with him at age 92, that left Mom alone in the house—save for Folly.

The dog became the focus of her life, and none of us doubted that Folly added the two more years she enjoyed before she died six months before our meeting with Nick and Shannon. When my parents expressed concerns about the possibility that they might outlive the dog—as they did—I'd promised them that Lori and I would always care for Folly. While I certainly meant to keep that promise, I knew that our regular travels to second homes in Alaska and then Arizona might be hard on her. Besides, we already had five dogs to care for, which would make it hard to provide Folly with the individual attention she'd enjoyed during the final years of my parents' life. So, when Nick and Shannon announced that they would really like to have Folly, I recognized a match made in heaven.

I would like to report that Folly came bounding out of the back of Nick's car that night, but it would be more accurate to describe her arrival on the ground as a graceful descent. She had spent a lot of time in our family duck camp during her younger days, although my parents' progressive debility had kept her away for several years. She seemed to recognize the place though, and her obvious excitement suggested recollection of the days she'd once spent there as a working retriever. Lori and I had kept my parent's ancient camper as a "guest house" for visiting friends. Folly immediately headed for it and began to scratch at the door of her old home.

She clearly recognized duck camp and all it meant to her when my parents were alive. We would have to wait until the following morning to see if she remembered what she'd once come there to do.

A Lab's lifespan resembles a human's, temporally compressed as if by Hollywood special effects. Like most parents, I look back on my kids' lives and wonder where the time went. One day Nick was a curly-headed toddler, and the next day he oversaw IT at a major Seattle company. That confused perception is even more dramatic for the dogs in my life, who seem to go from puppies to prime working dogs to old-timers in less time than it takes to tell the difference. Each of those stages of canine life requires special consideration from owners, none more so than the last, which concerns us here. Like aging parents, aging Labs face some special health concerns, but I will leave those matters to you and your vet. In this essay, I'm more interested in the intangibles of the changing dynamic between dog and owner as the dog ages.

The Labrador retriever was developed with a very specific purpose, as discussed earlier. The breed's character eventually made the Lab appeal to a broad range of owners holding widely varying expectations for their dogs. All need to recognize that aging Labs are different Labs.

This discussion begs a definition: What is an "aging" Lab? There is certainly no set numerical answer in years. I've had basically healthy Labs slow down as if they had hit an invisible wall at age nine. I've had others that couldn't wait to jump in the truck and go at age 12. Thirteen-year-old Rosy was snuffling around happily beneath my desk as I wrote this piece. This should come as no surprise.

Forty years of human medicine taught me that people age in startlingly different ways. Now in my mid-70s, I have longtime outdoor companions who just don't want to go anymore even though there is nothing specifically wrong with their health. On the other hand, I have friends ten years older than me who can still hike all day through the field behind their dogs. That's why it's so hard to use age alone as a cutoff for difficult medical procedures in people. I've sent 90-year-olds to the operating room for heart surgery and watched them enjoy years of happy life afterward. Better the right 90 than the wrong 60. The same principle applies to Labs.

Aging Labs, like aging people, above all else benefit from something to *do*. Life without purpose soon grows old—an interesting figure of speech in itself. It's normal for older Labs to spend a huge part of the day sleeping. An exceptionally athletic dog during his working career, Kenai eventually decided that his old age job description consisted of lying on his dog pad and holding the house down in case of a sudden windstorm. Even so, I made a ritual of taking him for an easy walk every day and throwing him one retrieving dummy on the lawn before we went back inside. He made it clear that one was enough. The instant I tossed that dummy he began to act like a puppy again. I think it made him feel better about the rest of his day. I know it made me feel better about mine.

Older dogs clearly benefit from regular exercise. The challenge is to make the amount you allow fall within the narrow window between too much and not enough. That's easy with younger dogs. They rarely need motivation, and absent unusual weather conditions or other exceptional circumstances one can safely allow the dog to set its own limits. Older dogs may require encouragement. Since dogs appreciate order in their lives, I tried to make Kenai's exercise ritual consistent by taking him for a regular walk along the same route at the same time every day. Consistency of timing allowed him to look forward to the outing. Sometimes he frolicked along the way, using his nose to look for the pheasants that occasionally inhabit our fields. (Even during hunting season, we leave our "house" gamebirds alone.) On other days, he simply shuffled along at my side. The choice was his to make, and I didn't push him to do more on a slow day or restrain him when he was feeling frisky. He always knew he was going to enjoy that one ritual retrieve before he retired for the day.

Older Labs frequently develop impaired vision and hearing. While consultation with a vet is always appropriate to exclude a treatable cause, adaptation usually helps more than treatment. Rosy was almost totally deaf during her last two years. Among other things, this meant that I never started the truck and headed from home without confirming that she was in a safe location. She'd never be able to hear a vehicle coming. When I praised her, I did so with touch rather than voice. When I had to scold her (she had an uncanny ability to get into garbage cans and strew trash across the floor), I simply held her head gently but firmly in my hands, got in her face, and stared. She knew what that meant, and my displeasure served as punishment enough... at least until she decided to explore the garbage can again. I cut old dogs a lot of slack in their behavior, perhaps because I'd like people to do the same for me when my turn arrives.

Impaired mobility is another common problem for aging Labs, usually involving the back legs because of arthritis or hip dysplasia. Veterinary evaluation may help, but the owner will still likely have to deal with a dog that has some difficulty getting around. Understanding and modification of the living environment help. Stairs can be a problem, and it may be wise to put everything the dog needs on one floor of the house. Getting the dog in and out of cars can become a problem. Be ready to assist, and if the dog is too big to handle, consider a ramp. Since some older dogs will balk when first introduced to a ramp, as Rosy did, it's wise to start the process early. Having the dog's daily food ration at the top of the ramp will help.

As caloric expenditures decline with decreasing exercise, an older dog will inevitably gain weight unless the owner modifies its diet. Obesity is common in older Labs, and it only makes other age-related problems worse. Old dogs don't tolerate cold (or heat) as well as they once did. We generally rotate all our dogs between kennel and house, but Kenai earned permanent housedog status in the winter. During the summer, we left the doors open and let the dog choose the environment that suited him best.

We're all familiar with the idea of comfort dogs for older people—a role Folly played admirably for my parents during their final years. I think old dogs benefit from regular canine companionship too. Since the rest of our working dogs—Rosy and two German wirehairs—were a bit too large and bouncy for the job when Kenai reached his dotage, that responsibility fell to Molly, our Jack Russell terrier. The way she doted on Kenai was both comical and moving, as she shooed the other dogs away from his food dish, barked warnings at him to compensate for his deafness, and curled up on the dog pad with him to keep him company at night. Old Kenai and our Jack grew up together since puppyhood and were nearly inseparable. Lucky Kenai.

Back in duck camp, Folly seemed a bit perplexed when I strapped her into a neoprene vest before we set off at dawn. The temperatures were moderate, and I didn't bother with insulating vests for my working Labs unless it was below freezing. However, I knew she hadn't been seriously wet in a long time and wanted to take every reasonable measure for her comfort. I deliberately took her to a blind I knew she'd hunted from years earlier. She seemed to recognize her surroundings. Then we settled in to wait for the ducks, and Folly settled in to whine.

It may be difficult for those who have never shared a cramped blind with a whining dog to realize what an obnoxious experience that can be. I was almost ready to walk Folly back to the truck when a lone wigeon appeared over the decoys and Nick dropped it. Because of my heartfelt obligation to recover every bird we kill I'd brought Rosy, then our hotshot, along in case a tough retrieving situation arose. Stone dead in the middle of the decoys, Nick's bird offered Folly just the chip shot she needed. I walked her out of the blind door and told her to *fetch*.

She certainly didn't exhibit the spectacular water entry I prize so highly, but I didn't expect her to. In no time, she was churning across the water investigating decoys—typically a puppy mistake. Then she zeroed in on the fallen duck, and all her dormant instincts began to kick in. She delivered the bird faultlessly and spent the rest of the morning scanning the sky without offering a single whine.

I could imagine my parents cheering her performance.

24.

All in a Day's Work

With some weighty subjects on the schedule in the chapters ahead I'm going to offer a bit of levity even if it does come at my own expense.

Not long after I first arrived in the rural Montana town that I would call home off and on for 50 years I met a delightful older gentleman I'll call Homer Jones. In addition to being a great raconteur and fund of local knowledge, he was a devoted bird hunter. Better yet, he always hunted with one of his black Labs.

That was a different era in the practice of medicine. We weren't working for salaries in a big clinic free from the hassles of running a business. We had no designated Emergency Room Doctors as most hospitals do today. The dozen physicians on the hospital's medical staff took turns covering the hospital after hours and the emergency room 24/7 (without pay). In retrospect I don't know how we did it. Being young helped.

The only time this responsibility really troubled me was when I had to cover the ER from Friday morning until Monday morning during hunting season. I didn't have to be on site physically, but I had to be available with 15 minutes of the hospital. Since these were the days before cell phones, I also had to be next to a land line. That was more than enough to guarantee a wasted, precious day of hunting season.

As I'd come to expect, my turn that October fell on a gorgeous Indian summer day. I was at home feeling sorry for myself and tossing bumpers for Sky when the phone rang. The ER nurse, whose competency I'd already learned to respect, seemed unusually flustered. "It's Homer Jones!" she shouted. "He's on his way in and he says you need to get here as soon as possible!"

"What did he say was wrong?" I asked.

"He wouldn't say. He just said you had to get here!"

With the weekend shot anyway I saw no need to debate the issue. After kenneling Sky I started for the hospital, although perhaps not quite at breakneck speed Homer seemed to expect.

Moments after arrival I saw Homer's rig pull in beside mine. When he jumped out, he looked remarkably hale and hearty for a middle-aged man having a medical crisis. Before I could get the first question out of my mouth, he opened the door to the back seat. Out hopped his big male Lab with his head framed by a dense corona of porcupine quills.

I made myself count to ten. Suppressing the urge to blow up, I reminded myself that the weekend was ruined anyway and I was already there. Besides, Homer was a nice guy, and the dog was a Lab.

Sophisticated medical evaluation was unnecessary. I mean, there was the Lab and there were the porcupine quills. The nurse had joined us by then and gratefully decided we didn't need to bother with forms and paperwork. After I asked her to go fetch a large Kelly clamp, I rigged up some crossties on the tailgate of my truck.

Then came the moment of truth. For this to work, the dog would have to remain calm and cooperative. Canine sedation is routine for those who do it all the time, but I didn't know the drugs and dosages. I wasn't about to inadvertently put Homer's dog down. Fortunately, with assurance from Homer the dog behaved like an angel and let me spend an hour pulling out quills without protest. After a final inspection to insure I hadn't overlooked anything in the back of the throat, I declared the procedure successful.

"How much do I owe you, Doc?" Homer asked after he returned the dog to his truck.

I scratched my head. This was one of those situations in which no amount of money could be worth more than a simple act of goodwill. Besides, the dog was a Lab.

"Forget it," I said. "Let's just go chase some birds together next time I have a day off. But I do have to ask you a question." I paused for dramatic effect. "Why didn't you call the *vet*?"

"Jeez, Doc," Homer replied. "I didn't want to bother *him* on a weekend."

All Creatures Great and Small? Wouldn't want to bother Dr. Herriot unnecessarily. I finally understood my position in the local health care hierarchy.

Homer and I did get out with the dogs the following weekend and shot a bunch of pheasants.

25.

The Wolf at Your Side

The 1940 discovery of the Lascaux cave ignited interest in the fascinating world of cave art, the remarkably sophisticated depictions of Upper Pleistocene fauna hidden in subterranean locations throughout Spain and southern France. Carbon dating indicates that the Lascaux artists worked around 17,000 years ago. The subsequent discovery of the Chauvet cave revealed even more dramatic paintings, created around 30,000 years BCE. The most dramatic finding at Chauvet may not have been on the cave's walls, but upon its floor.

There lay two sets of footprints, preserved with remarkable clarity. One, belonging to a boy around eight years old, is now widely regarded as the oldest set of human footprints ever found. The second belongs to a medium-sized canine. The tracks weave and wander together, as if the two that made them were traveling together as companions. Do the tracks represent evidence of the oldest known association between man and dog? Was the canine a wolf, a dog, or something in between?

Sometimes it can be hard to tell, even now. When I was still a student in Seattle many years ago, the Olympic Peninsula was a favorite outdoor destination. Steelhead were often the prime quarry, but we usually packed dogs and shotguns along and shot sea ducks on Hood Canal or brant on the spit at the mouth of Sequim Bay.

One such hunt took place in the company of my father, a good friend of his, and the friend's female Lab, who was not yet a year old at the time. Bluebird weather slowed the pace of the shooting that first morning. I did manage to drop a brant on the inside of the spit. Our friend's dog retrieved the bird with enthusiasm and style beyond her age.

We were staying at our friend's place on the east side of the bay. After we'd cleaned up and wiped the salt off our shotguns, we settled down on the deck overlooking the water without paying much attention to the dog's whereabouts. Suddenly, a commotion erupted in the dense brush above the waterline. We looked over the railing to see the dog chasing a young blacktail doe down the beach in front of us.

Our frantic shouts went unheeded as the deer plunged into the frigid water of the bay. Such behavior is not unusual in coastal blacktails, which are adept swimmers. In Alaska, I've encountered them swimming in salt water far from shore. Like caribou, they often use water as an escape route when pursued by wolves as they are the superior swimmers. When the deer jumped in and the dog hit the water in pursuit, the smart money was still on the blacktail.

We had a skiff hauled out on the beach below us. When the dog ignored more shouts and whistle blasts, we raced down the bank and launched it. By this time, the deer was a hundred yards offshore and the Lab was gaining. Before we could close the distance, the dog swam up the deer's back, grabbed both its ears in her mouth, and pushed its muzzle underwater. By the time we reached the scene of the disaster, the deer was dead by drowning.

In the decades since then I've spent a lot of time around apex predators of all kinds including grizzlies, cougars, and wolves, but I've never seen a more professional assassination. The dog wasn't even fully grown, and the deer outweighed her by a factor of two to three. She was a calm, quiet, well-trained dog, and nothing had taught her to behave the way she did. Something about the deer's flight had triggered instinctive behavior that made her act like a wolf. That's because all our calm, quiet, well-trained dogs *are* wolves.

Love them or hate them—and I have friends in both camps—wolves are remarkable animals. They are the world's largest canine and the only one found naturally in both Old World and New. While it is now generally accepted that all domestic dogs derived from the wolf—and that the dog is one of several wolf subspecies, *Canis lupus familiaris*—the details of when, where, and how some wolves became dogs have long been the source of confusion and debate. Those of us who really want to understand our dogs need to wade into the muddle in search of all the answers we can find.

To this end, Mark Derr's *How the Dog Became the Dog* (Overlook Duckworth, London, 2011) provides useful resource material and some interesting reading. I'm not offering a powder-puff book review. I don't always agree with Derr, and his obvious affection for both dogs and wolves sometimes seems to compromise his approach to the science. However, he certainly makes a valiant effort to sort through a wealth of often contradictory opinion and data.

The search for the origin of the dogs that became our Labs depends on two kinds of evidence: physical—such as bones or the footprints at Chauvet—and genetic. Study of the physical evidence has been going on for centuries, and unclassified canine bones lie tucked away in museum drawers all over the world. Genetic evidence reflects new science. Not long has passed since the first sequencing of the human genome was completed, but geneticists have now applied the same processes to dogs and wolves. While the details of the science are complicated, following DNA sequences from both animals back through the fossil record to a point of common origin should allow us to answer the question *when*.

One longstanding theory held that some wolves started to become dogs by scrounging food in and around human settlements. Some feel this may not have happened until early humans abandoned their original nomadic lifestyle in favor of developed agriculture around 5,000 years ago. However, early genetic studies suggested that dogs diverged from wolves between 11,000 and 16,000 years ago. At the other extreme, some believe this took place over 100,000 years earlier. The most recent genetic studies have settled on estimates between 30,000 and 40,000 years ago, a timeline most but not all authorities now accept. Despite the frustrating confusion, it seems most likely that the dog emerged from wild wolf lineage when humans were still wandering hunters during the last Ice Age. It's comforting to know that our dogs did not originate in garbage dumps, as many originally believed.

Although almost everyone agrees that the dog arose in Eurasia, the details of *where* also remain controversial, with various investigators arguing in favor of China, the Middle East, or the central Asian steppe. Others, including Derr, suggest that differentiation from wolves took place independently at multiple locations. However, geographic outliers like the African Basenji and Australian dingo have more gene sequences in common with other dogs than with any modern wolf, suggesting that a "melting pot" phenomenon took place long ago.

The *how* question may be the most interesting of all. The archaeological record establishes that the dog was the first wild animal to be domesticated by humans. What motivated this event, and what unique characteristics of the wolf allowed it to take place?

It is easy to see how wolves and early hominids, including the Neanderthal, could have benefited from each other's company during the Ice Age, when apex predators were concentrated in limited areas where local climate conditions allowed prey species to survive. Early wolf-dogs (or dog-wolves, as Derr calls them) helped humans by barking to alert their camps to potential danger and serving as mobile food sources themselves when prey was scarce. They also made us more effective hunters, by locating game, engaging in its pursuit, and holding it at bay. Numerous anthropological studies show that hunters with dogs bring more game back to camp than those without (as if we didn't know that already). The interesting point is that this principle holds true almost universally across a wide range of cultures, habitats, quarry, and means of take.

The kind of symbiosis proposed for wolves and early humans had to work both ways. Armed with bows, arrows, and spears, our ancestors helped wolves kill prey they had helped run down. Wolves shared the benefit of mass killing events like the slaughter at buffalo jumps, which came about because of organized human hunting strategies. Humans provided wolves with food in the form of carcasses and camp scraps, and warmth from fires during frigid Ice Age climate conditions. Deliberate control of breeding also freed selected wolves from the constant physical and nutritional stress of bearing young.

But why was the wolf the only wild canid our early ancestors successfully domesticated? Wolves are uniquely social animals with complex means of communication that they utilize constantly, just like people. Except for African painted hunting dogs, they are the only wild canid that hunts in packs. Wolves are naturally programmed to hunt cooperatively—a trait that must have facilitated early interactions with human hunters. Perhaps most crucially, wolves seem to like people (when we're not trying to kill them) and are capable of emotional bonding with humans—a trait eventually selected for and passed along to those wolves that went on to become man's best friend.

I've never fallen for the modern, politically correct representation of wolves as misunderstood lapdogs. However, it is difficult to reconcile a genetic basis for socialization between wolves and humans with a long cultural tradition suggesting otherwise. Think Aesop, *Little Red Riding Hood*, and *Peter and the Wolf*—not to mention a modern vocabulary full of phrases such as, a wolf in sheep's clothing, thrown to the wolves, and lone wolf terrorist. Yet a large body of behavioral studies shows that at least some wolves bond readily with people under the right circumstances, especially those raised as puppies. Their ability to engage emotionally with humans is unique among wild canids and rare elsewhere in the animal kingdom. No doubt those were the genes selected and bred for thousands of years ago when our human ancestors needed an alarm system to let them know when a cave bear was about to pay a nocturnal visit.

Whatever the circumstances that led to mutual tolerance, cooperation, and eventual affection between early wolf-dogs and humans, the path those original genes followed on their way to our Labs proved long and tortuous. At first glance, the phenotype—the physical expression of those genes—of a terrier, poodle, or even a modern hunting dog doesn't seem to have much in common with a wolf. Much of this divergence in appearance and behavior likely arises from human engineered selection for traits deemed desirable—obvious in the case of a retriever, less so, to me at least, in the case of a French bulldog (which recently replaced the Lab as the dog breed registered most frequently by the AKC). But if you get past the cover and look at the book inside, you'll still find the genes of a wolf.

Archaeological evidence suggests that domesticated dogs accompanied the first people to reach the New World by way of the Bering Sea land bridge near the end of the Ice Age around 15,000 years ago. These dogs played an important role in Native American life long before European contact, although, except for the Eskimo dogs', those animals' genes eventually disappeared. While the origins of both the Lab and Chessie are easily traced to our Atlantic Coast, their genes derived from imported dogs of European extraction with no contribution from the "native" dogs that arrived with North America's first human inhabitants. The late Richard Wolters' book *The Labrador Retriever* (Petersen Prints, Los Angeles, 1981) gives this confusing subject a particularly thoughtful treatment.

At the beginning of her second season, Rosy was admirably aggressive whenever a duck fell, but calm and demure the rest of the time—just like our friend's young Lab back at the mouth of Sequim Bay. More so, in fact, than I ever could have imagined.

Lori and I had spent a slow but pleasant morning in the blind. At least we had a few birds when I started to pick up the decoys and noticed that the dog had quietly disappeared. Surprised and not particularly happy with this behavior, I handed my unloaded shotgun to Lori and set out to find the missing dog. I was walking down the track we'd driven in on, blasting angrily on my whistle when a clatter erupted in a dense stand of Russian olive behind me. I turned around just in time to see a wild-eyed mule deer doe bearing down on me like a freight train.

I managed to sidestep the deer like a matador executing a *paseo*. The deer roared by so close I could have touched it—as did Rosy, hot on its heels. It took me thirty minutes to collect the dog, by which time I was having serious difficulty heeding my own advice about not applying discipline when you're angry. How could this potential calamity have taken place? I maintain a zero-tolerance attitude toward dogs chasing deer. That's usually an easy fix when you live in the country with a lot of deer around and own an e-collar. Although I had not neglected her training in this regard, Rosy had taken me right back to the Sequim Bay shoreline fifty years earlier. At least she didn't catch the deer, although not for lack of effort.

Once again, I'd been reminded of our dogs' origins, and how thin the veneer of domestication lies upon the genes of a wolf.

26.

Current and Banks

In the introduction to this segment, I explained that most of it would not be devoted to hunting. However, I also needed a place to discuss training, within the limitations acknowledged earlier. Some training topics are best illustrated by examples from the field, and this is one of them. I invite non-hunting readers to bear with me for a few paragraphs or skip them all together.

It was the week before Christmas by the time the first serious blast of arctic air—an Alberta Clipper, in local parlance—hit us that year. Temperatures were plummeting when I turned in the night before, and I didn't even need to look at the thermometer that morning to know we were in sub-zero territory. That kind of weather spells the end of the waterfowl hunting in most places. Not where I live, where ducks concentrate on spring fed creeks and sloughs once the rest of the local water is covered in ice. In fact, I'd been biding my time in the upland cover for weeks, just waiting for the right morning to tackle some mallards.

The weather certainly hadn't diminished the dogs' enthusiasm, and a chorus of excited barking greeted me as I approached the kennel. I hesitated briefly in front of Sonny's run and made an impulsive decision. Instead of calling for the old pro, I continued down the line and released young Rocky. He'd performed well since the upland season opened three months earlier, and he seemed ready to meet the creek.

By the time the sun's luminous crescent began to edge above the horizon we were tucked into a frozen tangle of reeds, shivering quietly and waiting for the first wave of mallards to return from the fields. A dozen decoys tacked back and forth in the current in front of us. This spring-fed creek never freezes, and I knew that hundreds of mallards would be returning to its open water sometime that morning. The brutal conditions practically guaranteed fast shooting—if we could endure long enough to enjoy it.

The wait proved mercifully brief that morning. I'd barely had time to get cold when the whistle of setting wings tore through the air behind me. Moments later a greenhead lay kicking in the decoys, but unlike the blocks it wasn't attached to an anchor. By the time Rocky hit the water, the dead bird had already begun to bob away downstream.

One of the strengths young Rocky had already demonstrated was marking ability. The line I gave him compensated for the current, but he had the vector to the original fall locked in his computer and wasn't about to change his mind. He headed upstream, the duck headed down, and I began to castigate myself for putting a young dog in a confusing situation without adequate preparation. The only smart thing I'd done was to hold off with my second barrel so the dog could concentrate on the single fallen bird. We eventually recovered it after a long downstream sprint together, but the experience nicely illustrated a principle I already knew: Dogs should be introduced to current before duck season.

A lot of Decembers and a lot of retrievers have come and gone since then. Because I do a lot of duck hunting over moving water, I've learned to avoid that scenario by working my young dogs in creeks during the off-season with specific training goals in mind. No amount of preparation will eliminate all the difficulties a dog faces the first time it encounters current and banks, but a little effort

CURRENT AND BANKS

over the summer has certainly made my life easier during the last month of duck season.

Never mind shotguns and waterfowl—I don't even bother with a training dummy on a dog's first trip to the creek. None of this should take place until the dog has proved comfortable and capable in still water. While retrievers may seem born with an innate ability to swim, current just isn't an intuitive concept for dogs. Pointed directly upstream in brisk current, even a strong dog may wind up going backwards at full speed ahead. Most dogs need to *learn* how to tack back and forth across the current, seek out the seams of quieter water, and otherwise navigate their way through water that just won't hold still.

The time to do that is during the summer, under controlled conditions. Pick a hot day, put on shorts, and jump in with the dog. I like to take my young dogs along when I fly-fish our local creeks, which happen to be the same places where we'll be hunting ducks by the end of the year. At first, I don't try to teach them anything. I just want them to get a feel for swimming in current and dealing with the banks on either side.

It will take most dogs some time to learn that the shortest distance from Point A to Point B may not be a straight line. Some may act panicky the first time current takes them in a direction they don't plan to go. That's why it's important to make this introduction under the right conditions: warm weather, water shallow enough for you to wade, no downstream obstructions. And no steep banks to negotiate—that will come later. My rule of thumb is that if I wouldn't feel comfortable swimming there myself, it's not the right place for a naïve young dog.

Once the dog appears comfortable—and mine quickly learned to look forward to trips to the creek—it's time for dummies and the most important lesson of all: *The dummy (or the duck) isn't going to be where it fell by the time you get there.* Paradoxically, it's the dogs with the best natural marking ability that have the most trouble with this concept. Again, pick a nice day and the right spot, plan to get wet, and prepare to be patient. Unless you like losing dummies, it may help to station an assistant downstream, since even the simplest retrieves may go awry at first.

Start in calf-deep water and smooth, even current with the dog beside you. Toss the dummy upstream, aiming for a position in the current that will bring it by you 10-15 feet away. Watch the dog to see if it is tracking the dummy visually. If so, give the *fetch* command as the dummy draws even with your position. If the dog completes the retrieve uneventfully, repeat the process while aiming to have the dummy pass by at progressively greater distances until the dog can track the dummy all the way across the creek.

Some dogs just won't get it at first. In that case, aim the next toss to bring the dummy right into the dog and make some encouraging commotion as it approaches. You may have to make these throws ridiculously short at first. The idea is to serve the dog a can't-miss situation.

With this step mastered, it's time to teach the dog to look downstream. In actual hunting situations a dead duck can drift a long way, especially if multiple birds are down in the water at the same time. Begin with the same basic setup just described, with a good hundred yards of open water straight downstream. Toss the dummy ten yards or so directly across the current and make sure it hits the water with an attractive splash. Then watch the dog. If it's tracking the dummy, let the drift continue for 20 yards or so and give the *fetch* command. If that goes well, let the dummy drift progressively farther downstream on successive tosses until the dog can handle 80-100 yards of drift.

If the dog has trouble at first, give it another slam-dunk. Tease the dog with the dummy to get it excited, slap the dummy down right in front of it, and let it drift straight downstream for a few feet before commanding *fetch*. If the dog can't track the dummy that far, it isn't ready to retrieve in moving water.

Once the dog appears comfortable with retrieving across current and downstream, get out of the water and start working from the bank, as you will in many duck hunting situations. Banks, like current, offer retrievers an element of challenge largely unique to hunting moving water, since lakes, ponds, sloughs, and marshes usually don't have them. As with current, steep banks are best addressed with some experience before hunting season.

Some dogs will launch off a steep bank like a missile the first time the opportunity arises, but some will balk initially. As in any training situation it's best to start low and go slow, at least initially. Pick a bank no more than a foot or so above the water in an area free of brush and other obstructions. It helps if the dog is already wet, so don't make this the first retrieve of the day. The dog should be solid on everything we've already discussed, so the only new element to the exercise is the bank. Give the dog an easy retrieve with plenty of time to track the dummy downstream and issue the *fetch* command when the dummy arrives.

If the dog responds with a spectacular leap and a geyser of spray, congratulate yourself for being a brilliant trainer. More often the dog will run the bank, which poses an immediate dilemma. You want the dog to complete the retrieve, but running the bank *for no good reason* (more on this later) is a bad habit that's easier to prevent than correct. When this happens, I keep the dog on a leash and pull it back to heel if it starts to run the bank. (Have an assistant standing in the water downstream to snag the dummy.) I repeat the process until the dog understands that to make the retrieve, it will have to jump off the bank. The natural urge to retrieve will usually overcome failure to launch.

But sometimes it doesn't, in which case I just make my own water entry with the dog in tow. (There's a reason why we go through all of this during warm weather.) That extra bit of encouragement is usually all it takes. If that fails, I'm not above physically pitching the dog off the bank as the dummy drifts by. That method sounds drastic and should only be used as a last resort, but that's the way my father taught me to swim at age three and I've loved the water ever since.

After a summer of this the dog will probably be treating you to good water entries from banks by duck season. Even so, some dogs just never get it, and you may have to accept that fact. Kenai, for example, spent his entire career hitting the water like a reluctant matron entering a cold swimming pool even though I put him through countless versions of the drills we've just reviewed. Kiska hated the water from the start and never grew to like it, a flaw I've never seen in another Lab.

Leaving the water in a stream with steep banks can be more of a problem for retrievers than entering it. Most dogs demonstrate a remarkable ability to claw and scramble their way up, but some circumstances—glare ice or overhanging banks, for example—just won't allow it. One obvious solution to this challenge is to set up in a location that won't require the dog to deal with difficult banks. Summer training can help, too. Start by pitching a dummy onto the opposite bank of the stream in a place where the dog can see it. Choose a location where the dog will have to face a bit of a climb to complete the retrieve. As the dog builds confidence, give it progressively steeper banks to climb. Remember that in brisk current the dog will usually reach shore downstream of the shortest line to the fall.

While running banks is usually regarded as a fault, those rules weren't written for running water under hunting conditions. A dog that spends a lot of time hunting creeks and rivers will eventually face a bank too steep to climb. That's why I like to give my dogs the freedom to improvise as needed, whether they're running the top of a bank looking for the best route to a floating duck or swimming in search of a good place to climb out. That's not the same as letting a dog run the bank just because it feels like it. I want to be the one to make the call, not the dog. That means being able to stop the dog with a whistle blast when I see it making poor decisions. Absent that ability, letting a dog get away with running banks on a whim will eventually lead to problems.

I've made the point before, but it's so important that it bears repeating. Canine safety is always a paramount concern, and currents and banks involve potential dangers not encountered elsewhere. Current running through obstructions beside a bank deserves attention. Dogs can handle a little brush and debris, but large sweepers are another matter. I assess the dog's ability during the summer, when I can get into the water too. Again, if I wouldn't feel comfortable swimming in a location, the dog shouldn't be there.

Ice shelves pose the greatest danger to a dog swimming in current. There's no way to practice dealing with them over the summer, but that doesn't really matter. The only safe way to avoid trouble with ice shelves above deep current is to avoid them completely if there is any chance the dog could get swept under. However, smaller ice shelves above still water are routine obstacles during winter hunting, just like banks. Dogs must learn to deal with them, either by breaking through ice too thin to support their weight or clawing their way up onto thicker ice. Introduce them to the concept in water shallow enough so you can get in and help them should the need arise.

Whatever the nature of the hazard, remember that in moving water danger always lives downstream. It's not enough to know that everything is safe right in front of you. Know the terrain below, and if there are any questions about its safety, set up the decoys somewhere else.

Creeks and rivers can provide great waterfowl hunting, particularly during cold weather when they offer the only open water around. That means great opportunities for the dogs, but it also means new challenges. Current and banks can make otherwise routine retrieves difficult even for seasoned retrievers. Introducing the dog to new challenges under controlled conditions during the off-season is always a wise training principle, and this is no exception.

27.

Bones and Beyond

The first thing a new Lab owner is likely to discover after cautiously turning the puppy loose upon its new home is that little Labs love to chew. They bring remarkable determination and persistence to the process. Owners may greet these dental exercises with responses ranging from amusement to anguish, depending on the value of whatever household object has just felt the sting of those sharp little puppy teeth. This kind of chewing differs in several ways from more controversial adult aspects of chewing we'll examine shortly. Puppy chewing has little if anything to do with nutrition, since dogs at this age are just as happy chewing objects of no food value as they are chewing organic matter. Think of it as analogous to teething behavior in a baby.

Puppy chewing does offer some potential benefits to the dog. Improved saliva flow and mechanical cleansing lead to a helpful oral environment as permanent teeth begin to erupt at around five months of age. The entertainment value of a romping puppy can improve socialization with members of the new household. If other dogs share the home, teething play can help to establish the natural pecking order that inevitably emerges whenever dogs share space and compete for resources.

Drawbacks to this behavior are few except for occasional anguish over the loss of some favored personal household item. Dogs' "baby" teeth are soft. Unless owners are careful about restricting access to hard objects, teeth can chip. As a rule, the chewed object should be soft enough to indent with your thumbnail. Occasionally, small objects can pass into a puppy's throat and obstruct breathing with potentially serious results. Don't deliberately let a puppy chew anything shorter than its jaw. If the dog is making the object smaller as it chews, remove it before it reaches this size. Puppy play can get out of hand as participants become possessive. Even mild-mannered older dogs can snap at a puppy hard enough to injure it given sufficient provocation. Monitor these interactions carefully especially when another dog new to the environment is involved. With these simple caveats in mind, let the puppy enjoy the modest benefits of chewing and don't worry about it.

Chewing among adult Labs is a more complex and controversial subject. On one end of the spectrum, some knowledgeable Lab owners consider bone-chewing important, healthy canine behavior that provides unique nutritional and social benefits. They may advocate allowing it with few if any restrictions. Meanwhile, others hold that chewing offers no objective benefit to adult dogs and that doing so exposes them to unnecessary and potentially serious health risks. Many Lab owners, who simply want to do what's best for their dogs, either haven't given the matter much thought or have become overwhelmed by contradictory opinions. As I try to sort this out, let me acknowledge that vigorous scientific evidence is rarely available to settle the matter. Reliance on opinion, personal experience, and anecdote will have to suffice.

Advocates of allowing adult Labs to chew cite a variety of real or perceived benefits to the dog. Of course, both the risks and benefits of this behavior vary with what the dog is chewing, and we'll visit that topic shortly. Let's start with bones as the prototype.

Some argue that this behavior should be encouraged because it is instinctive and provides dogs with natural sources of nutrition that may be lacking in some commercial dog food. There is no doubt that chewing was (and is) an important adaptive behavior for wild canids including our Labs' biological ancestors. An extensive fossil record of chewed bones wherever these animals gathered supports this theory. Wild dogs depended heavily on scavenging to provide food sources, which is why our own Great Plains once supported such robust populations of prairie wolves. Back when that habitat was home to 60 million bison, some were constantly tipping over for various reasons that had nothing to do with predation. In addition to their food value, these bone-chewing sessions likely contributed to social bonding, the formation of packs, and the eventual development of efficient group hunting strategies.

How important are the unique nutritional benefits ascribed to bone chewing then and now? Most of the discussion centers around bone as a source of calcium, ideally accompanied by phosphorous in a ratio ideally suited to encourage healthy bone formation. No one disputes that bones are an excellent source of calcium or that calcium is an important nutrient. However, wild dogs had few good alternatives, and our dogs do. Now dietary calcium does not have to come in the form of whole bones with their attendant risks. Ground bone meal can provide plenty of calcium, and most (but not all) commercial dogfoods provide adequate amounts. More is not necessarily better. If you really need to have your dog chew bones to meet its requirements for calcium and phosphorous, you need another dog food. Read the labels and consult your vet.

Some claim that letting dogs chew bones provides a more "natural" balance in the ratio between dietary calcium and phosphorus needed for healthy bones. Granted, the balance between these two important nutrients is complex. However, I'm skeptical about the theory that dietary balance has much to offer the dog. The mammalian kidney has remarkably complex mechanisms for maintaining homeostasis among key minerals during bone metabolism, upon which we will never improve. If the intake of calcium and phosphorous is adequate, the dog's body will sort it out barring unusual metabolic illness.

The dog's instinctive impulse to chew for nutritional reasons isn't all about calcium and bones. Predators and scavengers need calories even more than they need calcium. The wild environment offers no better source than fat-rich bone marrow. Having examined countless kill sites where a coyote, wolf, jackal, or feral dog has consumed a dead ungulate, it seems clear to me that most wild canids are more interested in eating what's inside the bones than the bones themselves. If it were all about calcium, bone fragments would be the first to go, but crime scene investigation usually shows that long bones are cracked open rather than consumed. Canine tooth and jaw structure is well suited to this task. Living in a home or kennel today, our Labs don't need marrow the way their ancestors did unless there is something wrong with their dog food.

One final potential benefit chewing behavior offers adult dogs is improved oral and dental health. Chewing stimulates saliva flow and mechanically cleanses teeth, although the overall contribution of these actions to the dog's oral health remains uncertain.

Other factors contribute to our dogs' fascination with chewing and our willingness to tolerate it. Most adult Labs love to chew almost as much as puppies do. We naturally enjoy seeing our dogs have fun and helping them meet their social needs. However, this enjoyment raises a central question. Are we encouraging dogs to chew for our benefit or the dogs'? It's hard to address that question without examining the downsides of this behavior—the risks in the ratio of risks to rewards. If there were none, we could just toss the dogs some bones from the butcher or buy them packages of chewies and be done with it.

Health hazards related to adult chewing come in two main forms, both of which involve harm to the digestive tract in various places and in various ways. The first arises from bone splintering, which can result in small, sharp bone fragments lodging anywhere between the mouth and deep in the intestinal tract. The injury may be trivial and result in nothing more than excess salivation or odd chewing movements, or it may lead to a deep perforation requiring surgery. The choice of what to let the dog chew can significantly impact the chance of such an event.

The second major health threat comes from the possibility of obstructing either the gastrointestinal tract or the upper airway with a bolus of foreign matter from the chewed object. In the case of intestinal obstruction, the problem may pass with nothing but supportive care, or it may require endoscopic removal or surgery. Airway obstruction can be an immediate life-threatening emergency, the reason the Heimlich maneuver was developed for people. I've never performed one on a dog, but I wouldn't hesitate to try in dire circumstances.

Obstruction hazards aren't limited to bones and chew toys. For reasons known only to the dog, a friend's Lab swallowed a large wool hunting sock. Fortunately, it went down the esophagus and not the trachea. It still required sedation, endoscopic removal, and a vet bill, which the owner was happy to pay given the good result. One of the first things I learned as a young father was that when a baby becomes a toddler every object in the house needs to be beyond reach. That's a good rule to follow when young Labs are indoors.

Even the most devoted advocates of letting dogs chew acknowledge that some chew objects are just too dangerous to justify. Bones with sharpened points head the list—a pork chop bone cut with a butcher's saw is a prime example. Cooked bones are always best avoided. Because they soften during cooking, they are more likely to splinter or grow smaller as the dog chews, making it easier for them to slide down the back of the throat and get stuck. Bird bones are ill-advised, much as your Lab would love to tear into the leftover carcass from that Thanksgiving turkey. Soft, hollow, and fragile even before cooking, they are problems waiting to happen. Furthermore, for Lab owners like me who train their dogs to handle birds delicately in the field, allowing them to chomp on bird carcasses is a step in the wrong direction.

In a roundabout way, we have just defined the kind of bones you should allow your dog to chew if you decide the benefits outweigh the risks. Firm, long, uncooked bones are preferred, hard enough to resist easy splintering but not hard enough to injure teeth (remember the thumbnail test). The bone should be longer than the dog's jaw, to minimize the chance of it sliding into the back of the throat. Since bones often get smaller as the dog chews them, it's wise to observe and take the bone away when it gets small enough to slide back into the airway.

Bones aren't the only possible choices for owners who decide they should give their Labs something to chew. At this point matters become even more confusing. Back when I began my relationship with Labs decades ago, a bone was a bone and that was about it. Now a wide variety of commercial products offers a range of alternatives, including competing claims about their safety and benefits.

These products divide into two general categories: those made of "natural" organic material and those made of something else.

Dried pig ears, bully sticks, and rawhide twists are good commercial examples of the first. Because of their composition these products have some nutritional value although their overall contribution to dogs' health is debatable. This is a good place to mention two other organic alternatives if only to discourage them. Labs love to fetch sticks, which are cheap and abundant. However, they make poor chew toys because of their tendency to splinter and fragment. Some people like to offer their dogs antlers from deer and other ungulates to chew on. After a bad winter, our dogs drag plenty of them up out of the coulee behind our house, but I confiscate them immediately. They are too hard for dogs to chew without risking damage to their teeth. This said, I have friends who routinely let their Labs chew shed antlers without problems.

The second general class of chew toys consists of variously shaped and textured items made of substances such as resins and rubber. They add nothing to the dog's nutrition but may (or may not) be safer. Their construction, at least in many cases, seems to reduce the possibility of fragmentation or aspiration into the airway. One problem alluded to earlier is that there is virtually no accurate information about the relative safety of any of these products—or even, for that matter, the overall incidence of serious adverse effects from chewing of any kind. It's mostly a matter of observation and conjecture, although every experienced vet I know seems to have stories to confirm that dogs really can get into trouble when bones and toys wind up in the wrong place. Some of these tales are humorous, but others are tragic.

There is more to the pros and cons of chewing than nutrition and gastro-intestinal injury. Some dogs become aggressive during this kind of play, which may make them hazardous to themselves and others. For obvious reasons, chewing is a highly undesirable trait for Labs that will be employed as retrievers in the field unless the trainer is a fan of pre-tenderized duck burger. Having spent decades teaching Labs *not* to chew, I find it best to avoid confusing them by encouraging this behavior in some situations while discouraging it in others.

What to make of all this confusion? Absent good data, the best I can do is point out some area of general agreement and describe what I do myself.

1. There is no compelling nutritional need for dogs to chew on bones or anything else.
2. Dogs should not receive bones that have been cooked, sawed, or come from birds.
3. Owners should observe dogs while chewing, especially when they are being introduced to a new object.
4. Organic chew toys like rawhide may be safer than bones and artificial toys may be safer yet, but under the wrong circumstances all can lead to problems.
5. Most Labs like to chew, but few of them need to.

After taking all these factors into consideration, I keep my dogs away from the bad stuff, feed them high quality dog food, supplement their diet with table scraps rather than bones, and toss them an occasional rawhide chewy under supervision. That approach seems to represent a reasonable compromise among all these competing recommendations.

When in doubt, consult your vet!

28.

The Lab in Winter

*...as he faced the firing squad, Colonel Aureliano
Buendia remembered the distant afternoon
when his father took him to discover ice.*
Gabriel Garcia Marquez
One Hundred Years of Solitude

That sentence earned the future Nobel Prize winning novelist credit for one of the great opening lines in literature, right alongside *Call me Ishmael.* The image deftly leads the reader into a remote tropical setting in which it is quite possible to grow up without ever seeing ice. I remembered that line poignantly on two separate occasions when visitors from tropical northern Australia and Zimbabwe marveled like children at our Montana winter landscape and even put snow in a jar in an effort to take some home. (It didn't work.)

I also remembered Marquez the first time Kiska saw snow. She was a spring puppy, and events would not have transpired as they did save for one of those Memorial Day blizzards for which our part of Montana is notorious. The storm was accurately forecast, and while I knew the big dogs would be fine in the kennel, I brought Kiska back inside the house the night before the storm struck. (Small dogs do not tolerate cold as well as big dogs, for reasons we'll discuss later.) The storm passed through overnight, and we awoke to a stunning winter landscape with a foot of pristine powder glistening in the sunlight. The temperature had risen well above zero by then, and I decided it was time to introduce the puppy to the conditions she'd face during her upcoming seasons as a working retriever.

Her first few steps through the snow were tenuous, as if she'd awoken on another planet, but that didn't last long. In no time, she was frolicking across the lawn, sending up geysers of fresh powder in her wake. Then she began to roll, shake, and burrow through the powder much as my friends and I used to do on similar mornings back when I was a kid. Joyous behavior like that usually goes best with company, so I sent Molly, our rambunctious Jack Russell terrier, out the door to join her. A short-legged, short-coated Jack, Molly immediately found herself buried in the snow. The only way I could keep track of her was by following the progress of her frantically wagging tail.

The subsequent game of tag went on for nearly an hour and probably would have lasted all morning had I let it. I finally walked around to the kennel and released the big dogs—Rosy, Kiska's older half-sister, and Max and Maggie, our seasoned German wirehair pointers. All three were seasoned field dogs who associated fresh snow with hunting trips. Ignoring the games on the lawn, all three of them headed immediately for the truck, practically begging me to drop the tailgate so they could jump into their dog boxes and let me take them hunting. In fact, bird season had been closed for months, but that's a difficult concept for eager hunting dogs to grasp. They finally gave up and joined Kiska and Molly in the riot in progress on the lawn.

Granted, nothing particularly noteworthy took place during this morning of manic frivolity, but these events illustrate an important point. Labs love winter no matter how uninviting the weather seems to us, and it is a mistake for their owners to deny them the opportunity to enjoy it, especially out of misguided concern for the dogs' safety and comfort. There are 12 months in every year, and it's a shame not to let our Labs be Labs for half of them just because it's often cold and dark outside.

Let's begin by reviewing some facts about our favorite breed's physiology. Labs began to become Labs as working dogs in the Newfoundland cod fishing industry during the 1600s. It's hard to imagine a background that would demand greater tolerance for cold than swimming around in the frigid water of the North Atlantic for days on end. Dogs incapable of dealing with this demanding environment were removed from the gene pool, whether by accident or design. The survivors passed their ability to function in extreme cold on to the dogs that eventually became our Labs.

With few exceptions, I consider Labs the best cold adapted dogs on earth today. Only a few dog breeds I know fare as well or better in cold weather. That short list includes sled dogs like malamutes and huskies, several of which inhabited our neighborhood back when I lived on Alaska's Kenai Peninsula. Their owners kept them outdoors even when the thermometer hit 30-below, and the dogs usually preferred to bury themselves in snow rather than retreat to their doghouses. That impressed me as extreme at the time, although the dogs didn't seem to mind. They survived on road-killed moose and loved to bark, especially when I was trying to sleep after a long shift at the local hospital. While I would never keep my own dogs under such conditions, there was method to the madness. When they were running the famous Iditarod sled dog race and sleeping indoors in front of a fire just wasn't an option, they needed to be adapted to those conditions before they hit the trail.

I'll also include another gundog breed in the elite group of cold tolerant dogs: the Chesapeake Bay retriever. In contrast to the Lab's, the Chessie's origin story is well documented and confirms their ancestors' ability to survive and thrive in the North Atlantic. In Alaska, I enjoyed hunting sea ducks on Kodiak Island with a friend's Chessies. Those experiences left me deeply impressed by the dogs' courage and enthusiasm in some of the least forgiving conditions I've ever seen.

That brings us to Labs. I recognize two components of the breed's ability not just to tolerate cold but, apparently, to enjoy it. The first is mental. I'm not sure that I can explain why, but Labs just seem to be delighted by the cold. They get excited when the temperature drops and snow begins to fall, perhaps just because they associate these conditions with going hunting—their favorite activity of all—just as Rosy did when young Kiska was romping on the yard that day. The second derives from the way they are built. Use your fingers and eyes to examine the structure of your Lab's coat. When temperatures drop below freezing, long guard hairs keep ice away from the dog's hide, while the dense, fluffy undercoat traps air, stays dry, and provides a remarkably high R-factor.

There are a couple of downsides to the features that make the Lab's coat so cold resistant. The first is that the same characteristics that allow Labs to function well in cold have the opposite effect when it's hot. My Labs are much happier and perform better at 10-below than at 80-above. You'll notice the second when it's time for the dog to shed and dog hair starts to cover the house. Thanks to that dense undercoat, nothing sheds like a Lab!

Since snow and cold are no excuse for ignoring a Lab's inherent need to remain active year around, let me share some ways my dogs and I have enjoyed winter together. Cross-country skiing was a favorite activity of mine for years. Our Kenai Peninsula home was located right on the edge of the national Moose Range with nothing but pristine wilderness outside the door. If you followed a line of latitude east from there, you would hit exactly one road (the Alcan Highway) before you reached the Atlantic. A nice little salmon stream named Funny River ran past our yard, and its surface was always frozen solid by Thanksgiving. Given a full moon and a fresh layer of powder, I'd strap on my skis, call Sky from the kennel, and ski on the ice for miles upstream toward the mountains. Since the terrain was inaccessible by foot, boat, or aircraft, I doubt that anyone else ever reached the terrain we visited. Thanks to Sky panting at my side, I never felt lonely even when no one was around for miles.

One caveat about skiing with Labs... Routine teaching of the command *heel* doesn't take skis into consideration, and Sky and I would often get royally tangled up on the first such adventure of the year. Fortunately, it seldom took him long to figure out that when I was on skis my "feet" were a lot longer than usual and learn to adjust his response accordingly when I told him to heel.

Alaska winters also provided great opportunities for dog owners who were pilots. Put skis on a Super Cub and you could land in places you'd never get to otherwise. My Labs loved to fly. Sometimes we went just to get out of the house, but by February the days were long enough to let us go ptarmigan hunting. (The season lasts through the winter in most parts of Alaska.) That really got the dogs wound up and gave them a chance to do what Labs do best. Since I was often on snowshoes, it also gave me an opportunity to start getting back in shape after two months of darkness.

You certainly don't have to live in Alaska to enjoy your Lab's company in winter. I think the best single activity you can engage in to maintain your Lab's mental and physical fitness is simply taking the dog for a walk, which is good for my own mental and physical fitness, too.

I used to do a lot of cougar hunting in the winter (much of it "catch and release," since I enjoyed chasing cats more than killing them). Of necessity, my canine company on those winter treks consisted of my hounds rather than my Labs. However, cat hunting left me with a deep respect for the mountains in winter, when virtually no one else was ever there to disrupt the solitude. It also taught me appreciation for the art of winter tracking, even when I wasn't hunting anything. The Labs provided perfect company on many of those outings.

Experienced trainers recognize the tendency of all dogs to regress and forget lessons they have previously learned absent constant reinforcement. (Humans suffer from the same problem.) It takes a lot less time and effort to remind a Lab of lessons it has already learned than to teach it something new. No matter how foul the winter weather, I could almost always find a few minutes to take Rosy and Kiska out to review the basics—a long blind retrieve or a few simple hand signals. Frozen pigeons buried under a layer of snow forced them to use their noses to locate them even when it felt too cold for them to smell anything. If it's truly awful outside, I can always put them through the fetch-hold-drop sequence right in my office while I'm trying to think up another brilliant idea for my favorite editors.

THE LAB IN WINTER

Labs are ultimately water dogs. Liquid water can only get so cold—32° F or 0° C—at which point it becomes a problem, not because of its temperature, but because it turns to ice. Readers from southern parts of the country usually won't have much trouble finding open water where their Labs can swim, but in Alaska and Montana, where I've spent my adult life, that's rarely the case during winter. The trick is to use your imagination, do some scouting, and keep some basic safety considerations in mind.

Since saltwater freezes at a lower temperature than fresh water, some readers may need nothing more than a convenient ocean beach nearby to keep their Labs swimming throughout the winter, as I did while living in Alaska. Here in Montana, I have several choices: spring fed creeks that run at a constant temperature warm enough to resist freezing; tailwaters below dams; and larger rivers that run fast enough to keep ice at bay throughout much of their length. Most of these options come with an important warning related to ice shelves. I realize that I've addressed this hazard before but keep returning to it after commiserating with friends who lost their dogs to ice shelves in moving water.

Some can be wide enough to drown a dog that gets swept beneath them, while smaller ice ledges that form along shorelines can be difficult for a dog to climb onto on the way back in. I have two simple rules to mitigate these hazards. 1. In moving water, never work a dog upstream from an ice shelf even if it's a long way away. 2. Never let a dog swim near a shoreline ice ledge unless you know you can extricate the dog if need be. If in doubt, keep the dog on shore or go somewhere else.

Opinions differ about the value of insulating neoprene vests when dogs are outside in cold weather. Even after a lot of Internet research and discussion with several respected veterinarians, I can't find a definitive, scientifically based answer. I generally avoid them unless temperatures are extreme, simply because I think they impede the Lab's ability to shake itself dry and fluff up that air trapping undercoat. However, I now use them far more often than I once did.

There is one important exception to this and other principles about Labs in cold weather that I've already mentioned: dogs at either end of the age spectrum. Like all warm-blooded animals dogs lose heat through their skin. Because puppies have a higher ratio of surface area to body mass than their adult counterparts, they get colder quicker. This doesn't mean that puppies can't go outside during the winter, but it does mean those excursions should be brief, the owner should be alert to signs that the pup is getting cold, and a reliable heat source should be nearby. I never introduce young dogs to cold water in the winter. Those initial swimming lessons will be far better received when they offer a respite from summer heat. We'll revisit the topic of canine hypothermia in detail shortly.

Does keeping your Lab kenneled outdoors help increase its cold tolerance? Once again, I could find no vigorous, scientifically tested answer. My father was a firm believer in conditioning dogs to cold by keeping them outside. Since I grew up with that principle, I still do the same. However, I provide my dogs with high quality insulated dog houses and shelter from the prevailing wind. For social reasons more than shelter from the cold, each of the dogs spends time in the house every day, and one of them also stays indoors every night on a rotating schedule. Puppies spend their days inside our heated garage during the winter. How much good does this cold weather conditioning do when it's time to work the dogs outdoors in zero-degree weather? All I can say is that when visiting friends from warmer climates arrive in the winter, their dogs don't seem to perform as effectively or as happily as mine. The same can usually be said of the hunting party's human members.

Thus far, this discussion has focused upon the Labs in our lives, but there's another side to the story. We need to get outdoors in the winter too, to keep ourselves in shape and enjoy one of the year's most beautiful seasons when, at least in my part of the country, I'll have the woods largely to myself save for the wildlife and the tracks it leaves behind. My Labs provide a wonderful combination of companionship and motivation then, and I know that I enjoy being outdoors far more with them than I would without them.

That's just one more reason why Labrador retrievers have become such an important part of our household, and that relationship shouldn't end just because it's winter.

29.

Forgive them their Trespasses

During the middle of March 2020, Lori and I were hunkered down safely in our rural hilltop home waiting for the coronavirus pandemic to run its course. The only positive step we could think of was volunteering to return to duty at our local hospital as physician and nurse should the need arise. Other than that, there was little to do but maintain a positive attitude and stay busy. I had stories that needed writing, and Lori can always find work to do on the photo computer. We spent a lot of time with the dogs and a lot of time cooking, which we both enjoy. With freezers full of wild game, we weren't worried about the developing shortages at the grocery store.

Rosy was in the house with us one bitter cold day when Lori, a skilled baker, decided to make a loaf of bread to accompany our evening meal. When the welcome aroma of freshly baked bread reached my office, Rosy left her dog pad and headed upstairs to the kitchen. With the bread cooling on the counter, Lori turned her attention to the main course, which, as I recall, was green chili pheasant. When she turned around several minutes later, the loaf of bread had vanished, apparently into thin air.

In response to her angry shout, I raced up the stairs. (Whenever Rosy misbehaved, she suddenly became *my* dog.) The bread, of course, had not vanished into thin air but into Rosy, as the guilty look on her face and the crumbs on her muzzle quickly established. The remarkable aspect of this act of larceny was that Rosy had pulled it off so stealthily that Lori didn't realize it was happening even though she was standing nearby in the kitchen.

My Lab, the cat burglar.

I assume that most readers of this book have established important relationships with Labrador retrievers. Little wonder—they are remarkable animals whether they are serving as household pets or working companions in the field or, as is in our household, both. However, the same intelligence, curiosity, enthusiasm, and ability to understand people that make them so welcome and useful in these settings also make them sly masters of mischief. Sometimes it is a wonder that we put up with them at all. Our tolerance for the mayhem they sometimes cause is a testament to the winning nature of their personalities.

After decades spent sharing my household with Labs, I've become something of an authority on their misdeeds and aggravations.

Food Thieves

Yeah, Rosy was good at it, but she was an amateur compared to her predecessor, Kenai. A big, athletic yellow male who charged through thick bird cover like a rhinoceros, he hardly looked like the kind of dog that could become an accomplished pickpocket. Looks can be deceiving. His accomplishments as a food thief eventually earned him the household nickname "Counter Surfer." The name didn't do him justice, for despite his weight, his vertical leap reached well above the level of the countertop when motivated by food.

He was an expert safecracker, too. After losing all sorts of inadequately secured breadstuffs to his nocturnal escapades, we started storing our loaves and pastries in an old wooden roll-top breadbox. His ability to climb onto the counter and open it proved surprising enough. Then after a series of early morning scoldings he started rolling the top back down after he'd emptied the larder, as if he were trying to cover his tracks. Faced with a choice between harsher punishment than I wanted to administer and a gluten-free diet, I eventually started putting him out in the kennel like a real dog every night.

But it was Sky, my first Lab, who was responsible for the Brinks Robbery equivalent of Labrador retriever food heists. As usual, I'd spent Thanksgiving Day in the field with the dog, and we both arrived home cold, tired, and hungry. I mixed Sky a bowl of food and left him in the garage with it while I went inside to make myself a little less unpresentable before our Thanksgiving dinner guests arrived. Unbeknownst to me, my then wife—who lacked Lori's enthusiasm for the field—had set the cooked turkey in a platter on top of the freezer in the garage to create more working space in the kitchen. When the doorbell rang and she asked me to go out and fetch the bird, I found no evidence of a turkey where she'd told me to look. What I did find was Sky, looking like a pregnant hippopotamus. Fortunately, our dinner guests were understanding Lab owners, and the traditional sweet potatoes, dressing, and gravy tasted fine all by itself.

Snap

Alert the media! Labrador retrievers can break things.

I've been fly-fishing even longer than I've been raising Labs. During a dinner table conversation with like-minded friends one evening, the subject of broken fly rods and their causes arose. "Electric car windows!" one party claimed. "I rolled the tip of my favorite bamboo rod up in one last year."

"Overhead ceiling fans," someone else said. "It's mostly just a problem in the tropics, but a fan can sure eat a rod."

"Small stuff," I said. "The real threat comes from Labrador retrievers." Then I related the following story.

Some years back, I modified the space beneath my pickup topper by building a sleeping platform under which I could stow my gear on trips lasting overnight. The foam padding on the bed also made a convenient place to lay fly rods when I didn't feel like breaking them down completely and casing them (as, yes, I know I always should have been doing).

Ever the optimist, Sonny always assumed that whenever I dropped the tailgate on the truck, I was about to take him somewhere. His vertical leaping abilities were almost as good as Kenai's. When I opened the truck one summer day to make sure my favorite fly rod was in place prior to a trip to our local trout stream, the dog went sailing past me and onto the sleeping pad. Broken down in two pieces still attached by line and leader, the rod was lying on the foam, and Sonny immediately became entangled in it. When I tried to call him to me, he assumed I was about to leave him behind and retreated to the back of the pad, dragging the rod all the way. Both sections had snapped by the time I finally got him under control.

That rod was made by Sage, which had an excellent replacement policy for broken rods. When composing the cover letter to accompany what was left of the rod back to its maker, I thought about inventing a wild tale involving a world record brown trout, slippery rocks, and a waterfall, but finally just told the truth. They replaced the rod at nominal cost. I've bought a lot of Sage rods since then.

The all-time record for the most destruction in a single incident, however, belongs to Rocky. The preponderance of male dogs in these stories simply reflects the fact that I was not smart enough to have girl Labs for years. When Rosy and Keta joined the family, the ladies quickly began catching up in the chaos department.

I don't remember who or why someone gave daughter Gen a chukar when she was a little girl, but Chuck adapted quickly to life inside a dog crate at the foot of Gen's bed. One day during my complicated life as a single parent I forgot to take Rocky out of the house and put him in the kennel before leaving for work. That afternoon, I picked the kids up after school, drove home, and opened the door to a scene of mass destruction.

Rocky retrieved gamebirds as well as waterfowl, and Chuck the Chukar was a gamebird. In his determined effort to retrieve Chuck, Rocky had eventually torn open the cage, leaving Chuck free to fly around the house with the dog in hot pursuit. Everything inside the house that a large Lab could knock over was on the floor and feathers were everywhere. We never recovered Chuck, although I was pretty sure I knew where he was. Since I didn't have the heart to tell Gen, I suddenly remembered that he had flown outside past me when I opened the door. I'm also pretty sure Gen was too smart to buy that, but she didn't have the heart to tell me either.

Querencia

This term may not mean much to readers unfamiliar with the work of Ernest Hemingway or my lesser known but still talented friend Steve Bodio, but I'll explain as I go along. The term derives from the Spanish verb *querer*—to want or desire—and refers to the common tendency of fighting bulls to select, apparently at random, a small portion of the bull ring to retreat to and defend. Labrador retrievers do much the same thing, albeit less aggressively.

I don't know why Labs pick these favorite spots or how they select them, but they all seem to do it. Once one has made up its mind about that location it is almost impossible to keep the dog from returning to it compulsively no matter how inconvenient that might be to human members of the household. Offering seemingly more attractive options rarely changes the dog's mind.

I too am a creature of habit. I always sit in the same place at the head of our table when we eat. Unfortunately, Rosy chose the small area of the floor directly under my chair as her primary *querencia*. While I don't allow our dogs to beg for scraps at the dinner table, I've always enjoyed their company while we're eating. But short of banishing her to the kennel, as I was sometimes forced to do, I could not keep her out of that spot whether I was trying to sit there or not. If I booted her out, pushed my chair back, or stepped into the open kitchen to stir a sauce or pick out a fresh bottle of wine, Rosy would inevitably be curled up on the exact spot my chair needed to be by the time I returned.

Rosy's secondary *querencia* was an overstuffed chair that Lori bought me for Christmas one year. Rosy didn't care whether I was sitting in it or not and would walk right across the dog pads we'd bought for her to climb into that chair. I spent more time than usual there when I was recovering from brain surgery, and Nurse Ratched was not happy about the proximity between the dog and my recent surgical incision. I considered the therapeutic value of Rosy's company to be more important than the theoretical risk of a wound infection.

Kiska's *querencia* was in our bedroom on top of our double bed. She could have chosen Lori's side, but that would have been too much to ask for. It didn't matter to her whether I was trying to sleep there or not. I always threw down two comfortable dog pads at the foot of our bed before I hit the hay. Rosy would stay on hers all night, but as soon as I started to doze off, Kiska began creeping slowly back into her spot, leading with her muzzle, followed by one front leg at a time, until I had a 60-pound female Lab sleeping on top of me.

These anecdotes are just random selections from a long list. Rosy snored and barked at nothing in the middle of the night. Kenai walked in his sleep. Rosy quickly taught Kiska how to excavate the lawn, whether to bury bones or dig up pocket gophers. They all knew how to turn dogfood into methane gas at the most socially awkward moments.

However, reviewing even these egregious examples of canine mischief forces me to make an honest admission: none of them were the dog's fault. Lori knew enough about our Labs' counter surfing abilities to avoid turning her back on Rosy and the bread, even for an instant. I should have broken my fly rod all the way down and put it in its case the way my father taught me when I was a kid. Who in their right mind allows their daughter to keep a live chukar in her bedroom?

More generally effective options were available then and still are now. I know how to make a Lab stop engaging in undesirable behavior, but just didn't feel like doing it in all those situations. They must deal with enough discipline when I'm teaching them to retrieve. All these problems could have been prevented by keeping the Labs in our comfortable outdoor kennel all the time instead of some of the time, but I didn't feel like doing that either. Why should I? Of course, they are all working retrievers, but they're friends and family, too.

At the conclusion of the events just described, we were still living in the coronavirus era and taking our social distancing obligations seriously. Since we missed seeing our many friends, an occasional missing loaf of bread or disturbed night's sleep seemed a small price to pay for enjoying those we could still enjoy.

Even if they were just Labs.

30.

The Power to Heal

To a physician, no experience feels as disorienting as a visit to a strange hospital as a family member or a patient. Despite my familiarity with the medical environment, I felt oddly intimidated as Lori and I walked down the corridor after the long drive to Seattle. I was no longer in charge of anything there and had no idea what to expect in the room down the hall. It occurred to me that if all doctors went through similar experiences more often, they might be more sympathetic to those under their care.

I had tried to prepare myself, but as soon as we opened the door to my father's room, I realized I hadn't prepared myself enough. He looked very sick and very old. A skilled surgeon had amputated his leg a few days earlier, but now he was battling his way through pneumonia, bleeding, and a litany of the other complications that routinely beset men his age who undergo major surgery. While it was easy to remind myself that he was almost 90, he was also the powerful figure who had led the way on so many outings and wilderness adventures. As he'd grown older, I'd learned to tell myself that he was only mortal, but this was the first time I had ever had to confront the true meaning of that realization.

"Why, Don!" he said after I'd roused him gently. He seemed surprised, although my mother had known we were on our way. Suddenly overwhelmed, I did what doctors always do when faced with emotional conflict in the hospital setting. I became a clinician and launched into a pointless discussion of his blood counts and antibiotics. Nurse Lori, no longer Nurse Ratched, quickly began a critical examination of the monitors and devices crowding his bedside.

"Is there anything I can get for you, Dad?" I finally asked once I'd convinced myself that all the right things were being done in all the right ways.

"Yes," he replied with more conviction than I'd heard all morning. "I really want to see my dog."

My father was no more a stranger to the medical environment than I was. The product of a hardscrabble upbringing in Depression-era Texas, he somehow found his way to Harvard Medical School. After completing his military service, he sat down as a newly trained hematologist and tried to imagine the greatest possible challenge in the field. After considerable thought, he concluded that developing the ability to transplant human bone marrow offered the theoretical possibility of curing fatal diseases like acute leukemia. Trouble was, at the time bone marrow transplantation seemed as daunting a project as sending manned space flights to the moon.

But against tremendous odds he kept at it, assembling a crack team of researchers and solving problems as fast as they arose. Four decades later, the techniques he developed were saving thousands of lives all around the world. In recognition of his accomplishments, he received the Nobel Prize in Medicine in 1990. As hard as he had to work throughout those long, trying years, he always had time for his wife and children... and his hunting dogs.

He was not an early fan of retrievers. As noted earlier, I grew up with shorthairs and Brittanies and didn't acquire my first Lab until I left home to complete my medical internship. Dad began to express interest in the breed after he'd hunted with Sky and Sonny, but his kennel always seemed too full to accommodate one of his own. When one of his Brittanies died of old age, I seized the bull by the horns and presented my parents with a female puppy from Sonny as a 50th anniversary present. Unusually belligerent for a female Lab, Goldie won a place in my parents' hearts even though she served them better as a watchdog than a retriever.

My father's first Lab might have been his last, save for a series of events that led to one of my own most inspired decisions. My parents were well into their 80's when Goldie and the last of their shorthairs died during the same year. "I don't know, Don," my father said when I called him to discuss the sudden emptiness in his kennel. "We've talked it over and decided that we're just too old to get another dog."

"No, you're not!" I protested, unable to imagine my parents living without a dog for the first time in my life.

"If we got another dog, it would probably outlive us," he replied. "What would happen then?"

"Your dog would always have a place with us," I assured him.

After a little more discussion and gentle arm-twisting, I placed a call to the Indiana kennel that had produced Rocky. A few months later, seven-week-old Folly was winging her way to Seattle. Over the next three years, she became the principal focus of my parents' household. She and my father became particularly attached. As his mobility decreased due to advancing age and associated health challenges, he could no longer hunt upland birds with the intensity he had once shown in the field. Trips to duck camp with Folly became the highpoint of his life. Every day during the off season seemed to begin and end with some backyard adventure involving the dog. All my increasingly frequent phone calls home concluded with descriptions of her latest accomplishments.

The dog had become both a substitute for three kids grown and gone to start families of their own and an emotional link to bygone days outdoors. It was clear to both Lori and me that Folly was keeping my father going at a time when he needed all the help he could get.

"You've got to get me out of here, Don," my father said as his various medical complications began to resolve.

"You're not ready," I pointed out. "You can't get in and out of bed yet, and Mom isn't strong enough to lift you." Lori and I would have been happy to take my parents back to Montana with us, but my father wouldn't hear of it.

"I just want to see my dog," he replied in the saddest tone I'd ever heard from him.

We talked to the nursing staff about bringing Folly to the hospital, but, as I well knew, there were rules against it and hospital rules were rules. I've certainly broken more than my share of them over the years, but Folly, although small even for a female Lab, was still too big to smuggle into my father's room undetected. At that point, with the worst of the medical crisis behind us and pressing matters of our own to attend up North, Lori and I had to depart for Alaska.

"It was a wonderful day!" my Mom practically shouted into the phone when I called a few days later prior to departure for an extended period of guide work in the Bush. "We got your father up in a wheelchair and took him down to the hospital entrance, where I had Folly waiting in the car. You should have seen the two of them! He looks like a new man now, and he ate a real meal for the first time all month." After that encounter, a sympathetic head nurse began to allow my mother to smuggle Folly in during night shifts.

The following week, my father moved to a rehab unit with a more relaxed attitude toward pets. Visits from Folly became the highlight of every day. And after he made it home, Lori stopped in on her way back from Alaska to supervise from a nurse's point of view. "You should see your father and that dog!" she said over the phone once I finally made it back to civilization. "They're inseparable. I think she was what he really needed when things looked so grim back in the hospital. While everyone was busy worrying about all the medical details, we just should have brought him his dog!"

Everyone loves a heartwarming dog story, but it turns out that solid scientific evidence supports Lori's assessment. A team from the University of Guelph, in Ontario, conducted a survey of 1,000 elderly Canadians, 286 of whom lived independently with either a cat or a dog. The pet owners showed a significantly greater degree of activity and mobility. They also reported significantly less psychological stress and depression during periods of crisis such as hospitalizations. A Medicare study showed that elderly patients who lived with a dog made fewer visits to physicians' offices and emergency rooms than matched controls with no dog in the house. A 2009 article in the *Journal of Psychogeriatrics* reported a significant reduction in anxiety scores among nursing home residents who had daily contact with "therapy dogs". Other studies have shown lower blood pressure readings, shorter hospital stays, and even longer survival among elderly patients who enjoy regular contact with a dog.

None of this was news to me, no doubt as the result of a lifetime spent enjoying canine company. At a local nursing home where many of my patients lived when I was working as an internist in a rural community, I encouraged a liberal attitude toward dogs. Families often brought dogs along when they visited elderly relatives. The nursing home even adopted a mutt from the local pound for residents with no dog of their own. Then one day someone brought a cat to visit. The dog spotted the cat and barked, the cat ran up a patient's leg, and a few minor scratches resulted. Given the liability climate, the subsequent ban on all pets in the nursing home was probably inevitable, even though the event sounded more like a reason to ban cats than a dog problem to me. That was around the time I decided to stop practicing medicine.

I can't cite any studies showing that any one breed makes a better "therapy dog" than any other. Most studies suggest that it probably doesn't much matter. My own personal biases should be obvious. Labs have been a big part of my life for over 50 years. I consider the Lab's personality ideally suited to the purpose. It's remarkable that a dog capable of such determination in the field can also express such loyalty, devotion, and responsiveness to human emotion around the house. Somehow Labs do, and those are just the qualities the elderly need to experience when faced with the demands of age and illness. The wistful notion of a return trip to the duck blind with Folly provided my father with a specific motivational focus that produced gratifying results as he pursued his rehabilitation

My father did remarkably well following his return home. The surgical wound healed, his appetite returned, and my mother's home cooking helped him regain the weight he lost in the hospital. When we called, he couldn't wait to tell us about Folly's latest backyard training accomplishments. During our visits she never left his side.

Naturally, we started talking about getting back to duck camp together. That was an ambitious goal, but ambitious goals are essential to the process of rehabilitation at any age. In the event, it proved too ambitious and never happened. My father died in the hospital later that year. The following year my mother's own health problems caught up with her. We were able to honor her wishes and let her die at home with Folly next to her on the bed. Lori and I kept our word and arranged for Folly's care with my son Nick and his wife Shannon. The dog couldn't have lived out her own life in better circumstances.

Nothing can change the fact of our mortality, but a loyal Lab can delay its inevitability and improve the quality of life's final days. Now that I have reached my mid-70s facing significant health challenges of my own these issues are no longer merely theoretical. I have made my own wishes clear.

My advance directives specify that the Labs will remain with me until the end.

31.

Don't Tread on Me!

Years ago, an occasional hunting partner was working a young Lab on early season Huns. Attracted by motion in a clump of sage, the curious youngster paused to investigate. Once he spotted the source of the disturbance, he did what Labs have been bred to do for generations. He tried to fetch it.

Unfortunately, the object of his attention proved to be a rattlesnake, which bit him in the tongue. Soft tissue swelling developed quickly, producing critical airway compromise. The dog never made it to veterinary care. Normal behavior on the part of both the dog and the snake had cut short a promising career.

Every upland hunter and Lab owner I know worries about their dogs sustaining a serious, or perhaps fatal, bite from a venomous snake. I'm especially concerned during Montana's early grouse and partridge season when temperatures are high and snakes are active. The thought of losing a loyal canine hunting companion this way can be frightening. Strategies for preventing and treating snakebites remain controversial, often hampered by lack of meaningful scientific data. In this chapter I'll discuss those options and try to present some practical guidelines. Be advised that the science may have changed by the time you read this. My own recommendations are influenced by my background in human medicine.

I introduced this chapter with a focus on hunting dogs just because they face an especially high risk of snakebite. However, Lab owners who don't hunt with their dogs face similar risks. The advice that follows applies to all dogs that venture outdoors in snake country no matter what their job description.

First, some reassurance. Fatal snakebites are like bear attacks in that we worry about them more than their actual frequency suggests we should. Your dog is far more likely to be killed by a vehicle than a snake. While there are no accurate records about the incidence of fatal snakebites in dogs, there are for humans. Although several thousand Americans are bitten every year, only around five die, a survival rate that is likely similar in dogs. Of course, if it happens to you or your dog such statistics offer little comfort.

Except for the reclusive and narrowly distributed coral snake, all North American venomous snakes are pit vipers, a family that includes copperheads and water moccasins as well as multiple rattlesnake species. Injected through hollow fangs, their venom is a mix of proteins so complex that its exact composition remains uncertain. Toxicity takes two forms. Local swelling around the bite can lead to tissue loss and compromise circulation to an extremity or even the airway if the bite is near the face or neck, a potentially fatal complication. As it absorbs into the circulation venom can cause cardiovascular collapse, and interference with the blood clotting mechanism can lead to serious bleeding.

Now more good news. Snakes don't want to waste good venom on creatures they don't plan to eat. In approximately 50% of bites no venom is injected, resulting in a so-called "dry strike." Since all snakebites can be contaminated by bacteria antibiotics may be indicated anyway, but a dry strike is not an emergency. However, it's a mistake to try to make that distinction in the field, since signs of envenomation may not appear for hours. A known or suspected snakebite should be treated as envenomation until proven otherwise. That calls for a rapid trip to the nearest veterinarian.

The proverbial ounce of prevention begins with an assessment of risk in the area you plan to hunt. Dry, rocky terrain should arouse caution. Snakes are not randomly distributed. In some locations I have encountered an unusual number of snakes during hunting season, suggesting a winter denning site nearby. I don't go back until temperatures drop and snow covers the ground. Time of year matters. Home to 12 (!) species of rattlesnakes, Arizona is a snake-bite hotbed, but in years of quail hunting there in December and January I never saw one. It may not have felt like winter to me, but it did to the snakes. On the other end of the risk scale, Montana's early bird season is prime time for snake activity.

I think that the most important preventive measure a dog owner can take against snakebite is an avoidance clinic conducted by a skilled and experienced trainer. I have put all my dogs through one except young Keta, and I'm looking for a good one for her. The best in which I've participated was conducted in Arizona by noted trainer and writer Web Parton, who spent an entire morning with eight dogs while gently conditioning them to identify snakes by scent, sight, and sound and then to avoid them. By the end of the session, handlers had learned to recognize behavior by a dog that detected a snake, adding to their own safety in the field. During the "final exam," one of my Labs not only recognized a rattler hidden in the grass but actively pushed me away from it. Parton told me that he has only seen this protective behavior in Labs.

It is important to realize that avoidance clinics vary considerably in quality and approach. In most, trainers use an e-collar to condition the dog to avoid the snake. In the clinic just described I never saw anything more than a mild twitch of the dog's head in response to stimulation. I observed another clinic in which an inept trainer hit the dogs way too hard with the e-collar. I found it frankly revolting. As Parton says, a dog that's hurting isn't learning. Seek opinions from friends who have been there before signing up. Some may balk at the idea of an e-collar, but a properly conducted clinic won't hurt the dog and is certainly preferable to a snakebite.

How effective are avoidance clinics? As with the next topic, solid data are lacking. Good trainers emphasize that no avoidance training is totally effective. I base my own recommendation upon observation of dogs' behavior around snakes during and after a clinic.

Now for what may be the most controversial topic in the discussion—immunization against snake venom. While this practice obviously won't prevent bites, it may (or may not) protect a dog from serious consequences. This ambivalence results from a lack of good scientific data, not surprisingly since meaningful trials would involve exposing a lot of dogs to venom.

The sole manufacturer developed the vaccine against venom from western diamondbacks. It has not been tested against venom from other snakes. Although generally safe, dogs sometimes experience allergic reactions. What studies have been done did not demonstrate protection from the vaccine, and expert opinion advises against it. I have not vaccinated any of my dogs. Since I first wrote this chapter the company that made the vaccine has withdrawn it from the market. I won't miss it.

With or without prior vaccination, the crucial element in treatment of a snakebite is antivenin, a biologic agent that neutralizes snake venom. Everything else—intravenous fluids, antibiotics, pain medications—is secondary. Antivenin must be administered under the direct supervision of a qualified veterinarian, and it's expensive. Total cost of treatment varies depending upon how much is required based on the dog's response but may run into thousands of dollars. If you are hunting an unfamiliar high-risk area, it's wise to locate the nearest veterinary clinic before going afield and confirm that they can treat snakebite. After initial evaluation don't be surprised if the clinic recommends keeping the dog under observation even if it appears well to you. Life threatening complications can develop long after a bite.

Most first aid measures once recommended for field treatment prove useless or harmful. Since pit viper venom binds rapidly to tissues, suction devices are ineffective. Some recommend giving over-the-counter antihistamines by mouth but there is no good evidence of benefit. I would only give antihistamines upon advice from a veterinarian and would not delay evacuation to do so. For a definitive, if somewhat technical, discussion of snakebite treatment, review the Unified Treatment Algorithm online (pubmed.ncbi.nlm.nih.gov and others).

Let's imagine a worst-case scenario. You're in the field, your dog yips and paws at a leg, and you spot a rattler nearby. What next? Here's a step-by-step guide.

1. *Secure the area.* Other snakes may be nearby, and you won't be able to give your dog best care if you are bitten too.
2. *Identify the snake if this can be done safely.* This can be important in areas with multiple dangerous snake species. Bites from the Mojave rattlesnake in our desert Southwest are often treated differently from other rattlesnake envenomations. However, if you can positively identify the offender as non-venomous you can save yourself and the dog a lot of inconvenience.
3. *Calm the dog down and keep it still.* This will help delay absorption of venom.
4. *If the dog is bitten on a leg, avoid moving the extremity as much as possible.* This may mean carrying the dog out of the field.
5. *Don't waste time on ineffective measures.*
6. *Get the dog to a qualified veterinarian as soon as possible even if it appears well.* A known or suspected bite is an emergency until proven otherwise. If you can, call ahead, give the clinic an ETA, and inform them of the situation so they can prepare in advance.

Above all, be vigilant in snake country, for the dog's sake and your own.

32.
From the Yard to the Field

Pheasants still lay a month away on the calendar, but I had already enjoyed two weeks of Montana's early season for sharptails and Huns. Grouse numbers seemed down, likely due to exceptional rainfall in early June when chicks were starting to hatch. However, that same rain had made the prairie bloom. The ground cover was in better shape than I'd seen it in years. With bumper hay crops baled and stacked, ranchers didn't need to graze their livestock as intensively as they had during the recent draught. Upland birds enjoyed plenty of room to thrive. Those same welcome conditions allowed the birds, especially the grouse, to disperse widely. Hunting the usual brush patches had largely been unproductive.

Lori and I had done all our hunting behind Max, our veteran German wirehair. I've found shooting over pointing dogs a special experience ever since I was a kid in eastern ruffed grouse country. Max is a highly capable retriever, but I still found the absence of a Lab unsettling given the circumstances. Rosy was turning 12, and if she were to hunt at all that season it wouldn't be on long hot days on the prairie. Kiska, her designated understudy, had just died unexpectedly in her prime. On a brighter note, we had picked up Keta the week before we lost Kiska, but she was still very much a puppy.

All this soap opera left me in a quandary. I've always believed in hunting young dogs earlier than many trainers recommend, but

I felt ambivalent about taking the puppy. Was I paying attention to Keta's development or responding to the gloom I felt following Kiska's unexpected demise? Lori had already taken the puppy under her wing, and she was the one who finally made the call.

As I loaded the hunting truck one more time during the last week of September, I put a second dog box in back and boosted Keta up and into it.

Most dogs get their early training under controlled conditions. We choose the time and place and the object of the day's lesson. We can work the dog on a lead if need be. Training in a familiar setting makes it easy to minimize distractions and keeps the young dog focused by reducing the impulse to explore.

Those of us raising our dogs to be hunters will eventually have to oversee the transition from the backyard to the brave new world of the field, where the controlled environment just outlined may be replaced by confusion in an unfamiliar environment. Young dogs will feel excited and enthusiastic in their new surroundings and enjoy their sense of freedom. (At least let's hope so.) The dog will likely recognize your loss of immediate control over its behavior and take advantage of it, just like our own teenaged kids. No matter how confident you feel about the dog's mastery of basic commands at home, obedience will be challenged in new circumstances. Expect these lapses rather than being surprised by them.

Since my dogs are raised to hunt, I've had my share of experience with this difficult transition and have made mistakes along the way. I also recognize that many experienced trainers will disagree with some of my decisions. However, I think most general principles outlined here are sound and reasonable in most situations.

A poorly thought-out first hunt can create disastrous gun-shyness. A young dog's first exposure to gunfire should not occur during a hunt. I never take a young dog into the field until I've addressed that potential problem under controlled conditions. There are many ways to do this, which I won't belabor here. The important point is confidence in the dog's tolerance of gunfire.

To the extent possible, a young dog should not have its first exposure to any potential problems while hunting. The introduction to water is another example. Taking a dog on its first duck hunt before it has proven comfortable in water is a mistake. There are valid benefits from having a dog's first hunt be from a duck blind as outlined shortly. Even so, a young dog shouldn't go duck hunting until it has demonstrated confidence while wading and swimming.

While you will inevitably cede some degree of control during the initial hunting experience, you can still determine the circumstances under which it takes place. Young dogs don't tolerate heat or cold as well as dogs in their prime, so avoid temperature extremes. In hot weather, even experienced dogs will have trouble scenting and holding birds when they are panting. Location also matters. Initial hunts shouldn't involve demanding terrain. Developing independence while starting to range from your side should be encouraged gradually. Since maintaining visual contact is important, I avoid brushy cover. On first duck hunts, stay away from ice and flowing water. Dealing with those variables can wait until the youngster has had more experience.

Choose your quarry wisely. I'm fortunate to live in sharptail country. Dog trainers have long recognized these cooperative grouse as ideal for a young dog's first exposure to upland game. They make an excellent choice for retrievers as well as pointing dogs. For as long as I have lived on the prairie, sharptails have almost always been the first birds my dogs retrieved in hunting situations. Quail and other grouse species can serve the same purpose elsewhere. Here on the prairie, Huns are more challenging to hunt (and to hit) than sharptails, but they are a perfect fit for a young dog's mouth. During the early season, I often picked one from my game vest after a hunt and worked Keta with it in the yard for a day before cleaning it for the table. Do not use a bird with exposed meat or blood, which can encourage chewing.

Early training should provide exposure to the scent and feel of gamebirds. Many of us have done this by fastening a bird wing to a small dummy for yard training. However, despite experimenting with various combinations of twine and duct tape, I always found it difficult to keep the wing attached to the dummy. To address this problem, I started to use zip-ties. Locating the tie over the strongest part of the wing bone and pulling hard on the tag end with a vice-grip created a strong bond that survived a lot of retrieves after placing another tie or two around the end of the wing. Trimming the stiff tag end to about a half inch made the finished package just prickly enough to discourage hard-mouthing without risking injury to the dog.

While pheasants are the upland species best suited to hunting with a flushing retriever, they are a poor choice for a dog's early hunting experiences. Their preference for thick cover, running ability, size, and belligerence when crippled combine to put them above a novice's pay grade and can lead to frustration and bad habits in dog and handler alike. Game farm pheasants aren't nearly as difficult, and they make a reasonable substitute for those without access to wild birds. Otherwise, leave the ringnecks alone until the dog has more experience on its resumé.

Sitting on a chair with your young dog beside you while pass-shooting doves sounds attractive but presents problems too. In Montana doves disappear as soon as cool weather arrives, which means we are usually hunting them on hot days. Dove feathers are loosely attached to the skin and dogs don't enjoy having a mouth full of them while panting. I leave young dogs behind for a season or two before introducing them to doves. The veterans in the kennel will enjoy the early season work.

Starting a youngster out in a duck blind has a lot to recommend under favorable conditions. The dog will be close and easy to control or correct. One can take a second, more experienced dog along to prevent unrecovered game. If neither dog is steady, and the young dog probably won't be, one or both can stay on a leash.

The hunter's attitude may be even more important than these practical considerations. My personal rule is simple. On a dog's first hunts, the focus needs to be on the dog rather than the shooting. If you're eager to shoot a limit of birds, leave the youngster behind until you can provide the dog with the time and focused attention it needs. If you are going afield with hunting partners, be sure they understand the dog's priority. Fortunately, this is easy for me now, since my regular wing-shooting friends have young dogs of their own, and Lori has a good understanding of a puppy's needs and limitations.

I don't want to launch into a debate about e-collars, but those who use them (and I do, albeit carefully and conservatively) will need to consider when to start using them in the field. Unless a dog is demonstrating behavior—especially behavior dangerous to the dog—that really needs correction, I leave mine behind during a dog's first season in the field. I would never give a dog its first exposure to an e-collar during a hunt. That can be done under controlled conditions while training in the yard. First hunts should be as pleasant for the dog as possible.

While young dogs love to romp, playing with other dogs—especially if they are also young—can be a tremendous distraction. However, this behavior is also an essential part of puppyhood. Should other dogs, especially young ones, accompany your young dog on its initial hunts? The simple answer is a *no*, usually followed by a *but...*

At the risk of sounding squishy, I think a strong emotional attachment between dog and hunter enhances every aspect of the relationship, whether as company around the house or performance in the field. The younger the dog is when that bonding begins, the stronger it will become.

From the start around the house, I teach young dogs the distinction between training and play, since each has a different purpose. Training is about obedience and my authority. Play is about having fun and creating enthusiasm. Making the dog understand the difference isn't difficult and can usually be done just through body language and tone of voice. If it's a training situation I don't let the dog get away with disobedience without gentle correction. When it's play time, I just let the dog have fun.

Which circles us back to essential questions: Why take a young dog hunting in the first place, and what should you expect from the experience? I prefer to let these outings fall under the category of fun rather than training. I can teach a trained retrieve in my front yard. The goal should be to encourage enthusiasm and excitement when you load the dog into the hunting truck.

No matter how well trained the dog eventually becomes, there's just no substitute for drive in the field. Old Rosy illustrated this principle well. Sure, she had a good nose, marked accurately, and took hand signals well, but so have a lot of my dogs. Her signature characteristic was always her absolute refusal to give up on a retrieve no matter what the obstacles. I honestly don't know if that trait is innate or learned, but I'd like to give every young dog that comes my way the best chance of developing it.

The cover we chose to hunt today was complicated. Its main attraction is thick brush along a meandering prairie creek that holds a lot of pheasants, but I'd frequently flushed both Huns and sharptails from the adjacent native grass.

Ten minutes from the truck, Max went on point in cover a bit thicker than typical Hun habitat, and I expected to flush either sharptails or a lost pheasant as I walked in behind him. However, the reward proved to be a large covey of Huns. I dropped one right in front of me and took my eyes off the falling bird to complete a double at longer range. Although I hadn't marked the first fall precisely, I felt confident we would find it. I sent Max after the second bird, which had fallen into thick brush beside the creek.

"I saw where the first bird fell," Lori said from behind her camera. "Let's see what Keta can do with it."

Despite some skepticism, I had worked Keta on dead birds in the yard enough to be impressed by her instincts and soft mouth. The open cover and good visibility seemed well suited to a dog's first live fire retrieve. I gave Lori the green light to walk Keta toward the general area of the fall to see what she could do. By the time Max was back at my side holding the long half of the double, Keta was sprinting toward us with a Hun in her mouth. The bird was in fine condition, although the puppy did have to dance around a bit and show it off before dropping it at my feet—hardly a picture-perfect retrieve, but we could work on the details back in the yard.

Small bird, small dog... it made a perfect fit.

33.

The Big Chill

One recent evening after a long day of hunting, a friend shared a story that I found both frightening and inspirational. While those emotions don't always transfer well to the printed page, it left such an impression on me and illustrated so many important points of information for retriever owners that I've decided to give it a try.

The weather in the Pacific Northwest that day wasn't anything you'd see on a tourist brochure advertising the region's charms, but it wasn't anything to frighten a party of serious duck hunters either. Temperatures were above freezing, but not by much, and a 20-knot wind blew from the west. Michael and three friends had set up on a lake large enough to provide plenty of long-distance retrieving opportunities. The ice had just started to open up after a long freeze, and the water temperature was cold. The only dog in the blind was Michael's six-year-old male black Lab.

To no one's surprise, the great duck hunting weather produced great duck hunting. Everyone was shooting well enough to knock down plenty of birds, but not always well enough to leave them kicking in the decoys. The dog spent the morning churning up and down the lake in pursuit of cripples. Late in the morning, someone dropped the last bird they needed to complete four limits. The duck fell in a tree all the way across the lake. Michael could still see it, and he set off with the dog while everyone else started picking up decoys.

In retrospect, Michael acknowledges that the dog wasn't acting himself on that last retrieve, ignoring hand signals and heading in the wrong direction when the wind finally blew the duck out of the tree so the dog could fetch it. He didn't make much of this at the time—a mistake, he now admits—and he and the dog finally made it back to the blind without incident. He was helping with the last of the decoys when he turned around and spotted the dog floating lifelessly behind him, apparently supported by nothing but the buoyancy of his neoprene vest.

Two members of the party had already left to get vehicles, but the other hunter helped carry the dog to dry land. He was a trained EMT, and when he couldn't detect a pulse or corneal reflex, he immediately began cardio-pulmonary resuscitation (CPR). Details of this potentially lifesaving technique are beyond the scope of this discussion. Multiple resources are available on-line, and your veterinarian can likely direct you to one of the classes that teaches canine CPR.

By the time one member of the party returned in an ORV, the dog had been through several cycles of CPR with no evident response. The EMT had told Michael that the dog was dead. Fortunately, they had already considered hypothermia as the cause of the dog's collapse and knew enough to keep trying. An adage in human medicine holds that no suspected hypothermia victim is dead until it's warm and dead. With the dog wrapped in heavy coats, they raced back to Michael's nearby house with CPR in progress. By the time they got the dog inside, it had a faint pulse and was breathing spontaneously, although it was barely arousable. They confirmed the diagnosis of hypothermia with a thermometer. After an hour wrapped in an electric blanket, the dog was standing up and walking around the room. The EMT had been right. The dog *was* dead at that point, but skill and determination had brought it back to life.

THE BIG CHILL

That's the frightening part of the story. The inspirational aspect is that the dog recovered completely and went on to enjoy several more years of happy life and duck hunting, with no apparent sequelae to its near-death experience.

Why did all this happen? The dog was in its prime, with no underlying health problems. Its baseline level of care was excellent, and weeks into a busy hunting season it was in fine physical condition. The weather was not exceptionally cold, and the dog had tolerated colder conditions frequently. However, that day the dog had made multiple long retrieves in cold water, and the wind was blowing hard enough to drop the chill factor into the dangerous range for a wet, exhausted dog. Michael later acknowledged that he had simply lost track of how hard the dog had been working all morning. As the lone retriever for four capable guns in a large body of water, it had been losing heat to a perfect storm of environmental conditions faster than its body had been able to produce it. There are lessons here for all of us.

I have never personally had to deal with hypothermia in a dog. What I know about the subject is largely derived from experience with the problem in people, and after a 40-year medical career in rural Montana and Alaska, I've had my share. Since the basic mechanisms of hypothermia and approaches to its recognition and treatment are similar in dogs and people, I'll let that background carry me through the discussion that follows.

Like all mammals, dogs (and people) are warm blooded. Their bodies are meant to operate within a narrow, well-defined internal temperature range no matter how hot or cold the environment. When body temperature falls outside that range in either direction, organ systems begin to malfunction quickly. Death can ensue if the internal body temperature isn't corrected. In this discussion we'll ignore the problem of hyperthermia, or heat stroke in its various forms, even though that may pose a greater danger than hypothermia in cold-adapted breeds like retrievers. I'll address that in a later chapter.

Understanding how hypothermia develops is the first step in preventing it, a far better option than diagnosing and treating it after the fact. The mammalian body has complex means of regulating its internal temperature to keep it within its optimal range. When a dog loses heat to the environment faster than its body can compensate, hypothermia will eventually develop.

Cold ambient temperatures are an obvious risk factor, but what matters is not the air temperature alone but the rate at which the dog loses heat to the environment. Air moving over the body surface promotes heat loss. Most of us by now are familiar with the concept of wind chill factor. If, for example, the air temperature is right at the 32-degree freezing point (all temperatures in this chapter are expressed in degrees Fahrenheit) and a 20-m.p.h. wind arises, the body will lose heat as if the air temperature were 15 degrees. Unfortunately, the best duck hunting usually takes place when the wind is blowing.

Moisture is an equally important environmental risk factor. Because water conducts heat better than air, surface moisture reduces the insulating ability of most protective garments, whether it's a down parka or a dog's coat. The process of evaporation itself consumes heat. Since water is denser than air, immersion in cold water creates heat loss at a greater rate than a dog would experience sitting on dry land in the same air temperature. Exertion also increases heat loss by multiple mechanisms, including the need to breathe more cold air. All this means that a hard-working retriever in and out of cold water on a windy day is facing most of the major risk factors for hypothermia no matter what the air temperature.

The principal reason more dogs don't succumb is that the retrieving breeds have been selectively bred for generations to tolerate such conditions. Most chihuahuas wouldn't last a day in the conditions my dogs face routinely. Retrievers' ancestors were chosen for their ability to work in harsh conditions conducive to hypothermia. Their build features a high ratio of body mass to surface area, which helps promote heat retention. Their coats provide excellent insulation, repel water, and dry off quickly. While these factors allow retrievers to work comfortably in conditions that would overwhelm many dogs, they do not make them immune to hypothermia.

Everyone who has shared a duck blind with a retriever knows about the "shaking off" ritual dogs perform when they exit the water. While this behavior can be a nuisance, especially when performed next to you in a confined space, shaking off is a complex adaptation designed to ward off heat loss. Scientific studies show that the motions a dog goes through as it shakes off are precisely calibrated to maximize dispersal of water droplets from its coat. So, don't get mad when your dog anoints you and your favorite shotgun with pond water. It's just trying to keep in shape for the rest of the day.

Over the years, I've changed my mind about one common means of averting hypothermia in retrievers. I once avoided insulating vests because I thought they might interfere with the natural water-shedding quality of the dogs' coats and their ability to dry off by shaking. I've now decided that isn't the case and noted that my dogs, particularly the older ones, hold up better when wearing one. Neoprene insulating vests offer another advantage: improved floatation. Dogs appear to expend less energy swimming while wearing them, and if a dog gets in real trouble, as Michael's did, a vest may keep it from going under completely. The vest must fit properly. Too tight and it will interfere with swimming, too loose and water will get inside and defeat its original purpose.

Even in cold-tolerant breeds like Labs, some factors make individual dogs more susceptible to hypothermia than others. Puppies are at particular risk because of their high ratio of surface area to body mass and their lack of experience with compensatory behavior. While I'm always enthusiastic about getting young dogs into the field early, I leave them behind whenever conditions raise the possibility of hypothermia. Old dogs are also at risk because their bodies can't generate heat as fast as they once did. Almost any chronic medical condition can also increase the risk of hypothermia. Be conservative about taking a dog in any of these categories into the field on cold, wet days.

Early recognition of developing hypothermia is important, because it's much easier to treat before it reaches advanced stages as Michael's dog did. Unfortunately, early hypothermia can be hard to detect in people, and it's even harder in dogs. Shivering is one obvious sign, but it's important to realize that shivering is a normal response to cold and does not necessarily indicate hypothermia. Shivering is a means of generating body heat by inefficient muscle contraction, roughly equivalent to revving the motor in an idling car. We've all done it without progressing to hypothermia and so have our dogs. Shivering actually ceases as frank hypothermia develops, and that is an ominous sign. If a dog appears to be shivering uncontrollably or much harder than usual, I'd consider getting the dog out of the field, but normal shivering should not be cause for alarm.

Measuring body temperature is the only definitive way to diagnose hypothermia, but that is usually impractical in the field.

However, it could be useful once you have the dog in a secure environment and are trying to decide if an emergency trip to the nearest vet is indicated. (If in doubt, call the vet.) If you do use a thermometer, remember that dogs run a bit hotter than people. Their normal temperature is 101-102 degrees as opposed to our own 98-99. A dog with a core temperature of 99 is in the early stages of hypothermia.

Close observation of the dog's behavior is the most practical means of detecting early hypothermia in the field, especially if you know the dog well. Loss of usual enthusiasm, inattention, and sudden difficulty performing routine tasks can all indicate falling internal body temperature. The important point is to be aware of the possibility. As with most difficult medical diagnoses, if you don't think of it, you won't recognize it. If environmental conditions are right and you observe unusual behavior in the dog, consider hypothermia until proven otherwise and take appropriate action.

Treatment of known or suspected hypothermia in the field is roughly the same for dogs and people, simply because options are limited. Get the dog out of the water, dry it off, check for a pulse and respirations, and begin evacuation. If the dog is cooperative, upon reaching dry land I would cradle the dog next to me and wrap us both in warm clothing while sending a hunting partner (if available) for a vehicle.

In both dogs and people, most cases of mild to moderate hypothermia can be managed by external rewarming. Severe cases may require more aggressive internal rewarming by administration of warm IV fluids or mechanical ventilation with warm air. These techniques require the services of a capable veterinarian, and one should be consulted if the dog doesn't respond promptly to external warming as described below.

Once the dog is in a controlled environment, be sure it is dry and apply warm (never hot) heat sources against its skin. Your own body heat may suffice as described earlier, but a heating pad under an insulating blanket or an electric blanket will be easier. Be sure the heating source is not hot enough to be uncomfortable on your own skin and rotate its position frequently. If the dog is capable of drinking, offer it warm water. Never force fluids into the mouth of a lethargic dog. Meanwhile, someone should be contacting the nearest veterinarian for advice about management and the need to transport for professional care.

Michael's experience represents an extreme example of canine hypothermia, but its happy ending illustrates another important point about its management. Paradoxically, hypothermia can protect many organ systems from the damage caused by low tissue oxygen levels during cardio-respiratory arrest. Human medical literature confirms many cases in which a patient has arrived at a hospital profoundly hypothermic with no pulse or respirations for an unknown period of time, only to be successfully resuscitated. No matter how bad it looks, don't give up on the dog too soon.

Hypothermia is a complex subject, and a lot of the advice I've presented has not been confirmed by rigorous scientific study. Our dogs' remarkable ability to thrive in conditions conducive to hypothermia is why we don't have to confront it more often, which explains why we don't know more about it. Some veterinary professionals may disagree with some of what I've written, in which case I'd be glad to hear from them.

However, I think some points are beyond dispute. We should recognize environmental conditions that can lead to hypothermia. Since our dogs are retrievers and not lap dogs, they will inevitably be called upon to perform in such conditions. We should remain alert to the possibility of hypothermia, be able to identify its early signs, and know what action to take if we do.

We owe that much to the dogs that serve us so well.

34.

September Heat

Montana delays its version of the British Isles' Glorious Twelfth until September first, the traditional opening day of our season for grouse and partridge. The days leading up to the opener arouse intense anticipation reminiscent of the way I felt on Christmas Eve when I was a kid. Shotguns appear from gun cabinets, boots get oiled, and shells go from boxes into game vests as if these rituals could somehow make the date circled on the calendar arrive faster. Somehow the dogs seem to sense what's coming, perhaps by some ingrained awareness of the sunlight's angle prior to the equinox.

Most of us are accustomed to rising in the dark to hunt ducks, but *grouse*? Here's the situation. Although our house sits nearly a mile above sea level, daytime September temperatures on the nearby prairie can threaten or sometimes exceed triple digits. Today's forecast calls for something close to that by late morning, and that's just too hot for the dogs, not to mention for Lori and me. Anticipating the need to leave the field early, I want to be ready to start hunting by the time legal shooting light arrives half an hour before sunrise. Since the ranch we plan to hunt lies nearly an hour's drive away, the moon is still shining overhead as we start down the road.

The lead role in the team riding in the dog box falls to Maggie, our experienced and talented female German wirehair. I know this book is about Labs, but no worries. Today we've also brought Rosy.

While her star always shines brightest in the duck blind, she can also be helpful in upland cover, which she loves to hunt. She is with us today primarily because she needs the exercise and we enjoy her company, but she has proven helpful on early season sharptails and Huns for years.

When we arrive at our friends' ranch I turn off the county road and stop while Lori hops to out to wrestle with the one gate between us and the bird cover. It's a tight one and Lori's only five feet tall, but as a fourth-generation product of an old Montana ranch family she has an innate ability to manage taut barbwire that's at least equal to my own.

After stopping the truck at the base of a long, steep coulee, we put the time before the seasons' official opening to good use. Out come the dogs, quivering with excitement. E-collars and whistles, check. Game vests and 20-gauge shells, check. Wallets with hunting licenses, check. Camera, check. Water bottles and folding dish for dogs, check. Shotguns with chambers empty for now, check.

Then it's time to find some birds before the sun's radiant heat drives us from the field.

Having just reviewed some thoughts about the way cold weather can impact our Labs, it seems appropriate to discuss problems at the other end of the temperature scale. Labs are more susceptible to overheating than many breeds. As reviewed in an earlier chapter on the breed's history, generations of their ancestors were selectively bred for cold tolerance. The genetics that make them capable of working in cold water during waterfowl season can become a liability during early season upland hunts. Lab owners should understand how hot weather can affect their dogs as much if not more than they need to understand hypothermia.

In some parts of the country hunters seldom have to worry about the demands hot weather places on their dogs. Overheating certainly wasn't a problem when I lived in Alaska even though I did most of my ptarmigan hunting in August. By the final days of Montana's upland season weather can challenge anyone's cold tolerance, but I know how to dress for it and the dogs are more comfortable in cold weather than hot. We'll take zero in December over 90 in September any day. One obvious solution to scorching early season days is simply to stay at home and wait for the first frost, but on *opening day?* C'mon.

However, no one's eagerness to get back in the field after the long off-season layoff should compromise the well-being of the dogs. We are supposed to be able to anticipate uncomfortable or dangerous situations and alter our behavior accordingly, but dogs, especially hunting dogs, don't enjoy that ability. No matter whether they're pointers or retrievers their default position will be to keep hunting, leaving us responsible for their welfare in difficult environmental conditions.

Two paragraphs ago I scoffed at the idea of staying at home to avoid hot weather hunting, but I didn't mean to sound casual. I pay more attention to weather forecasts in September than I do in December. At some point on the thermometer, controlling your own enthusiasm and staying out of the field becomes the unpleasant but responsible course of action. If there were one fixed temperature limit defining how hot is too hot, making the call would be easy. There are too many variables in addition to the air temperature to make that possible, including the difficulty of the terrain and the individual dog's heat tolerance.

Heatstroke represents the worst-case scenario for a dog hunting in hot weather. This potentially fatal condition arises when the dog is generating more heat by exertion or absorbing more from the environment than it can lose it by panting. This most commonly happens to dogs confined in closed spaces. We've all heard horror stories about dogs dying while left in closed cars on hot sunny days.

However, heatstroke can occur under field conditions if the dog is working hard on an exceptionally hot day. Large, heavy coated dogs (such as retrievers), are more susceptible than smaller breeds, as are dogs that are old, de-conditioned, or otherwise ill. Warning signs include increased (or, paradoxically, decreased) panting, in-coordination, vomiting, tremors, and a fast or irregular heartbeat. Initial care includes reducing or eliminating exertion (which may mean carrying the dog out of the field), getting the dog into the coolest, shadiest place possible, and sponging the dog down with room temperature (not frigid) water. Heat stoke is a potentially fatal emergency. If the dog doesn't respond promptly to these basic measures, it should receive professional veterinary care as soon as possible.

Heatstroke occurs when a dog's internal body temperature rises from the normal 101° to 105° or beyond. Heat exhaustion is a more common but less serious problem that may not involve any dangerous increase in core body temperature. The dog may simply lie down and stop hunting. Offer the dog water and get it out of the field and into a cool, shady place as quickly as possible. If it still seems lethargic or reluctant to stand, seek veterinary care.

All of us have seen our working dogs pant even on cool days. Since dogs don't sweat, panting is a normal cooling mechanism and the dog's primary means of disseminating body heat into the external environment. It should not be a cause for alarm unless it seems excessive for that dog or is accompanied by other signs of heatstroke or exhaustion.

Dehydration can be both a cause and a result of heatstroke. Even in the absence of serious complications, it can compromise performance and lead to unnecessary discomfort for the dog. Fortunately, it is easy to prevent and treat. Thirst is the first symptom, but dogs can't tell us when they're thirsty. The solution to that communication failure is to provide frequent access to water and let the dog respond to its own internal cues. In familiar areas I keep track of surface water locations and on hot days frequently go out of my way to provide dogs access to them. Creeks and ponds are obvious sources of water, although they can dry up suddenly during a drought. In ranch country I remember the location of stock tanks and water troughs. If livestock are in the area, they're getting water somewhere.

You may not have that kind of local knowledge in unfamiliar terrain. This means carrying water for the dogs. During the early season I don't leave the truck without plenty of it. Plastic bottles are light and easy to carry but are prone to rupture or leakage. Although they are heavier, I prefer metal canteens with secure lids. A collapsable bowl from a backpacking supply outlet will reduce spillage when the dog is drinking. How much water to carry depends on multiple variables, but you can't carry too much.

Complications of excess heat exposure aren't the only hazards dogs have to face during the early season. In most locales, that is also prime time for encounters with venomous snakes as discussed in an earlier chapter. Cold blooded vertebrates are always more active during warm weather. Species that engage in communal denning, like our prairie rattler, may be concentrated in large numbers in some good upland cover. Since I've covered this topic earlier, I won't go into detail except to say that I think the best way to avoid a disaster is to put the dogs through a good snake avoidance clinic.

One can always alter the hunting agenda to avoid troublesome heat without having to stay out of the field completely. Possibilities vary considerably in different parts of the country, but doves are a great option in many places. They are one of the few gamebirds that I think can be hunted responsibly without a dog, but a retriever can still be useful on long falls or when several guns have multiple birds down at the same time. Furthermore, they make good company while you're waiting for birds to start flying, just as they do in a duck blind.

Because the dog's job description on a dove hunt doesn't involve much exertion, heat shouldn't be a big problem even on hot days. Furthermore, some of my favorite places to pass-shoot doves lie beneath shady trees, next to surface water, or both. As noted earlier, feathers detach more readily from doves than from other game birds. A panting dog with a hot, dry mouth may be reluctant to hold them. Keeping the dog rested and well hydrated will help, but in these circumstances, I don't try to correct the dog for dropping a bird prematurely. I also avoid hunting doves with a young dog on hot days until they have acquired some retrieving experience.

Another option is simply to hunt in cooler places. Where I live that usually means abandoning the prairie and heading for the mountains to hunt to hunt ruffed grouse or blues. With several isolated mountain ranges within an hour's drive of home I have lots of terrain to choose from. Temperatures can frequently be 10 to 15 degrees cooler than they are on the prairie below, and dogs are often hunting in breeze and shade. The terrain may be tougher on me and the shooting slower, but on hot September days this option may offer the only possibility of getting the dogs into the field.

SEPTEMBER HEAT

Opening day offers young dogs their first opportunity to hunt after summer training. In my part of the country sharptails provide a wonderful introduction to hunting, for retrievers as well as pointers, because of the open terrain they inhabit, docility, and reluctance to run when crippled. Both Huns and sharptails are easier on young retrievers than pheasants. Most of my dogs have learned their first lessons in the field on these two species. However, youngsters don't tolerate heat as well as mature dogs and are likely more naïve around snakes. Don't push too hard, offer plenty of water, and hunt as far from known snake habitat as possible.

Meanwhile, back at the ranch... We have just spent an hour walking up the first coulee without finding a bird. At least the air has remained cool and comfortable in the bottom of the draw. Maggie shows no signs of fatigue as she ranges ahead while Rosy tags along at heel.

One paradox of early season sharptail hunting is that conditions that make them easiest to locate also make it harder for the dogs to hunt them. As temperatures rise mid-morning, sharptails usually retreat to the shade inside scattered copses of brush such as hawthorn, chokecherry, and especially silver buffaloberry. Later in the day, hunting those isolated, easily recognizable patches of cover should eventually produce birds, but early in the morning they can be anywhere. Thus far, we've investigated some brush with no results while letting Maggie range widely through the open grass, where we have fared no better.

Then Lori alertly notes Maggie on point beside some buffaloberry above us near the coulee's rim. Why dogs always seem to go on point uphill remains a mystery, but she is still locked up when we reach her after the climb. I want her to hold the point, but the birds, which I assume are sharptails, aren't going to flush without some encouragement. When I line Rosy up and give her a line into the tangle she accepts the challenge readily. After a detonation of wingbeats, Lori and I each have a bird down. We let the dogs split the retrieving responsibilities.

By now the sun has crested the coulee's rim and the temperature is rising right along with it. Sometimes a trickle of water runs down that draw, but I've already determined that whatever moisture was there earlier hasn't survived the long, hot summer. However, I know that a stock tank lies just over the ridge. We decide to baptize the dogs before hunting our way back to the truck.

Although Maggie needs the cool-down more than Rosy after all the ground she's covered, she has never been a water dog. She doesn't look happy when I boost her into the tank. Rosy, being a Lab, appears to love it when her turn comes. Even after that refreshing interlude, it's time to get the dogs out of the field.

As we near the vehicle, I have started to unload my shotgun when Maggie screeches to a halt right in front of us. After reloading, Lori and I walk in ahead of the dog. Since we parked next to an abandoned barn beside a stubble field—classic Hun habitat—I'm not surprised when a tight covey explodes in unison from the edge of the grain. They flush at the edge of shotgun range as Huns often do on the initial covey rise, but each of us drops a bird before they disappear into the coulee behind us.

After a routine retrieve by each dog, we break our guns again and discuss options. I have a reasonable idea where the covey has landed, and letting Maggie go to work on scattered, tightly holding singles sounds attractive. However, the air temperature has risen steadily and both panting dogs have retreated to the shade beneath the truck. While I drop the tailgate and reach for the 5-gallon water jug I always carry with me at this time of year, Lori climbs into the cab to check its thermometer. "80 degrees," she calls back.

"And still climbing," I point out. "We're done."

With two dogs ready to call it quits even if they don't know it and one gamebird dinner already in our vests, the rest of the Hun covey can wait until another day.

35.

A Dog for All Seasons

When the sun finally cleared the eastern horizon old Sky looked dressed up to match our surroundings, with a layer of sparkling frost framing his muzzle in the clear morning light. As I stomped out a nest in the snow and settled back against the fallen cottonwood that had served me as a blind for years, he began to scan overhead for ducks. You can't teach a dog that kind of enthusiasm. When you're with a good one you don't have to.

Soon the sound of whistling wings rose from the darkest corner of the sky. By the time we saw the mallards approaching the decoys the birds already had their flaps down and their landing gear extended. The shooting itself was kid stuff. By the time the ejectors spat the empties into my gloved hand one drake lay stone dead in the snow across the creek while a second bobbed gently away on the current.

I whistled Sky off the easy mark and gave him a line on the floating bird. He hit the water in a geyser of spray and zeroed in on his target like a heat-seeking missile. When he returned with that bird in his mouth, I accepted the delivery and sent him again. Within minutes of the first flock's arrival, we were back in place waiting for the second.

What remains remarkable about this brief canine performance turned in years ago by a dog no longer with us? Nothing and everything, which happens to be the theme of this chapter. Different Lab owners entertain wildly varying expectations for their charges. A few minutes one dog spent retrieving a pair of ducks on a brisk winter morning could mean different things to any of them.

I view training goals for a Lab as falling into one of three categories: field trial competitor, hunting dog, or household companion. While some training principles apply to all three, others are more specific. Field trials require the dog to perform complex, challenging tasks and require rigorous training. Goals for hunting Labs vary considerably from lax to advanced, with appropriate differences in the approach to training. Simpler regimens usually suffice for those interested in a household companion. (Notice that I did not say *just* a household companion.)

Even after decades of living with Labs and hunting them as much as seasons and circumstances allow, I remain an outsider to a hard core of the retriever community simply because I don't field trial my dogs. I acknowledge that field trials define admirable standards for the working retriever. Whether they realize it or not, all Lab enthusiasts owe the field trial process a measure of gratitude. A century of such tradition, not always recognized to the extent it deserves, is what separates the dogs we know from mutts.

No system of standards remains infallible, and those of us who hunt with Labs should reserve the right to break the rules when indicated. As noted earlier, running a bank may represent a fault in field trial and hunt test circles. However, when I've sent one of my own Labs into flowing water after a mallard I want the dog back on dry land as soon as possible, for reasons ranging from more efficient duck hunting to canine safety. If I must challenge orthodoxy to achieve this result, so be it. I'll trade adherence to someone else's ideals for a safe, happy dog any day. Those are the standards I've set for my Labs under the conditions we spend our time together. While I'm not offering an anti-field trial screed, I do acknowledge the ability of hunting Labs to improvise and the value of allowing them to do so.

While some might cite lack of discipline in their critique of Sky's performance that morning others might complain about its excess. The thermometer hovered just above zero. Conditions were miserable *before* I issued the command to fetch and sent him plunging into the water. How could anyone who cares about dogs have asked such a thing? To which I would respond: How could I have asked him not to?

Let's remember how today's Labs evolved, and I choose this verb in the Darwinian sense, as described in an earlier chapter. By accident or design, dogs that could not adapt to that harsh environment disappeared from the gene pool. Labs destined to survive fetched buoys and nets and returned aboard fishing boats by being hauled up while grasping a line in their teeth. A modern Lab hitting frigid water with a splash isn't avoiding punishment. It's expressing its genetics.

Asked to summarize the Lab's distinctive personality in one word, I'd reply: *enthusiasm.* One of the breed's most remarkable traits is the ability to demonstrate enthusiasm towards almost anything from a duck hunt to a walk in the park. Finding ways to enjoy whatever's happening still differs from doing what one is born to do. Jumping into a river on a cold winter day may not be our idea of a good time, but Labs feel otherwise. Non-hunting Lab lovers willing to keep an open mind should find ways to invite themselves along on some of those outings. A morning or two in a duck blind with the right dog is the best way to understand the essential character of the Labrador retriever.

Given the increasingly broad base of the breed's popularity, the appearance of more Labs in non-hunting households shouldn't be surprising. These newer generations of Lab owners demonstrate attitudes toward hunting ranging from unfulfilled interest to indifference to downright antagonism. As with politics, religion, and similar issues of impassioned principle, tolerance for opposing views benefits all. Perhaps love of Labs will provide a badly needed catalyst for reconciliation between hunters, non-hunters, and even anti-hunters. It's certainly hard to imagine a better-qualified ambassador of goodwill than an enthusiastic Labrador retriever.

While I'm all for patience and understanding among Lab owners with different interests, a few concerns remain. In the years ahead, more Lab litters will be bred to satisfy the interests of owners removed from the breed's original hunting background. The fact that Labs make great house pets doesn't mean the breed should be reduced to its lowest common denominator. One tampers with success at one's own risk. Perhaps to a greater extent than any other hunting breed, the Lab has found ways to satisfy the needs of non-hunting owners, which may be the dogs' greatest accomplishment. Remarkably, this transition has come to pass without compromising the Lab's ability to perform in the field... so far. We all owe it to these remarkable animals to keep it that way.

Another Lab, another season. Dry grass crunches underfoot and the whole prairie feels as if it's sizzling beneath the Indian summer sun. Cold water and late season duck hunts seem as far removed as the Lab's original stomping grounds on the shores of the North Atlantic. No matter: Sonny's never met a hunting trip he didn't like.

How the dog can smell anything under such miserable scenting conditions remains beyond me, but we've both learned a trick or two about hot weather hunting over the years. The first is to save the dog from its own nearly hysterical early season enthusiasm, which is why he's plodding along at heel against his wishes. The second is to remember Sutton's Law and concentrate our efforts where the money is. That's why we're heading for the buffaloberry bushes.

Silver-leafed and spiny, the first dense clump of brush offers the only shade we've seen since we left the truck. Flushing birds single-handed from its depths would be an exercise in futility. Even if I could fight my way through the thorns, I'd never be able to get a shot off on the rise. That's where the dog comes in, and Sonny knows it.

Positioning myself on the rise overlooking the brush, I cluck softly to the dog and the long off-season's worth of tedium comes to a glorious end. Sonny bounds down the hill and launches himself into the cover as if it owes him money. Moments later, the first bird of the year erupts into the azure sky and crumples at the shotgun's report. Finally, it's time for the dog to do what he's been bred to do: retrieve.

As Sonny charges back up the hill with the bird in his mouth, I pause to consider the wonderfully variable job description the breed commands today, from field trial champions to civilian pot-lickers. Because I live in good hunting country that offers a long menu of outdoor experiences, I sometimes think I've exposed my dogs to all the variety they could ask for, but I've just scratched the surface. From the pressures of the field trial circuit to laid back evenings in front to the fireplace with the kids, Labs have found ways to do it all, without changing their essential character.

We owe it to the dogs to keep it that way.

36.

The Amphibious Lab

No element of performance illustrates the Labrador retriever's nature quite like a great water entry at the beginning of a retrieve. Whether the immediate goal is a duck, a stick, or a dummy, the moment of transition from land to water tells more about the breed in seconds than any amount of prose ever could. None of my dogs illustrated this principle as reliably as Jake.

An otherwise undistinguished member of the kennel family, Jake positively attacked the water whenever I released him from heel at the start of a retrieve. While his list of faults was lengthy, he redeemed himself whenever I gave him a line into the water by virtue of nothing more complicated than his eagerness to get wet. Hardheaded and an uninspired performer on dry land, water invariably turned him from a toad into a prince as if by magic.

And that's the way I'll always remember him. Jake died before his time but in contrast to Julius Caesar, the good he did was not interred with his bones. Each in his own way, all my Labs have probably taught me more than I ever taught them. In Jake's case, the lesson was simple:

Labs belong in the water.

As always in biology, an appreciation of the Labrador's aquatic instincts begins with an understanding of the animal's physical structure. The Lab is something of an anomaly in the dog family. While most wild canids can swim, few do so with much skill and enthusiasm.

A critical look at the Lab's design helps to explain the breed's distinction in the water from other dogs both wild and domestic. Consider the Lab's coat. Adequate insulation is paramount for warm-blooded animals to function in cold water. While long, thick hair like a wolf's is well adapted for insulation on dry land, it substantially increases drag in the water and compromises swimming ability. The Lab's coat, on the other hand, more closely resembles the fur of mink, beaver, and other aquatic mammals that inhabit cold climates. It's short and sleek for hydrodynamic purposes and coated with natural oils to facilitate the air-trapping necessary to inhibit heat loss when wet. Among domestic breeds, only the Chesapeake retriever sports a coat that rivals the Lab's in these crucial respects.

Around the house, a Lab's tail may seem a useless appendage at best and a nuisance at worst, especially when it's fueled by canine enthusiasm and busy knocking breakable items to the floor. In the water however, that same aggravating structure becomes a useful instrument. Take the dog down to the nearest pond on a warm summer day and watch that tail in action once your canine friend hits the water. Perfectly positioned behind the dog's center of gravity, its broad, powerful strokes contribute significantly to propulsion. The long lever angle provides steerage just like a ship's rudder, facilitating maneuverability in tight quarters. Design and function are wedded throughout nature. Just as a fox's bushy tail provides insulation to the vulnerable nose and face when the animal is curled up in snow, the Lab's is designed to help the dog fulfill its own unique job description: swimming.

No discussion of the Lab's suitability to the water would be complete without a look at the dog's feet. Strong webbing stretches nearly all the way to the end of each toe. Practically unnoticeable on dry land, this webbing turns each paw into a paddle wheel once the dog hits the water. The best way to appreciate this is to watch the dog swim in clear water from a raised vantage point like a high bank or low bridge. While swimming, the dog's paws seem to expand to twice their normal size as they help it churn through the water.

The soul of the water dog depends on mental attributes as well as physical, and the breed's background defines those traits as surely as its physique. Remember the breed's history as described earlier. The Lab's ancestors had to be mentally tough to survive the North

Atlantic. Today's Labs reflect the genetics of the survivors. No wonder they amaze us with their natural ability in the water today.

We should keep in mind the biological and historical basis for the breed's aquatic fitness when it comes time to get pups into the water. Conventional wisdom holds that it's best to introduce young Labs to the aquatic environment gradually, coaxing them into the water one step at a time until they are accustomed to feeling solid ground disappear beneath their feet. The measured introduction to new circumstances represents a sound training principle. With one exception I've never seen a Lab puppy demonstrate any reluctance to plunge in at the first opportunity. Kiska was the outlier for reasons I never could understand.

Granted, a puppy's first excursion into a pond may look comical as it performs the vertical dog paddle, a swimming stroke thus named for a reason. Genetics should ensure that the dog will figure it out quickly. Teaching a Lab to swim would be like teaching a bird to fly. I'm certainly not advocating introducing young Labs to water by throwing them off a dock, but the transition from land to water is one element of the training process that, with common sense, should be easy.

The usual problem isn't getting Labs into the water but keeping them out. Eastern Montana is dry country, but even rain showers measured in fractions of an inch can produce puddles deep enough to attract Labrador retrievers. Labs love to broadcast the news of welcome rainfall by leaving muddy footprints everywhere. I can't count the number of times I found old Sonny lolling in a remote stock tank during an early season hunt. Rocky wasn't above exploring the hot tub whenever our backs were turned. Most of our dogs eventually became enthusiastic companions on fly-fishing trips. Jake, when denied access to the creek, would amuse himself for hours on the lawn by dragging the sprinkler from one end to the other. None of those water-obsessed dogs could help themselves. They were just busy being Labs.

As described earlier, at any given air temperature moisture contributes to heat loss by several mechanisms. Labs don't just endure cold water. They thrive in it, thanks to their innate enthusiasm and the remarkable design of their coat as described earlier. In bitter cold conditions I learned years ago that I will usually cry uncle before the dogs, even when they're wet and I'm dry.

Because Labs are such superb swimmers, it's easy to regard them as invincible in the water. However, certain water conditions can cause them problems with consequences ranging from frustrating to life threatening. Because Labs are programmed to jump in first and think later (if at all), it's imperative that handlers learn to anticipate those situations and keep their dogs out of harm's way.

Strong current isn't necessarily dangerous for Labs, but it can sure be confusing. As discussed earlier, correcting for moving water's vector and momentum just isn't part of the Lab's instinctive makeup. Learning these skills always goes best under controlled conditions. If there's any possibility that your Lab will be called upon to negotiate current, introduce the dog to the concept of moving water during a warm summer day, on a stream with low banks and no obstructions. Be prepared for some initial confusion, even if the dog is a veteran.

Obstructions can cause even an experienced Lab real trouble in moving water. "Sweepers" along undercut banks on the outside edges of creek bends can get the best of even the strongest swimmer, canine or human. The degree of danger depends on the water depth, current strength, and nature of the obstruction. When in doubt, I use the rule of thumb mentioned earlier. If the water contains a sweeper that I couldn't swim clear of myself, I keep the dogs on dry land. I'm even more conservative if the dog is a youngster.

I know I've mentioned this before, but it's so important I'm bringing it up again. The combination of ice and open leads of moving water is especially dangerous. The thought of losing a dog under an ice shelf should be terrifying to any responsible handler. I simply won't let my dogs enter moving water if there are ice shelves downstream. Remember that a working Lab's enthusiasm will always trump the dog's judgment in these situations, so you will have to be the one to make the safety call. An eager retriever in strong current can cover a lot of downstream territory quickly, so be sure you know what lies around the next bend.

Ice on top of still water isn't nearly as dangerous but still needs to be treated with respect. While experienced Labs can become remarkably adept at scrambling back and forth between water and ice, breaking through a layer of ice in a large pond can still be dangerous. Since a dog's weight is distributed on four legs rather than two and most of us outweigh even the heftiest Labs, dogs should be able to cross any ice we can without breaking through. Anytime water is over waist deep, I won't let my dogs work on ice I haven't tested first. Always assume that in a worst-case scenario you might have to retrieve the retriever. If that thought makes you uncomfortable, you should keep the dog on the shore.

Sweepers, ice, and current... wouldn't it make more sense just to leave the dog at home? Ultimately, that depends on the nature of the working relationship between handler and dog. My Labs clearly enjoy their job description, which includes healthy measures of all these challenges. I find that denying them the opportunity to express their inherent enthusiasm for the water evokes images of caged birds. Point is, whether the Lab owner's goal is a heart-stopping retrieve or a summer romp in the nearest frog pond, the human component of the team needs to assume responsibility for canine safety. That means understanding the dog's abilities, desires, and limitations.

37.

Beyond Words

Come, sit, heel, stay—most of us are familiar with the basic commands our Labs should learn whether they're house dogs or hunters. However, it's important to recognize the limitations of any dog's ability to grasp commands. When a Lab sits on command it's not because it understands the concept of sitting. It is obeying the command because it has been conditioned to behave in a specific way in response to a specific stimulus. The dog would behave in the same way if you used the word "broccoli" instead of "sit" in the training process, as long as you did so consistently. Since the actual choice of words doesn't matter, it's important to recognize two nonverbal components of the training process: tone of voice and visual cues varying from specific hand signals to nonspecific body language.

Just as little kids learn to distinguish their "outside" voice from their "inside" voice, I teach my dogs the difference between my "play" voice and my "command" voice. There's nothing wrong with a "Good girl!" at the end of a well-done performance, but it's just affectionate chatter to the dog. The dog doesn't know the meaning of either word. Verbal praise can certainly be used to reenforce desired behavior, or simply to express your pleasure with the dog. Both goals are best achieved with tone of voice rather than choice of words. I use a soft, happy voice to communicate praise. By using it consistently, often accompanied by a pat on the head or a food treat, the dog learns to associate it with desired behavior.

I admit that discussion of the play voice sounds cold and heartless, as if the only reason to employ it is to modify the dog's behavior. Untrue! One of the loveable features of the Lab's personality is that they are, well… loveable. Labs aren't the only breed that craves human attention, but I can't think of a breed that craves it more. The phrase "one man dog" needs gender neutral updating, but the concept is sound. No matter what the performance goal, it will be achieved more readily and enjoyably with a strong bond between dog and handler. I use my play talk voice with my dogs all the time even though I know they have no idea what I'm talking about. It's the tone of voice that delivers the message.

Now on to the work voice, which should be reserved for specific commands. Whatever the word, it should be delivered with a clipped, assertive tone of voice. While mine is louder than my play voice, shouting is unnecessary and probably counterproductive as long as the dog is close enough to hear me clearly. When used consistently it should send a clear message independent of the word spoken: Whatever I just said, it's a *command.*

A command is not a suggestion, nor is it the start of a debate. It should be concise and delivered in a tone of voice that sounds as if you mean it. "Don't you do that!" is word salad to the dog. A firm, abrupt "No! will be far more effective as a deterrent to unwanted behavior, especially when used consistently.

A whistle can be an invaluable aid to training and obedience. Hunting partners who don't use them drive me crazy by constantly yelling at their dogs, who usually ignore them. A whistle has several benefits as a means of non-verbal communication. It is abrupt and audible at distances the human voice can't reach clearly.

I only have two "words" in the whistle vocabulary I use with my Labs: *Come* and *Sit.* The value of the first is obvious. The ability to have the dog sit to whistle is invaluable in the field and essential when teaching the dog to handle. I teach it at an early age by making the dog sit to a whistle blast at feeding time when it is under my immediate control with a strong enforcement right under its nose. The dog doesn't get to eat until I tell it to, by saying its name. Once that behavior is established, start progressively increasing the distance between you and the dog.

The dog will need to be able to distinguish between the two whistle commands readily. There are several options. My sit command is just one sharp blast. When I want the dog to come to me, I give a long trill followed by three short ones. Because it's a bit complex, it helps avoid confusion when a companion is whistling to another dog nearby.

While visual commands are useful around the house, they are essential when handling a dog in the field. I'm not going into detail about teaching the dog hand signals to direct it to the location of a fallen bird or cast in a specific direction in upland cover. I use several hand/body signals in everyday situations that should be useful for non-hunting Lab owners.

Sit may be the single most important command in the Lab's working vocabulary. If the dog won't sit promptly and stay seated until told otherwise all basic training will be more difficult. A single raised forefinger is an easy way to enforce this command. As with all hand signals, the dog will have to be looking at you for it to be effective. If necessary, get the dog's attention by calling its name.

Stay is an especially important command around the house. In addition to the spoken command, I reenforce it with an extended open palm, like a cop stopping traffic. There is lots of opportunity to teach and enforce this command. At feeding time, I use this signal to reenforce the message that it shouldn't eat until I tell it to. This is an effective teaching moment as the dog is under your control with a strong reward in plain sight (and smell). I also teach them to stay before crossing an open doorway in a building or a vehicle. This will keep them from barging ahead into places you don't want them to be or knocking someone over. The dog should stay in place until told otherwise, which I do simply by calling its name and pointing in the direction I want it to go.

While those are the two most important situations in which to use visual signals to reenforce a verbal command, I do use several others. When calling a dog in from distance I bend at the waist and spread my arms in a welcoming gesture. No need to maintain that posture once the dog has seen you and started in your direction. Dealing with a particularly excitable dog like Keta, I bend low and establish eye contact before letting her out of the kennel. This seems to communicate the idea that the time has come to stop bouncing around purposelessly and pay attention. I don't open the kennel door until she has settled down. Since she always looks forward to walks and training sessions, she knows that a reward is just around the corner, as long as she earns it.

One benefit of teaching a dog to respond to visual messages arises late in the dog's life. Impaired hearing commonly develops in dogs as they grow older. By the time she reached age 14 Rosy was almost totally deaf. Because she had previously been trained to hand signals it I still had a way of getting her to sit and stay.

This discussion raises a fundamental question for Lab owners who don't want to field trial or hunt with their dogs. Why bother training them at all? Labs are like teenagers in that they enjoy a little direction. Training provides an opportunity to bond that otherwise might not develop as strongly. Trained dogs are safer dogs. If one heads for a busy road and you anchor it with a whistle you may have avoided a disaster. Finally, Labs are Labs because they have been bred for generations to be obedient and tractable. I think of an untrained Lab as an unfinished work of art.

Maybe that's just me.

38.

The End of the Road

When Lori and I first met Kenai, he was the largest male in a litter of eight yellow puppies wriggling around a whelping box trying to hog the milk output from a friend's beleaguered dam. By this point in my long relationship with Labs I had begun to appreciate the value of small size and female sex in a working dog, but Lori was having none of it. "I want that one," she announced. It was love at first sight.

Over the years, he fulfilled most of the promise Lori saw in him as he turned into a big, athletic dog for whom no water was too cold and no briar patch too thick. I'd trained Labs that marked and handled better, but he became a favorite based on size, energy, enthusiasm, and personality. In some ways he remained a playful puppy, greeting visitors warmly and making them respond to him just as Lori had the day she first saw him.

Then it became hard to remember the accomplishments and the good times. By age 13, his eyes and ears were nearly useless (although he could still hear dry dog food hitting the metal bottom of his dish from surprising distances). He identified people and our other dogs with his nose. Spinal cord problems for which there was no cure limited his mobility and made it hard for him to get up and down. Save for a brief daily walk, he became a fulltime resident of his dog pad on the living room floor. We are facing some hard decisions.

This piece is not about Kenai specifically. It is difficult to write about the emotional turmoil one faces near the end of a dog's life, because the dog will never mean as much to others as it does to its owner. An adage in the business of writing about dogs recommends avoiding the topic completely. I've broken that rule before, but I'm revisiting it because of all the turmoil I've watched friends endure during a favorite Lab's final months. In human medicine, preparation always trumps ignorance in such difficult times.

Don't worry—I'm not going to drag readers through a tear-stained replay of *Old Yeller* or *Where the Red Fern Grows*, although I found those stories deeply moving and can recommend them both. Instead, I'm using Kenai's situation as a springboard for a discussion of a broader issue that most dog owners will eventually have to face. How do we best deal with a Lab's final days?

It's easier to predict when those days will come for dogs than for people. Since small dogs generally live longer than large dogs and hybrids live longer than those with pedigrees, Labs start with two strikes against longevity. Barring trauma or illness, most Labs live between 10 and 14 years, with a 12-year average lifespan. A British Lab named Adjutant, born in 1936, lived for over 27 years, but that is truly exceptional. Almost all my own Labs have died right around age 12, making Kenai the longest lived of the lot.

My own approach to this difficult topic is strongly influenced by my experience in human medicine. During decades spent as a rural internist, I cared for many patients and families facing terminal illnesses for which maximal efforts to prolong life were not appropriate. I learned that when presented with an honest, candid explanation of what was likely to happen and what alternative means of dealing with the inevitable were available, most patients and families valued comfort and dignity more than a few extra days of poor-quality life.

The medical profession now recognizes certain principles to help guide these decisions. One of the most important is patient *autonomy*. This simply means that whenever possible the dying patient—not the family, caregivers, or medical professionals—should decide what kind of terminal care to provide. That may seem obvious, but confusion arises when the patient can't make those decisions, as in the case of a minor child or a mentally impaired or comatose adult. In such cases, *surrogacy* comes into play, preferably by informed prior agreement but occasionally by court order if necessary. At this point, the medical surrogate becomes responsible for decision-making.

Dogs can't tell us just how they feel or when they would like to let go of their lives, although careful observation can provide important clues. By default, we will usually assume the role of medical surrogates for our Labs. How well we fulfill that position depends on understanding a few more key ethical principles.

Beneficence implies the obligation to do what is best for the dying patient, in this case the dog. Proper care implies providing maximal comfort and placing the dog's best interest above the interest of others, including your own. *Nonmaleficence* simply encodes the ancient Hippocratic concept of doing no harm. Whatever decisions you make should be guided by the welfare of the dog and not your own convenience. Of course, determining exactly what is beneficial and what is harmful to the dog isn't always as easy as it sounds. Then making that distinction often becomes a real dilemma.

While I think these guidelines from human medicine do provide valuable information about caring for dogs near the end of their lives, there is one important difference. In canine medicine, these decisions often revolve around a simple choice: put the dog down humanely, or let it continue its compromised quality of life. (Despite political bluster to the contrary, there is no such thing as a "death panel" in human medicine.) That decision can be emotionally wrenching for all involved in the dog's care. The key is to remember your obligation to do what is best for the dog.

There are basically two errors to be made in the decision about when to put an old, ailing Lab down: too soon, or not soon enough. In my experience, the second is more common, no doubt because of the degree of affection that develops between Labs and their owners.

I must stress that nothing in this discussion is meant to substitute for proper veterinary evaluation and care. Every dog and every situation are different, and decisions about when to put a dog down always need to be individualized. When a dog starts to fail, a professional opinion often can help lead to a better-informed decision. The younger the dog and the more abrupt the decline, the greater the chance of discovering something treatable. I've seen friend's Labs recover from major cancer surgery and go on to live several more years of happy, productive life. When in doubt, talk your vet.

The hard decision comes when everyone understands that the dog is dying and that there is nothing to be done about it. As the dog's surrogate, you must make the call, and that can be difficult. Age alone should not be a deciding factor, in dogs or in people. It all comes down to doing what's best for the dog. The clearest indication for putting the dog down is to end suffering.

Elisabeth Kubler-Ross's book *On Death and Dying* had a major impact on the way doctors and nurses approach dying patients. She famously divided the psychological aspects of dying into a succession of five stages: denial, bargaining, anger, grief, and acceptance. While parallels between human and animal behavior certainly aren't exact, I think this model can be useful when dealing with a dying dog. My own observations indicate that animals reach the acceptance stage a lot more quickly and easily than people do. The conflicting emotions surrounding a dog's impending death and the question of whether or not to hasten it arise within owners and families rather than within the dogs themselves.

Dogs may not be able to talk, but that doesn't mean they are incapable of communicating. Aging or terminally ill Labs instinctively seem to know when they have reached the end of the road. When one stops showing interest in its usual enjoyable activities like taking its daily walk or fetching a dummy on the lawn, it's sending an important message. In the absence of acute illness or injury, refusal to eat is an even more specific indicator that the dog has reached the stage of acceptance.

Human caregivers have long noted the ability of dying patients to "hold on" until some significant date has arrived and passed—an anniversary or a child's birthday, for example. I've seen Labs do the same thing too often to dismiss these events as coincidence. One of mine waited until I had returned from a trip before jumping up to greet me, lying down on the lawn, and dying quietly. Another waited until the evening of the last day of its last hunting season. Labs know more about death and dying than we think they do, and we should learn to listen to them.

While aging dogs almost always seem to accept the inevitable gracefully, their owners don't. Part of this dissociation stems from our own conflicted cultural attitudes toward death and dying. Despite recent changes, many of us are still frankly uncomfortable with the subject, and too often the medical system's default position is to prolong life as long as possible even when doing so is not in accordance with the patient's wishes or best interest. That's why I spent so much time discussing end of life decisions with my own patients well in advance of the event. Furthermore, we are often called upon to take (or not to take) an active role in the dog's death, an inherently stressful choice.

A note on semantics… Work by Kubler-Ross and others encouraged doctors and nurses to talk openly and honestly about death and dying rather than hiding behind a lot of traditional hospital euphemisms, the point being that if we were going to learn how to deal with it better, we should begin by learning how to say it. Fair enough, but I have never found an adequate verbal description for taking a dog on a final one-way trip to the vet. "Put to sleep" sounds evasive and inaccurate. "Euthanize" sounds cold and clinical. Any version of "kill" can be blunt and to the point but it's not accurate either, since the intent is not to kill the dog but to relieve suffering.

I'll continue to use the less than satisfactory "put down" until someone provides a better alternative.

Unless your Lab gets hit by a car or you die of a heart attack, you will probably have to face the subject. That's the way the biological clocks of dogs and people work. How best to deal with the human elements of loss? A good place to begin is right where Kubler-Ross told us to, by talking about it, candidly and well in advance of the event. For children especially, the loss of a pet often represents a first encounter with death. Just as fear of the unknown contributed so much to the discomfort of obstetrical delivery prior to the era of "prepared childbirth," uncertainty about what is happening and what to expect only makes the death of the family Lab more difficult for everyone.

I've been through the process of losing Labs far more times than I care to relive, and there isn't much I can say to make it easier. However, it has been my personal experience that having a younger dog around helps blunt the sense of loss. I've been fortunate enough to spend my adult life in rural environments with room for plenty of dogs, and I realize that not everyone enjoys this luxury. But if you have room for a younger dog, get one. My first advice to friends who have lost an older Lab has always been the same: Get a puppy, as soon as you can find the one you want. Everyone who has done so has thanked me later for nudging them in that direction.

What about Kenai, the subject that began this difficult essay? Some knowledgeable friends suggested that I put him down sooner than I planned, reminding me of my own recent advice to a friend who, in my opinion, waited too long. But I couldn't establish that Kenai was in pain or had reached the point of letting go. He responded enthusiastically to company and enjoyed his daily walk, even if we no longer walked very far. His appetite remained robust. We still had to help him up off the floor from time to time, and we knew that the trip back to Montana from our Arizona winter home would be difficult.

Perhaps reflecting my own sentimental streak, I liked to think he wanted to make it back to the place he knew as home. He did, and shortly thereafter he died quietly in his sleep. I took the other dogs for a long walk, remembered the good times, and started letting life go on.

And yes, I followed my own advice. In addition to spending a little extra time with Rosy, Max, Maggie, and Molly, we soon acquired a puppy. Lori says you can't name a puppy until you see it, but I was considering Kathy before we picked up the little female in Oregon. Lori didn't have to know about that old girlfriend, but it was still probably best that I let her settle on West Wind's Tundra Rose, quickly shortened to Rosy.

www.ingramcontent.com/pod-product-compliance
Lightning Source LLC
Chambersburg PA
CBHW062056290426
44110CB00022B/2611